INTERVIEWS

Gloria E. Anzaldúa

ENTREVISTAS

GLORIA E. ANZALDÚA

INTERVIEWS
ENTREVISTAS

EDITED BY AnaLouise Keating

ROUTLEDGE

New York and London

Published in 2000 by
Routledge
29 West 35th Street
New York, NY 10001

Published in Great Britain in 2000 by
Routledge
11 New Fetter Lane
London EC4P 4EE

Printed in the United States of America on acid-free paper.
Design: Jack Donner

We are grateful for permission to reprint revised versions of chapters 4, 7, and 9.
A different version of chapter 4 was published as "Writing, Politics, and las Lesberadas:
Platicando con Gloria Anzaldúa" in *Frontiers: A Journal of Women Studies* 14 (1993):
105–30; a different version of chapter 7 was published as "An Interview with Gloria
Anzaldúa" in *Iowa Journal of Cultural Studies* 14 (Spring 1995): 12–22; and
a different version of chapter 9 was published as "Toward a Mestiza Rhetoric:
Gloria Anzaldúa on Composition and Postcoloniality" in *JAC: A Journal of
Composition Studies* 18 (1998): 1–27.

Library of Congress Cataloging-in-Publication Data

Anzaldúa, Gloria.
Interviews/Entrevistas / Gloria Anzaldúa ; edited by AnaLouise Keating.
p.   cm.
Includes index.
ISBN 0–415–92503–7 (hb) — ISBN 0–415–92504–5 (pbk.)
1. Anzaldúa, Gloria—Interviews. 2. Women and literature—United States—History—
20th century. 3. Authors, American—20th century—Interviews.
4. Mexican American lesbians—Interviews. 5. Lesbians—United States—Interviews. 6.
Mexican American authors—Interviews. 7. Mexican Americans in literature.
8. Lesbians in literature. I. Title: Entrevistas. II. Keating, AnaLouise, 1961–   III. Title.

PS3551.N95 Z464 2000
818'.5409—dc21
[B]   99–055530

para almas afines

Contents

Acknowledgments   xi

Risking the Personal   1
An Introduction

1. Turning Points   17
An Interview with Linda Smuckler (1982)

Early Writing Experiences; Grade School; High School; A Sense of
Difference; College; "My Task": Making Face, Making Soul,
Making Heart; Sexuality/Spirituality/Writing; First Turning Point:
Teaching (and) Chicano Culture; Second Turning Point: Entering the
Feminist Movement; The "Path of Writing"; Third Turning Point:
Becoming a Full-Time Writer; Another Turning Point: Teaching
"La Mujer Chicana"; *This Bridge*; Audience and Voice; Publishing
and "El Mundo Zurdo"; Writing the Body, Becoming a Mouth; Other
Influences

2. Within the Crossroads   71
Lesbian/Feminist/Spiritual Development
An Interview with Christine Weiland (1983)

Early Life; Bodies and Health; Religions; "Yoga of the Body"; "Off
the Rational Track"; Meditations, Making Love to the Divine;
Spirituality and Power; Becoming Lesbian?; Ethnic Pride, Worldwide
Oneness; "The Gathering of the Tribe"; "La Facultad"

3. Lesbian Wit 129

Conversation with Jeffner Allen (late 1980s)

Labels; Shapeshifting, Changing Identities; Bridges, Rainbows, Coalitions; Reading; Compartmentalized Identities; Imaginal, Psychic Identities; Lesbian Writings and Audiences

4. Making Choices 151

Writing, Spirituality, Sexuality, and the Political

An Interview with AnaLouise Keating (1991)

This Bridge and *Haciendo Caras*; New Interconnections: Moving from Unity to Solidarity; Spirituality: "Roots," Masks, Essentialism; Becoming Lesbian?; Always on the Other Side/del otro lado: Differences, Lesberadas; Representation: Individual and Collective "We"

5. Quincentennial 177

From Victimhood to Active Resistance

Inés Hernández-Ávila y Gloria E. Anzaldúa (1991)

Claiming Agency; Resistance; Originality; The New Tribalism; Mestizas as Bridges; "Las Tres Madres"

6. Making Alliances, Queerness, and Bridging Conocimientos 195

An Interview with Jamie Lee Evans (1993)

Making Alliances; Shifting Power; Anthologizing Alliances; Identity: The Power of Self-Invention; Conocimientos

7. Doing Gigs 211

Speaking, Writing, and Change

An Interview with Debbie Blake and Carmen Abrego (1994)

¿Queer Conference?; The New Tribalism; Knowledge, Conocimientos, and Power; Fighting/Theorizing Racism; Coalition Work: Bridge, Drawbridge, Sandbar, Island; Revisionist Mythmaking; Essentializing, Universalizing, and the Autobiographical; Lived Experience/ Representation; Making Soul: Writing the Coatlicue State, Nepantla, Llorona; Impact on Readers; "Doing Gigs"

8. Writing 235

A Way of Life

An Interview with María Henríquez Betancor (1995)

Chicana Writers; Identity-in-Process: A "Geography of Selves"; Relational Identities; "Autohistorias, Autohisteorías"; Language Conflicts; "On The Edge, Between Worlds"; The Ethnic Test: Who's the Real Chicana?; Writing/Reading as Survival and Healing

9. Toward a Mestiza Rhetoric 251

Gloria Anzaldúa on Composition, Postcoloniality, and the Spiritual

An Interview with Andrea Lunsford (1996)

Early Memories of Writing; Nos/otras; Postcolonial Studies, Composition Studies; Writing: Difficulties and Practices; Teaching Composition: Assimilation, Resistance, Liberation; Language, Domination; Composing the Work, the Self, the World; Claiming Author(ity); Style; Activism, Working for Change; Additional Bits

10. Last Words? Spirit Journeys 281

An Interview with AnaLouise Keating (1998–1999)

Dealing with Criticism and Controversy; Ignoring the Spiritual; Shapeshifting; Interconnections; Anger; Physical Health, Bodies, and Identity Formation; The Importance of Listening

Primary Works Cited   293

The Interviewers   295

The Authors   298

Index   299

Acknowledgments

Interviews involve a tremendous amount of work. Before the actual interview, you must track down and contact the person whom you hope to interview and, assuming he or she's willing, arrange a time and place for the interview; you need to acquaint yourself as thoroughly as possible with the interviewee's life and work—reread her writings, look at what other scholars have said about her words, read other existing interviews, and so forth; you must then compose provocative questions designed to generate enriching dialogue that will enhance a reader's knowledge of your interviewee; and you must obtain and test the necessary equipment (a high-quality tape recorder, additional microphones if possible, tapes, and so forth). During the interview, you must keep your attention closely focused on the conversation, listen carefully yet be ready to ask follow-up questions to further enrich the dialogue. (Don't get distracted, don't let your mind wander, think quickly and make connections between interviewee's comments and her writings.) You also need to keep an eye on the recorder (is the tape still running? should you turn it over yet?) and make sure you're not overly exhausting your subject (does she seem tired? bored? distracted? should you cut some of the questions and wrap it up early?).

And the work isn't finished once the interview itself has taken place. You still need to transcribe the tape(s) (listening carefully to the tape, stopping after every sentence or two, rewinding to listen again to unclear words or phrases). When you've got the first draft of your transcription, you must proofread it carefully, checking the manuscript against the tape; you might need to contact your interviewee for clarification (accurately spelled places and names, missing dates, inaudible words, additional information, and so forth). This process takes much longer than the interview itself.

I know these details from my own work as an interviewer, and I want to thank the people whose words are collected in this volume for their time-staking work. Linda Smuckler, Christine Weiland, Jeffner Allen, Inés Hernández-Ávila, Jamie Lee Evans, Debbie Blake, Carmen Abrego, María Henríques Betancor, and Andrea Lunsford: My thanks for completing the tasks described above; thanks for your support, for your interest in this project, for your willingness to share transcripts with me. Jeffner and Inés: Special thanks for taking the time to look over your conversations with Gloria. Debbie: A special thanks to you also for sending me copies of your interview.

I can only imagine the other side of the interview process. I don't know firsthand what it's like to be interviewed, to be an interviewee. But I do know from conversations with Gloria and from the interviews I've conducted with her that, while enjoyable, granting interviews takes a lot of effort. First, you must rearrange your own schedule (put aside writing projects, time with friends, the books you're reading, and so forth). Very possibly, the interview will become your work for the day. If your interviewer sent you questions in advance, you'll probably look them over, think of possible responses, jot down some notes, and maybe do a little outside reading. When the person interviewing you arrives, you won't just dive into the interview and engage in a series of formal "Questions and Answers." Instead, you'll try to put your interviewer at ease, show her or him around the house, chat awhile, perhaps sharing intimate details of your life. Because you see interviews as a "community-making ritual," you'll try to get to know your interviewer, try to break down some of the barriers that so often inhibit effective communication. During the interview itself, you need to remain focused for several hours, listen carefully to the questions, and think—quickly!—of the best ways to respond. You might take a break from the interview—maybe prepare some food and have a meal together, perhaps go for a walk. And then, refocusing your energies yet again, you go back to the interview. It's exhausting! And so, Gloria, I thank you for the time you've put into these interviews—not only the original interviews included in this volume but also for the time you've spent on the interviews we've done together, for the time spent hunting down transcripts, looking for contact information, discussing the interviews with me, carefully reading the edited transcripts, making revisions to enrich your words. Thanks for reading my introduction twice and making very useful suggestions for changes; for your encouraging words; for being always available (even when the diabetes was acting up and you were clearly in pain, you answered my phone calls and talked at length); and for mentoring me through this process.

There are other people who have played important roles. Mi familia, of course: Thanks for your patience as I worked on this project, rushed to meet deadlines, spent time on the phone instead of with Jamitrice, and so on and so on. Margaret Estrada: Thanks for putting aside your other work and transcribing the interview tapes so quickly; this project would have been delayed for months without your assistance. Jesse Swan: Thanks for talking with me about the interviews and for offering your perspective on the interview process. Renae Bredin: Thanks for your encouragement. Aida Hurtado: Thanks for helping us contact Annie Valvo. Bill Germano, Amy Reading, Nick Syrett, and others at Routledge: Thanks for working with Gloria and me on this project; thanks for your useful suggestions; and thanks for your flexibility.

Risking the Personal

An Introduction

AnaLouise, I read and like your Introduction, especially the section on spirituality. I think the intro would be stronger if you put *yourself* into it more. Maybe put yourself and your body in my setting—driving down to Santa Cruz, sitting in my study, looking at the spiritual things—altars, candles, statues. Maybe talk about how you physically sense my presence. Put your feelings and observations in a bit, your reactions to the first interview and to this recent interview: What was the same? What was different?

—Gloria Evangelina Anzaldúa

Originally, I had planned to write a fairly conventional introduction to this collection of interviews. I'd begin with a brief analysis of the important role interviews have played in Gloria E. Anzaldúa's life since the early 1980s and claim that, for Anzaldúa, interviews are another form of writing. I'd then summarize the innovative ideas contained in this volume, explore the ways they elaborate on and revise those found in her published works, and provide brief summaries of each of the interviews. And perhaps in a few paragraphs I'll return to this conventional format. But if I do so it will be with hesitation, for when I sent a draft of this introduction to Gloria,[1] she responded with the comment I've used as the above epigraph.

Although I was not surprised by Gloria's suggestions, I groaned when I read them. Since I first met Anzaldúa almost ten years ago and asked her to read a chapter draft from my book in progress, she has encouraged me to put myself into the words I write. And still, I resist. My academic training, coupled with my love of privacy, make me fear self-disclosure. If I incorporate the personal into my words, perhaps I won't be respected as a scholar. Or maybe you'll think that I'm vain, egocentric, and selfish; after all, you picked up this book to learn more about Gloria Anzaldúa, not about AnaLouise Keating. Or maybe my family will read what I write and reject me. Or maybe I'll sound stupid, unsophisticated, naive. *I fear these risks!* But one of the most important things I've learned from reading and teaching Anzaldúa's works is the importance of risking the personal. Throughout her writings, Anzaldúa draws extensively on her own life—her early menstruation; her campesino background; her childhood in the Rio Grande valley of South Texas; her experiences as a brown-skinned, Spanish-speaking girl in a dominant culture that values light-skinned, English-speaking boys; and her sexual and spiritual desires, to mention only a few of the many private issues woven into her words. And you'll find this same willingness to risk the personal—to disclose intimate details, beliefs, and emotions—taken to a further extreme throughout the interviews collected in this volume.

As one of my students suggested last semester when we were reading *Borderlands*, Gloria's willingness to reveal the intimate details of her life is, in some ways, almost a violation of her own privacy.[2] At times, we squirm as we read her words. Although it often makes readers uncomfortable, this use of the personal is central to Anzaldúa's power as a writer. By incorporating her life into her work, Anzaldúa transforms herself into a bridge and creates potential identifications with readers from diverse backgrounds. She models a process of self-disclosure that invites (and sometimes compels) us to take new risks as we reflect on our own experiences, penetrate the privacy of our own lives.

And still, I resist the personal.

So what should I say? Should I describe my first interview with Gloria back in 1991, when I was a new assistant professor and a great fan of her work, and tell you about my nervous excitement when I first met her? (I wish I could recapture in words my astonishment upon first meeting her: She looked so short! Her words are so powerful that I had expected a much taller person.) Should I discuss the interview process and describe how Gloria transformed the conventional question-and-answer format into a conversation between equals, a conversation that has continued (somewhat sporadically at times) during the past nine years? Should I tell you that I was struck by her openness, her vulnerability, and her willingness to discuss her ideas at length—often veering off into insightful tangents that touch on current writing projects and national/international events? Should I describe the setting of our recent interview—Gloria's house filled with paintings of beautiful brown women, images of la Virgen de Guadalupe, and the little altars in her bathroom, her bedroom, and her study? In a sense, I *am* telling you these "personal" things as I ask my rhetorical questions, and I'm tempted to leave it at this, to return to my original plan and complete my formal introduction.

I am a product of the U.S. university system. I have learned to mask my own agenda—my own desires for social justice, spiritual transformation, and cultural change—in academic language. I use theory as a vehicle for extending the personal outward and making new connections among apparently divergent perspectives. Because it seems to hide private feelings, desires, and deeply held beliefs behind rational, objective discourse and abstract thought, theory can be more persuasive for some readers. As you'll see in the following pages (if you choose to read them, that is), while I've partially unmasked myself— let the mask slip, as it were—I cannot entirely remove it. I now replace my mask, a mask which doesn't fit quite as well as it did before I wrote the words you've just read.

> It's so rare that we listen to each other. The interviewee and the interviewer are sort of a captive audience to each other. I like to do one-on-one talks because I discover things about myself, I make new connections between ideas just like I do in my writing. Interviews are part of communicating, which is part of writing, which is part of life. So I like to do them.
>
> —Gloria E. Anzaldúa

> When I'm speaking it's kind of like I'm writing in process, orally, so that I have to expose myself.
>
> —Gloria E. Anzaldúa

The above quotes illustrate Gloria Anzaldúa's perspective on interviews, an intimate genre she clearly enjoys. In the past twenty years she has given well over one hundred interviews to a wide variety of people, including friends, undergraduate and graduate students, university professors, community activists, and others. She has granted interviews over the telephone, on the radio, at her home, in hotel rooms, in airport terminals, and during speaking engagements on university campuses across the country. In each instance, she made it clear to the interviewer that at some point she wanted to collect the interviews and publish them in a volume. (In fact, it was her comment to me back in 1991 when I first interviewed her that led me to call her last summer and ask her if she'd like me to edit an interview volume with/for her.)

3

For Anzaldúa interviews are another dimension of writing—oral writing, as it were. But because interviews occur within a specific time frame and consist almost, if not entirely, of dialogue and conversation, they have an immediacy rarely found in written work and a potential openness and self-exposure that perhaps even exceeds the openness Anzaldúa strives for in her publications. There's no chance to call back the words that reveal too much or seem poorly spoken. This spontaneity gives readers unique insights into Gloria's published words and an intimate picture of the ways her mind works. And because Anzaldúa meticulously revises each piece many times and refuses to rush her words into publication, the interviews collected in this volume provide readers with new information concerning her most recent theories and her numerous works in progress.

Spanning two decades, these interviews allow readers to follow the development of Anzaldúa's writing career from the publication of *This Bridge Called My Back: Writings by Radical Women of Color* to *Borderlands/La Frontera: The New Mestiza*, to *Making Face, Making Soul/Haciendo Caras*, *Friends from the Other Side/Amigos del otro lado*, *Prietita and the Ghost Woman/Prietita y la Llorona*, and beyond. Anzaldúa provides extensive discussions of her motivations for writing and anthologizing and gives us additional details about her writing process and her goals as a writer. In the interviews from the 1980s, you'll find early formulations of ideas like *la facultad*; *mita y mita*; "Tlapalli, the black and red ink" as the path of writing; lesbians' and gays' roles as mediators; and *making face, making soul*—ideas that later appeared in print. In the interviews from the 1990s, you'll read about Anzaldúa's most recent concepts and her works in progress, which include a collection of short stories, a novel-in-stories, a writing manual, a book on theories and writing, a book of daily meditations, and a novel for young adults.

Readers unfamiliar with Anzaldúa's work will find useful summaries of her perspectives on *This Bridge*, *Borderlands*, and *Haciendo Caras*. Readers familiar with Gloria's writings will find new information as well, for the interviews contain insightful discussions of a number of issues and theories that Anzaldúa has not yet put forth in published form, including her theory of *convergence* as a method of writing in which "the sexual, the mental, the emotional, the psychic, [and] the supernatural" converge, creating another form of stream-of-consciousness writing that expands previous definitions; her concept of *culture karma*; her beliefs concerning the fluidity of sexual identities and desires; her theory of the *yoga of the body*; her discussions of

4

multiple, interlocking, and overlapping realities; her concept of a *geography of selves*; her theory of *nos/otras*; and her responses to the reception of *This Bridge* and *Borderlands*.

The interviews also contain discussions of ideas and themes Anzaldúa has only briefly touched upon in her publications. In a number of the more recent interviews, Anzaldúa explores the intersections between postcolonial theory and her work; describes what she calls *conocimientos*, or alternate ways of knowing that synthesize reflection with action to create subversive knowledge systems that challenge the status quo; and explains her use of the term *New Tribalism* as a disruptive category that redefines previous ethnocentric forms of nationalism. Significantly, Anzaldúa does not reject ethnic-specific identities but instead expands them outward, to acknowledge the various forms of cultural fluidity and *mestizaje* we experience today.

In several recent interviews Anzaldúa presents her concept of *nepantla* as both an expansion and a revision of her well-known concept of the *Borderlands*. I find her discussions of nepantla especially exciting, for they enable Gloria to underscore the psychic, spiritual, trans-formational dimensions implicit in her earlier theory of the Borderlands. As she asserts in the 1991 interview with me, "There's more of a . . . spiritual, psychic, supernatural, and indigenous connection to Borderlands by using the word nepantla." For Anzaldúa, nepantla has multiple meanings that overlap and enrich each other. Nepantla represents liminal spaces, transitional periods in identity formation, or what she describes in the interview with Debbie Blake and Carmen Abrego as a "birthing stage where you feel like you're reconfiguring your identity and don't know where you are." This in-between space facilitates transformation; as the boundaries break down, the identity categories that before were so comfortable—so natural, as it were— no longer work; they dissolve, compelling us to find new ways to define ourselves. Nepantla also functions as a metaphor for forbidden knowledges, new perspectives on reality, alternate ways of thinking, or what Gloria describes in the interview with Andrea Lunsford as the "liminal state between worlds, between realities, between systems of knowledge." These discussions of nepantla, conocimientos, and New Tribalism illustrate the exciting developments in Anzaldúa's thought since the publication of *Borderlands* (1987) and *Haciendo Caras* (1990).

Not surprisingly, given Anzaldúa's well-known emphasis on the personal, the interviews are also extremely autobiographical. No matter what Gloria discusses—whether it's ethnicity, sexuality, politics, reading, writing, or spirituality—she anchors her perspectives in her

5

own body and life. While readers might be familiar with some of this autobiographical information, Anzaldúa offers new details—such as her early sexual experiences and later sexual attractions, the development of her spirituality, her role in Cherríe Moraga's coming-to-Chicana-consciousness, and the impact diabetes has had upon her life—that will expand and revise previous interpretations of her work. Through reading these interviews, readers will also gain important insights into aspects of Gloria's personality—her intense vulnerability, her openness to other people's pains and perspectives, her desire for social justice, her interest in creating new forms of connection among apparently distinct peoples, and her optimism.

Some of this new information might be rather shocking and will invite readers to reevaluate previous conceptions of Anzaldúa and her works. I must admit that when I first read Anzaldúa's comments to Christine Weiland concerning her sexual fantasies—especially her "intense sexuality" toward her father—I was astonished. "Damn!" I said to Jesse (one of my favorite intellectual compadres):

> What will people say if they read this interview? Gloria talks at length and in positive terms about erotic fantasies involving herself and her father. Surely her feminist values will come under suspicion and perhaps even attack. This is—I hate the term, but—it's so politically incorrect! And then there's the matter of sexuality. You know she identifies herself and is categorized as lesbian/dyke/queer, but if people read this material they will have to question their interpretations of these labels. In some of these interviews she talks about her relationships with and attractions to *men* as well as her attractions to women— and to animals and even to trees. Anzaldúa's perspective is definitely polysexual. And the *drugs!* What will people think when they read about the role drugs played in her life? Yes, I know that Gloria has never been one to follow external standards—whether imposed by the Catholic Church, by Chicano culture, by feminism, or by lesbianism. But this might be too much!

As always, Jesse offered sound advice: "Well, why not ask her how *she* feels about including these things?"

And so, I picked up the telephone and called Anzaldúa to make sure that she really wanted this material included in the book: "Hola. Gloria. Listen, you talk about some pretty radical stuff in these interviews: your erotic fantasies about your father, doing drugs, your attractions to and experiences with men. People might react negatively and surely they'll have to rethink their conceptions of 'Gloria Anzaldúa.' Are you *sure* you want me to keep these things in the book?"

The response was typical Gloria: "Yes. I think so. If I've exposed it to myself, I can expose it in the writing. Self-exposure is the hard part." (I'm paraphrasing, of course, but this was the gist of our conversation, and you'll find a similar attitude expressed in some of the interviews.) Because some of Anzaldúa's comments are so very startling, I felt it necessary to be absolutely certain that she was willing to risk such self-exposure. So I sent her copies of what I considered to be the most potentially explosive statements. Again, she told me to go ahead and keep this material in the book. I'm pleased that Gloria has agreed to include her provocative statements, and I'm eager to see readers' reactions to her words. Tell me, reader: Will you revise your conception of Gloria Anzaldúa, the Chicana dyke, or will you skip over the conversations that challenge your views of Anzaldúa and her words?

These interviews also provide Anzaldúa with opportunities to clarify her positions and "talk back" to the critics who have tried to define her and classify her works. In several interviews she insists on a broader definition of her concept of the Borderlands than those suggested by some scholars, who focus primarily on the geographic, ethnic-specific dimensions of the term. In other interviews she intervenes in debates concerning essentialism and social constructionism by elaborating on her statement in *Borderlands* that she "made the choice to be lesbian." In the conversation with Jeffner Allen, she takes issue with scholars who have focused too closely on a single aspect of *Borderlands*, thereby enacting a form of "character assassination" that diminishes the text. She also worries that the spiritual components might turn off some readers. As she explains in a 1993 interview, scholars have ignored the more dangerous, metaphysical dimensions of her work:

> The "safe" elements in *Borderlands* are appropriated and used, and the "unsafe" elements are ignored. One of the things that doesn't get talked about is the connection between body, mind, and spirit. Nor is anything that has to do with the sacred, anything that has to do with the spirit. As long as it's theoretical and about history, about borders, that's fine; borders are a concern that everybody has. But when I start talking about nepantla—as a border between the spirit, the psyche, and the mind or as a process—they resist.[3]

This resistance to the spiritual components of Anzaldúa's work occurs for at least two reasons. First, "spirituality" and "spirit" are slippery terms that defy logical explanation. As Dona Richards explains, "Spirit is, of course, not a rationalistic concept. It cannot be quantified, measured, explained by or reduced to neat, rational, conceptual categories as Western thought demands. . . . We experience our spirituality often, but the translation of that experience into an intellectual language can never be accurate. The attempt results in reductionism."[4] I am fully aware of the irony here: in the following pages, I will attempt to explain a nonrational concept in at least partially rational terms. However, I see no alternative. Gloria's insistence on the spiritual—reaffirmed in almost every interview—is one of the most striking characteristics of this collection. These interviews demonstrate that Anzaldúa's spiritual vision is central to her lifework and cannot be ignored. Indeed, I would argue that Anzaldúa's long-standing belief in the interconnections among body, mind, and spirit is a key component in the theories for which she is best known.

Scholars' reluctance to examine the spiritually inflected dimensions of Anzaldúa's work occurs for another reason as well: Because the spiritual is so often assumed to refer only to the nonmaterial dimensions of life, spirituality can easily be conflated with religion and dismissed as an apolitical, ahistorical form of escapism that inadvertently reinforces the status quo. At times, in fact, the interviews collected in this volume might seem to confirm the belief that spirituality is another form of escapism: Anzaldúa's conversations often take on a distinctly "New-Ageish" tone, with talk of near-death experiences, meditations, astrological signs, spirits, and extraterrestrial beings. But, for Anzaldúa, the metaphysical components of life are never divorced from politics, sexuality, writing, and daily living. Unlike those people generally labeled "New Age," who use their metaphysical beliefs to focus almost exclusively on personal desires and goals, Gloria anchors her metaphysics in her deeply held desire for personal, social, and global transformation.

For Anzaldúa, spirituality is a highly political, always embodied endeavor that has nothing in common with conventional forms of religion. Both in her published writings and in several of these interviews, she rejects organized religions as highly divisive systems filled with restrictive categories and rules that separate people from each other and from themselves. In the interview with Weiland, for example, she asserts, "The spirit evolves out of the experiences of the body. . . . Spirituality has nothing to do with religion, which recognizes that spirit and then puts a dogma around it. . . . Religion eliminates all kinds of growth, development, and change, and that's why I think any kind of formalized religion is really bad." Not surprisingly, given this belief that the spiritual simultaneously evolves from and is one with the body, Anzaldúa especially takes issue with conventional religions' rejection of the (female) body. As she explains in the interview with Linda Smuckler, it was this rejection of the physical, coupled with her own very early, extremely painful menstruation, that led her to disassociate herself from her own body and view it as other. Only when she recognized that "[m]atter is divine," that the spirit so often identified exclusively with the nonmaterial disembodied dimensions of life is itself a vital part of the material world, could she accept this alien other as a part of herself. She explains that she experienced "a type of conversion" during her hysterectomy, when she realized that the body itself is divine. This insight transformed her: "When I found myself, it was the beginning of my spirituality, because it was like getting in contact with who I really was, my true self. My body wasn't dirty." Clearly, for Anzaldúa spirituality begins with and is rooted in the body.

Anzaldúa's spiritual theory and praxis is based on a metaphysics of interconnectedness that posits a cosmic, constantly changing spirit or force that embodies itself in material and nonmaterial forms. As she explains in an interview with Kim Irving, "Everything has a meaning. Everything is interconnected. To me, spirituality and being spiritual means to be aware of the interconnections between things."[5] Similarly, in the interview with Weiland she states, "Spirit exists in everything; therefore God, the divine, is in everything—in blacks as well as whites, rapists as well as victims; it's in the tree, the swamp, the sea. . . . Some people call it 'God'; some call it the 'creative force,' whatever. It's in everything."

Whether this spiritual-material essence "really" exists—and how could we possibly prove its existence except, perhaps, by referring to David Boehm or a few other twentieth-century physicists—is far less important for us here than the pragmatic, performative functions it serves in Anzaldúa's lifework. On the collective level, Anzaldúa's belief in a divine cosmic force infusing all that exists enables her to create a new identity category and a theoretical moral framework for social change. By positing a universal commonality she can insist that—despite the many differences among us—human beings are all interconnected. As she explains in her 1991 interview with me, she believes that we are *almas afines,* or "kindred spirits," and share an interconnectedness that could serve as "an unvoiced category of identity, a common factor

9

in all life forms." This recognition leads to an ethics of reciprocity. As Anzaldúa states in the interview with Weiland:

> I'm a citizen of the universe. I think it's good to claim your ethnic identity and your racial identity. But it's also the source of all the wars and all the violence, all these borders and walls people erect. I'm tired of borders and I'm tired of walls. I don't believe in the nationalism. I don't believe that we're better than people in India or that we're different from people in Ethiopia. . . . [P]eople talk about being proud to be American, Mexican, or Indian. We have grown beyond that. We are specks from this cosmic ocean, the soul, or whatever. We're not better than people from Africa or people from Russia. If something happens to the people in India or Africa—and they're starving to death and dying—then that's happening to us, too.

On the personal level, Gloria's belief in an underlying constantly changing cosmic energy allowed her to develop a highly positive self-image that affirms her personal agency. Ana Castillo makes a similar point in her discussion of what she calls "espiritismo." According to Castillo, the

> acknowledgment of the energy that exists throughout the universe subatomically generating itself and interconnecting, fusing, and changing . . . offer[s] a personal response to the divided state of the individual who desires wholeness. An individual who does not sense herself as helpless to circumstances is more apt to contribute positively to her environment than one who resigns with apathy to it because of her sense of individual insignificance.[6]

I want to emphasize the pragmatic dimensions of this spiritualized worldview. Anzaldúa's increased sense of personal agency empowered her to resist the various forms of oppression she experienced both from the dominant culture and from her own culture. As she explains in her conversation with Weiland:

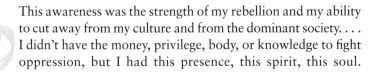

> This awareness was the strength of my rebellion and my ability to cut away from my culture and from the dominant society. . . . I didn't have the money, privilege, body, or knowledge to fight oppression, but I had this presence, this spirit, this soul.

> Spirituality—through ritual, meditation, affirmation, and strengthening myself—was the only way I could fight the oppression. Spirituality is oppressed people's only weapon and means of protection. Changes in society only come after the spiritual.

But what does it mean to describe spirituality as a "weapon" capable of effecting social change? What forms does this spiritual weapon take? Do we simply meditate our way into a better world, a world in which social justice has—somehow—been achieved? As later interviews reveal, Gloria does not believe that ritual, meditation, and affirmation *in themselves* bring about collective transformation. They are simply the first steps, steps which give her the vision, the desire, and the energy to work actively for social change.

More specifically, Anzaldúa embodies her spiritual vision and the metaphysics of interconnectedness upon which it relies in her writing. She offers an alternate mode of perception, a holistic way of viewing ourselves and our world that empowers individuals to work for psychic and material change on both the personal and the collective levels. As she asserts in the interview with Jamie Lee Evans, "Writing is a form of activism, one of making bridges." Anzaldúa makes a similar point in the interview with Debbie Blake and Carmen Abrego. After drawing an analogy between contemporary women and the Aztec mythic story of Coatlicue's daughter Coyolxauhqui, who represented such a threat to Huitzilopochtli (one of her four hundred brothers) that he cut off her head, chopped up her body, and buried the pieces in different places, she explains:

> [T]o me [Coyolxauhqui's story] is a symbol not only of violence and hatred of women but also of how we're split body and mind, spirit and soul. We're separated. . . . [W]hen you take a person and divide her up, you disempower her. She's no longer a threat. My whole struggle in writing, in this anticolonial struggle, has been to . . . put us back together again. To connect up the body with the soul and the mind with the spirit. That's why for me there's such a link between the text and the body, between textuality and sexuality, between the body and the spirit.

As this statement indicates, Anzaldúa views writing as a form of activism, an effective tool to bring about material-spiritual change. She is a modern-day Coyolxauhqui, a writer-warrior who employs language to "put us back together again." Because she believes that "[m]yths and fictions create reality," she seizes the existing myths—the stories that disempower us—and rewrites them, embodying her spiritual vision—her desire for social justice—in her words. Her writing invites us to see ourselves differently, to recognize the connections between body and text, between the intellectual, spiritual, and physical dimensions of life, between self and other. This recognition can transform us and motivate us to work actively for social change.

In many ways Anzaldúa's spirituality and the ethics of inter-connectedness it entails resembles the "visionary pragmatism" and the "passionate rationality" Patricia Hill Collins associates with African-American women's spirituality. As Collins explains, in their quest for social justice many black women have developed moral frameworks and spiritual worldviews that combine "caring, theoretical vision with informed, practical struggle."[7] Their desire to achieve social justice is infused with deep feeling, or what Collins describes as "passionate rationality," which motivates them and others to work together for social change. According to Collins, "This type of passionate rational-ity flies in the face of Western epistemology that sees emotions and rationality as different and competing concerns. . . . [D]eep feelings that arouse people to action constitute a critical source of power."[8] Like the African-American women Collins describes, Anzaldúa attempts to gen-erate this passionate rationality in her readers.

Given Anzaldúa's growing importance as a contemporary thinker and cultural theorist, I find her emphasis on this passionate rationality, or what she sometimes describes as "spiritual activism," especially exciting. This past year, when I was on the job market, a number of schools told me that applicants for positions in women's studies, American studies, and multicultural U.S. literature referred to Anzaldúa more frequently than to any other theorist. And two days ago a friend sent me an e-mail informing me that, at a conference she had recently attended, *Borderlands* was repeatedly cited as "*the* text of third-wave feminism." It is my hope that at least some of the many scholars who read Anzaldúa's words will adopt this passionate rationality as their own. Talk about transformation!

This almost finished product seems an assemblage, a montage, a beaded work with several different leitmotifs and with a central core, now appearing, now disappearing in a crazy dance. The whole thing has a mind of its own, escaping me and insisting on putting together the pieces of its own puzzle with minimal direction from my will. It is a rebellious, willful entity, a precocious girl-child forced to grow up too quickly, rough, unyielding, with pieces of feather sticking out here and there, fur, twigs, clay. My child, but not for much longer.

—Gloria E. Anzaldúa

I borrow the above statement from Gloria's description of *Borderlands*. To be sure, I cannot claim that *Interviews/Entrevistas* is my own precocious girl-child—since most of the words are Anzaldúa's, not mine. Despite this major difference, however, I see many similarities between Anzaldúa's perspective on *Borderlands* and my own feelings toward *Interviews/Entrevistas*. Like Anzaldúa's text, this collection of interviews is a "montage," a "crazy dance" around a number of recurring themes. And like Anzaldúa, I do not feel that I'm in control of this crazy dance. This collection has a life of its own, a life that will change—shift shapes, as it were—with each new reading.

But before I let *Interviews/Entrevistas* go, I'll attempt to tie up a few loose ends by telling you a little something about the process of editing this collection. While a few of these interviews have been previously published, in each instance I went back to the original transcript and incorporated material omitted from the published versions. Generally, this new material concerned issues related to Anzaldúa's spiritual-imaginal vision. Its inclusion here adds an important dimension to the published versions and provides a more complex view of Anzaldúa and her works.

My goal as an editor was to make the interviews compelling and readable—to make them flow—while remaining true to the spoken word, to the oral rhythms, and (of course) to the original meaning. To achieve this goal, I broke several grammatical rules and tried to punctuate the dialogues in ways that replicate how we speak. I also tried to avoid excessive repetition. Almost all of the interviews began with questions about Anzaldúa's life—her childhood, adolescence, and family background. Although the words vary, Anzaldúa's responses generally follow the same format. I have cut some (but not all) of this repetition out. These deletions were made at the suggestion of Anzaldúa herself who took time out of her busy schedule to read and comment at length on the entire manuscript.

I have organized these interviews into a format that in some ways mimics Anzaldúa's own defiance of rigid boundaries. The interviews are arranged in chronological order, beginning with the earliest and ending with an interview between Gloria and myself that summarizes and expands on the earlier interviews. But threaded through this chronological organization are portions of a 1998–1999 interview I conducted with her: At the beginning of each interview I've included questions that allow Anzaldúa to return to and elaborate on the issues raised in the interview itself. This arrangement serves several purposes. First, it connects the present with the past, enabling readers to see the changes in Anzaldúa's ideas and life; second, it offers readers a preview of the upcoming interview; third, it allows Gloria to explain herself more fully; fourth, it answers questions readers might have as they read the interviews; and fifth, it breaks down the boundaries between the interviews themselves. Readers interested in tracing the development of key ideas like the Borderlands, mestizaje, nepantla, conocimientos, or nos/otras can read selectively by utilizing the subheadings and the extensive index.

I hope you will enjoy reading this collection and learn as much as I have.

Notes

1. Throughout this introduction I shift between "Gloria" and "Anzaldúa" when referring to Gloria/Anzaldúa. I recognize the danger in referring to women authors by their first names, and I worry that referring to Anzaldúa simply as "Gloria" might seem like name-dropping—another form of showing off. But despite these reservations and in keeping with my decision to risk the personal, I've decided that shifting between "Gloria" and "Anzaldúa" replicates the ways my own mind works.

2. My thanks to Randall Robbins for allowing me to include this insight.

3. "Working the Borderlands, Becoming Mestiza: An Interview with Gloria Anzaldúa," conducted by K. Urch, M. Dorn, and J. Abraham, *disClosure* 4 (1995): 75–96, 85. Quoted from transcript. See also Marcus Emberly's assertion, "[A]nother accusation leveled at [*Borderlands/La Frontera*] is that it is full of 'New Age'-type passages, although these charges are the quietest and most pernicious, because they directly contradict the idiosyncrasies of the text that have been so widely celebrated" (89). In "Cholo Angels in Guadalajara: The Politics and Poetics of Anzaldúa's *Borderlands/La Frontera*," *Women and Performance: A Journal of Feminist Theory* 8 (1996): 87–108.

4. "The Implications of African-American Spirituality," in *African Culture: The Rhythms of Unity*, ed. Molefi Kete Asante and Kariamu Welsh Asante (Trenton, N.J.: Africa World Press, 1993), 207–31. Quoted in Patricia Hill Collins, *Fighting Words: Black Women and the Search for*

Justice (Minneapolis: University of Minnesota Press, 1998), 245. Collins makes a similar point, noting, "Thus, spirituality not merely a system of religious beliefs similar to logical systems of ideas. Rather, spirituality comprises articles of faith that provide a conceptual framework for living everyday life" (245).

5. Due to space limitations, we were unable to include this unpublished interview in the volume.

6. Ana Castillo, *Massacre of the Dreamers: Essays on Xicanisma* (Albuquerque: University of New Mexico Press, 1994), 159.

7. Collins, *Fighting Words*, 188.

8. Ibid., 243.

1

Turning Points

An Interview with Linda Smuckler (1982)

(1988–1999)

ALK: You talk about some pretty wild stuff in this interview and even more extensively in the following interview with Christine Weiland—an "extra-terrestrial spirit," different spirits entering your body, past-life regression, reincarnation, psychic readers, and more. How do you feel about these ideas being out there, in print?

GEA: I think it's about time for these ideas to be in print. I went to psychic readers and workshops in psychic development right after one of my near-death experiences, and these saved my life. It really helped me get in touch with who I was and what I wanted to do. I'm happy it's going to be in my interview book. People should know about this aspect of me and my life.

ALK: Don't you think it's going to make you less respectable and less reputable—because a lot of scholars don't believe in such things?

GEA: Tough shit! Once I get past my own censorship of what I should write about, I don't care what other people say. Some things were hard for me to reveal but my strong vocation for writing makes me more open. To be a writer means to communicate, to tell stories that other people haven't told, to describe experiences that people normally don't find in books (or at least in mainstream books).

ALK: This is just a different kind of risk-taking?

GEA: Yes. As you said, I'll be ridiculed and some academics will lose their respect for my work. A small number—one-half of one percent—will applaud me for talking about these things. Scholars connected to universities—what I call the "dependent scholars," dependent on their discipline and their school in order to survive—will object to this material, while independent scholars like myself who aren't tied up to any institution will applaud my discussions of spiritual realities, imaginal realities, and the inner subjective life.

The scientific story—which has no way of measuring subjectivity—is losing validity. It has created an industrial consumer society that's exploited the environment and put us in this crisis situation where we're running out of resources. Many people live by the paradigm that progress means to produce and therefore consume more, so we're in this race to consume and expand, to grow and to control the environment. As everyone knows, it's not working. Science has to change its story: it must accept information that goes beyond the five senses. So right away you get into subjectivity, the inner life, thoughts, and feelings. You get into intuition, which is a very maligned sense; in fact, people don't even think of it as a sense.

ALK: Are you saying that some of your statements—which might strike readers as "way out there"—are actually alternate ways of knowing that you've accessed, ways of knowing which have enriched your writing and which provide alternatives for all of us to think about?

GEA: Right, and I think these ideas will find legitimacy after the turn of the century. But there's a lot of resistance when people are changing the way they perceive reality, the way they look at relationships and their environment. People want the old familiar ways. Traditional science has such a grip on us, it's become the *only* way to describe reality. Every other way has been trivialized. I talk about this in *Borderlands*, where if you believe in some of these other ways you're labeled superstitious. Once the century turns, more people will believe in the existence of something greater than the physical world. If you think of reality as a continuum or a spectrum, the reality we see with our eyes, hear with our ears, smell with our nose, and touch with our fingers—that spectrum is a skinny little territory. Parts of a person are unknown to that person or to the culture but are known through dreams, imagination, spiritual experiences, or intuitive feelings. If science is going to continue as the reigning paradigm, it will have to change its story, change the way it controls reality, and begin acknowledging the paranormal, intuition, and subjective inner life. A few physicists, like Fred Allen Wolfe, have already begun this exploration. The ideas I talk about and am currently writing about will probably be frowned upon during the next couple of decades, but if my writing lasts, it will eventually be respected.

ALK: May your words be prophetic. In this interview you associate your early menstruation with your theory concerning your four death experiences, when different spirits entered your body each time you died. Do you still hold this theory or has your perspective changed, and if so, how?

GEA: I still hold this theory. I checked it out with a Russian psychic reader in San Francisco and with Luisah Teish, and they both agreed with my theory. Luisah Teish did a pretty detailed reading for me (she told me my mothers are Yemanja and Oya). Aurora Levins Morales also did a very good reading; she went into a trance and told me some things I'd been thinking about: that I felt scattered and needed to put myself together again, very much like my reading of Coyolxauhqui. I felt a calling to be an artist in the sense of a shaman—healing through words, using words as a medium for expressing the flights of the soul, communing with the spirit, having access to these other realities or worlds. At that time I felt pulled away from my calling as a writer because so many people around me needed some kind of healing. (People saw me as a healer; one person even said, "¡Tú eres una curandera!") I was doing tarot and psychic readings for other people, and it was taking up a lot of my energy. I thought, "Do I want to be a healer or do I want to heal through other means?" I backed away from those other types of healing and concentrated more on the writing. When Aurora Levins Morales did her reading, I was at that juncture, at that turning point, where I needed to rededicate myself to being an artist, a writer.

I have a piece called "Resisting the Spirit," based on an out-of-body experience I had in Austin. Like a lot of other people at that time I was experimenting with drugs, but I was using them to gain access to other realities. One night I mixed alcohol with percada, a downer, and my body had a reaction. I thought I was dying. My soul left my body. This story may or may not go into *La Prieta, The Dark One*. Some editors and publishers may censor the drug stuff because drugs have become a major addiction in our society.

As to my bleeding at the age of three months—doctors could never figure it out; it's a very rare hormonal disturbance or dysfunction. As far as I know only two people—including myself—have ever been diagnosed with it. Dysfunction is not due to the physiology of the body alone, other things impact on it. In my case some other entity or spirit had entered my body. This spirit was not used to incarnating in human bodies. (I do believe that we incarnate into different bodies, different races, different genders. Most of the souls in people originated from and have lived on the earth, but other souls or spirits come from *beyond* the earth). I got this idea early on but I couldn't make sense of it and thought, "Gloria you're going crazy, entertaining such ideas." When I talked about it to people they looked at me like I *was* crazy. But as I grew older I began exploring it—through psychic readers, books, meditation—and following my intuition. I realized that it didn't really matter whether an extraterrestrial spirit had actually entered my body or I had made it up. Human beings' whole struggle is to give meaning to their experience, to their condition, and this was my way of giving meaning to my early bleeding. People shape their experience, that's how reality is created. There's no such thing as objective truth. It's similar to how I create a story or a poem. The universe is created jointly by all the human minds and the universal intelligence in the trees, the deer, the snakes, and so on. By jointly, I mean all forms of consciousness, not just human. Even the rocks have a certain kind of consciousness, the trees, everything. I see the world as a text created by this collective consciousness.

ALK: You make a very provocative comment in this interview when you claim that "there are a lot of Indian souls inhabiting white bodies." This statement is very antiessentialist (or perhaps essentialism done differently, taken into the spiritual). Do you still believe this, and if so could you explain in greater detail what you mean? Your statement could be seen as a different form of appropriation, because there are so many New Age people who claim to be Indian.

GEA: This belief is similar to my idea that the universe is a text. An individual is multiple and has multiple personalities and multiple little selves, along with the big self. I'm an individual but because I inhabit many worlds I can go from being at my mom's little pueblito to an academic classroom to a lesbian musical event to a writer's conference, and in each instance I can experience what the other people present are experiencing.

ALK: I'm not sure I see the connection between these examples, where you as an embodied individual move from one location to another, and your statement about "Indian souls" inhabiting white bodies.

GEA: It's the same movement but instead of a concrete physical movement it's the movement of the soul. The soul has little souls, just like the self has little selves, and these little souls can manifest in people who are white, black, men, women . . .

ALK: So you don't really mean "Indian" souls. You mean souls which were in "Indian" bodies, now occupying "white" bodies. The souls themselves don't have any kind of ethnic marker like "Indian" or "white."

GEA: Right. I also believe we bring knowledge from previous existences with us each time we're born. You're not born as a blank slate; something from your previous lives bleeds through. If you're incarnated as a black person for many, many times, when you become Russian or European, or Japanese, it kind of leaves a little trail.

ALK: It's a form of growth?

GEA: Right! If I look at my experience with you and say, "Oh, she's so typically Chinese," or "Oh, she's so typically Indian," it just means that behind that soul is the other. Does that make sense to you?

ALK: Yes! It makes a lot more sense than the way you said it in the interview. In this early interview you discuss creating a "writing of convergence"—the coming together of "[t]he sexual, the mental, the emotional, the psychic, the supernatural." That's almost twenty years ago! Have you developed this theory and style of writing, abandoned it, changed it?

GEA: I've developed it in personal essay form and fiction. It's integral to my teaching, my guided meditations, and my writing exercises. I believe that we're very complex beings. We can't just divide the mind from the body in sexuality, or creativity and rationality from intuition. One of the tasks I've chosen is to blur these boundaries. I try to do this with some of the *Prieta* stories where one reality bleeds into another, where fiction bleeds into concrete reality with dreams and visions, and the energy from sexuality is very much a part of mental thought and feelings. It's not so much that I've written down the ideas rationally or concretely or theoretically, it's more like I'm fooling around with stories and the impact the stories have on the reader. It's very hard to paraphrase a story because when you read it and you're experiencing the characters' emotions—whether it's elation, anger, or fear—your body is experiencing an emotional and psychic process. At the end of the story, you can't sit down and say, "This is what the story really means" because it impacts on your unconscious in a way that you can't articulate in your conscious mind. It's very hard to get these ideas across fiction-wise; it's much easier to explain rationally. But fiction has a greater impact on the whole psyche than theory does.

"Turning Points"
An Interview with Linda Smuckler (1982)

Early Writing Experiences

LS: I'd like to start by asking you to discuss your writing experiences as a child. What do you remember—any beginning stories of when you wrote?

GEA: I grew up listening to both my grandmothers tell stories about the old days. All the members of my family were storytellers. Most Chicanos are storytellers, especially those who haven't had much schooling. They pass on their stories orally. I was the only one who really listened to my grandmothers and took everything in. But what made me decide to tell stories was that I wanted to be an artist. I thought that I was going to be either a writer or an artist, but first a visual artist. I started with sketching, especially—I loved horses. (Since then, I've come to realize that horses are symbols of the primal instincts—sexuality and desire.) I'd go up to the horse, look at it, stroke it, and make up stories about it. The first book I read about a horse was *Black Beauty*. Then I read *Call of the Wild*, and I'd make up stories about dogs. Having decided I was going to be a visual artist, I became attentive to light, movement, shadow, and shapes, and I'd try to recreate them.

When I was a child I told my sister stories as a bribe. At a very early age I started reading. I loved to read. But there was so much work to do on the farm that I didn't have time during the day. At night, when everybody was asleep, I'd read with a flashlight under the covers. My sister would threaten to tell my mother unless I'd tell her a story. After a while, she wanted two stories. In the middle of the night—one, two, three o'clock—I'd be telling her these stories. I got to the point where

I'd build up to a climax and stop until the next night and leave her hanging. I'd do an episode a day.

LS: Did you tell your family you were going to be an artist? Did you talk to them about it?

GEA: Yes. I think my father approved, but my mother wanted me to do practical things. See, no one in my family had ever been to high school much less college. My father got as far as the sixth grade, and my mother the eighth. And this was a little primitive ranchito. The first seven years of my life I lived in a tiny ranch settlement or ranchito in two different adjoining ranches: Jesús María Ranch and los Verjeles, in houses with no electricity or running water. Los Verjeles translates into "the gardens." I grew up with the land, animals, woods, and coyotes. I was a strange kid. When we moved into town, I realized I was even more different. I'd started bleeding at three months old, menstruating at the age of three months.

LS: I read that in the *Conditions* story; it was amazing.

GEA: Being different was really right for being an artist or writer because you start dealing with all the other levels of reality besides the physical, concrete level. To protect myself I had to invent this whole new world, the world of symbols and the imagination.

I did a lot of things with my hands. I got into leathercraft. I'd make my sketches and put them on the leather. I made a belt once that had a jungle scene: elephants, tigers, giraffes, and trees. At the same time, I'd be making up little stories in my head; sometimes I'd tell them to my sister. I connected the visual with the word.

LS: How did you get from the story in your head to the paper?

GEA: During my first eight years of school, there were no Anglos; they were shipped to another school. When I got to high school I took a placement test and placed very high. So I was the only Chicana in all my classes except P.E., health, homeroom, and study hall. That segregation, even more, cut me away from friends because the white kids didn't want anything to do with me and the teachers weren't used to having such a bright Chicana. To keep from being bored I'd have the textbook open, but hidden under it I'd be writing in my journal. I'd make up ideas about stories and plot them.

I started writing short stories in 1974, in Indiana. I had a really good writing teacher named Elaine Hemley. The first story I wrote was about a man who commits suicide: He has recurring images of Aztec sacrifices and is pulled back to what he called his "racial karma." He figures out a way to cut his heart out and flush it down the toilet while he's sitting on it. His name was Sabas Q. After that, the characters in my stories had last names like "Q" or "de la Cruz." The people in my fiction are related or are friends, though they're in different stories.

Elaine Hemley said, "I want you to start writing a novel." She gave me a lot of encouragement, and so did the people in the class. The novel I conceived was about Chicanos who were making their ancient Aztec and Mayan cultural roots come alive in a political, unifying way. Right now the Chicano communities are split because of regional differences: the Chicanos in California are different from the Chicanos in Texas, from East Chicago. I wanted a common denominator that all Chicanos could plug into. This commonality is our cultural roots—being mestizo, half white and half Indian, or whatever proportion. I wanted this novel to be about a modern-day group of Chicanos plugging into their roots. Halfway through planning the novel, the protagonist turned from male to female. In '75 I started writing it again and ended up with a first chapter with Andrea as the main character.

LS: Oh. So that's where Andrea came from.

GEA: Andrea really came from a novella I wrote for my Poetry of Decadence class. (Graduate courses required papers, but I always asked the professors, "Can I try to do this in a fictive mode?" I got away with it twice—in the Poetry of Decadence course and in my criticism class.) For the Poetry of Decadence class, I wrote a story about two Chicano maricones and Andrea. She was cousin to Joaquin, one of the main characters, and brother to Heche (He/she), the novella's protagonist. I put all the decadent elements I could into the story. This novella was the longest piece I'd written.

LS: Where did Zenobio come from? Is he a faggot?

GEA: Yes. He just came from that story. He's not a major character.

Grade School

LS: Let's back up to your grade school experiences. You spent your first eight years of school with Chicanos. What was that like? Were the teachers white? Did you get support for your writing?

GEA: Hargill [Texas] is just a little ranch town, part of the Edinburg

24

Independent School District. All the teachers were white, and except for two or three, we got the dregs. All the best teachers were at Edinburg, teaching the white kids. We didn't have any music or art; we just had writing, reading, and arithmetic. But even the basics weren't taught that well. What saved me was that I started reading very early; the first book I read was a western that my father bought—

LS: The twenty-five-cent pocket book, I remember.

GEA: Right. I'd read everything in the library. Everything: encyclopedias, dictionaries, Aesop's Fables, philosophy—I started reading all these heavy books. I literally went through all the shelves book by book.

LS: How did you feel reading these books? Did you feel any sense of identity? Did you know that your life wasn't in a lot of those books?

GEA: Oh yes. I also knew that in the westerns—and in some of the other books where they portrayed Indians and Mexicans—we were portrayed like animals; we weren't really humans. But I was also reading stuff from Europe and other races, which weren't as prejudiced against blacks and nonwhite cultures.

LS: Is there anything you read, besides all the racist shit, that stands out, that helped you get a perspective? Anything you remember that really affected you as a child, beside the twenty-five-cent books?

GEA: Some stuff about Eskimos struck me because the doctor had told my mother that I was a throwback to an Eskimo and that was why I was bleeding. So I kept reading about Eskimos. In the children's books, sometimes there would be a story about an Eskimo fishing for whale or whatever. Those stories were the only ones with positive Indian or dark-skinned people. One character I could identify with was *Jane Eyre*. She was short; she was little. She was stubborn and deviant. She was a governess—no parents, no money.

LS: Would you say that the origins of your spiritual involvement began during grade school, or was it even earlier?

GEA: My awareness of a spiritual dimension started when I began differentiating between who I was as a little kid and who my mother was, what the table was, what the wall was. When I was about three years old, I was sitting on the floor and above me, on the table, were some oranges I wanted but couldn't reach. I remember reaching for the oranges; I could feel my arms getting really long. I really wanted them, and suddenly there were three bodies, like I was three of me. (Like an ear of corn, which has all these coverings on it like sheaths: there was me and then from my center there were these three ears of corn and they were like my bodies, but they all came from one place.) I don't remember if I really got the oranges or not. Right after that experience I began to feel apart, separate from others. Before this point, I couldn't differentiate between myself and other things. I'd feel like I was part of the wall.

But as a little kid I was wide open—like a sponge; everything came in. I had no defenses, no way of keeping anything out, so I was constantly bombarded with everything. Once when I was in Prospect Park in Brooklyn for a picnic everyone was smoking cigarettes and putting them out in the grass. My whole body reacted: I could feel the pain of the grass. These people were turning their live cigarettes on it.

LS: Do you remember anyone in your family who was an ally or did you feel alone in this?

GEA: My brother Nune understood a little, but sometimes he used that understanding against me. I was most vulnerable to him because he was the one who got in the most and so could hurt me. (He still knows me pretty well.) But, no, I didn't feel that I had an ally. The land was my ally, but I also felt the dangers there. The physical and psychic energies there could also harm me. I'd hear people say that evil spirits, mal aigre, rode the wind, and that when a person got sick it was because the bad air had gotten in. When I grew up I scoffed at these ideas, but now that I'm older I know it's true. Bad vibrations come in the air; when someone is thinking bad about you—feeling envy, jealousy, or whatever and directing it at you—you get the evil eye; people really get sick. Mexicans heal the evil eye with an egg. We let the egg absorb the jealousy, envy, whatever emotion another person is directing at you. But I found that out later. You can be in a really horrible mood and I can be on top of the world and, if we're sitting here, after a while I start to absorb your stuff. Well, what happened with me was not only this type of one-to-one influence, but sometimes I'd feel depressed. I was grieving—not from anything that had to do with me or with anyone around me. I was grieving for the world. It was so strange.

LS: It also sounds as if you had a feeling of becoming one with everything happening around you. It sounds like this still happens to you now.

GEA: Yes, it comes and goes: at times, I feel a real unification with people, real identification with someone or something—like the grass. It's so painful that I have to cut the connection. But I can't cut the connection, so instead of putting a shield between myself and you and your pain, I put a wall inside, between myself and my feelings. For a long, long time I had a really hard time getting in touch with what I was feeling—especially around pain because I had very severe menstrual periods. Instead of walling people out, I'd censor my feelings within my body. So the origin of my belief that there's something greater than myself came both from that empathy and identification I had with things and from the isolation when I didn't have it. When I had too much identification, I couldn't process the feelings; it was too painful. I'd be sitting here feeling the subway, the birds, what you were feeling, the people below . . . I was like a tape recorder, picking up everything. You and I are listening to each other and you're focusing on what I'm saying and other sounds fade, but with me it was different; everything came in at the same volume.

LS: Did you go through a process of protecting yourself?

GEA: Yes. I needed a lot of time by myself. I was a very studious little kid and used books as my refuge, a little cave I could enter—a cave with a door through which I could go into other worlds. I also had my imagination. I'd make up stories at night for my sister, fantastic stories about the coyotes, this little girl named Prietita which was my nickname, dogs, and horses. I had those two retreats: the books and the knowledge. I could sit for hours and do all kinds of stuff. I could be the heroine. You know when you're a little kid, school is so unbearable; that's the only way I made it through school, by daydreaming and books. Under my English book, I'd be reading *Jane Eyre* or *Robinson Crusoe*.

High School

LS: So then you go to high school, and you get in the more advanced classes.

GEA: I wanted to be a doctor.

LS: So did I.

GEA: The counselor said no. It would be better to be a nurse because it took so many years of schooling to be a doctor—and this counselor was a woman! But I took physics, microbiology, chemistry, and other sciences. I'd always been a straight A student. I got to be valedictorian. I had trouble with P.E. and a little bit of trouble with arithmetic. I really concentrated on subjects I was weakest in—algebra, calculus, etc.

LS: What about English class? What do you remember?

GEA: I was in the "plus" section, the "genius" section. A few teachers made an impression on me. Mr. Dugan, who taught history, made an impression on me, so I started to read a lot of history and stuff. Mrs. Dugan, his wife, taught advanced English. I was the only Chicana in her class, and I was virtually ignored. She concentrated on all the other kids, so I didn't get very much help from her. We had a difficult book on how to improve your vocabulary. My first semester with her, I made a 70—which is like a C—almost failing. (I don't remember if it was the first semester or the first test. But anyway, it was a 70.) And I realized, "Shit. It's going to be harder for me to be the head of my class than before." They were all "brains"—these white kids who had privileges and stuff.

LS: How was your English?

GEA: I always spoke with an accent. I scored really high on the Iowa tests and the entrance and yearly exams. I always got better grades on those exams than I did on my report card. Every year I'd get a little statue for academic achievement. My mother still has them. School was easy for me. But I never did what they wanted me to do. The same thing happened in college. If I was interested in a particular thing, I'd concentrate on that and not worry about whether I should study for the trigonometry test or not.

LS: But you managed to do well anyway.

GEA: Yes. I did very well.

A Sense of Difference

LS: What about support for your interest in art? Did you take art classes in high school? Was it OK for you to do visual art? To do leather?

GEA: No. There was no art that I remember until I got to college. I did art on my own. My mother didn't want me to do it, 'cause it took me away from household chores. No one wanted me to do this stuff.

LS: How about friends?

GEA: No. Doing art just made me seem more strange. In grade school
a girl named Ophelia would always copy what I did.

LS: She was probably in love with you.

GEA: If I got a particular colored notebook, she'd have her mother
buy her that particular colored notebook. (I always spent money on
pens, paper, and notebooks—not on clothes. My mother made our
clothes.)
   My father was the only one who said that I was going to college,
but he died when I was twelve. Nobody else in the town read. Well,
maybe once in a while they'd have a Bible. My grandmother had some
old Spanish books in her chest. Some of my father's sisters read, but
they lived elsewhere. No one had any books, magazines, or dictionaries
of any kind; I'd end up reading the labels on cans.

LS: I wonder if you even know what made you want to go on to college,
to go on to write, to go on to do these things?

GEA: Well, I knew that there were other worlds out there, and I found
it out through books, through writing, and through my imagination.
There were other worlds out there that were different from this Chicano
community where I was a total alien—because I was different.

LS: Why else did you feel different in your own community?

GEA: The bleeding was the main thing. It made me abnormal. Reading
was the other one. Through books I knew things other people didn't
know. Also, I was different because I wasn't interested in boys. A lot
of the girls in my class were knocked up by the time they got to the
sixth grade. They'd drop out by the seventh grade and get married by
the eighth grade. They'd be having kids by the time I got to high school.
They had to sneak out to do that. I never did that.

LS: So your sexual identity emerged differently?

GEA: Yes. I had no sexual identity because this whole part of my body
was in total pain all the time. Once a month I'd get fevers of 106,
tonsilitis, diarrhea, and throwing up. Sometimes it would go on for
seven to ten days. So I withdrew all feeling from my genitals; from the
time I was little it was always a smelly place that dripped blood and
had to be hidden. I couldn't play like other kids. I couldn't open my

29

legs, my mother had to put a little piece of rag there. My breasts started growing when I was about six, so she made me this little girdle. I was totally alienated from this part of my body. I felt very much alive with my other body. I've always sensed things through my body. The sexuality was dead, but not all the time because I remember masturbating when I was really little. I remember my first orgasm. The sexual would make me feel different from the other girls because I wasn't out there fucking behind the bushes by the lake like they were. And I didn't really think men were all that great.

LS: Did you have any close girl friends during that time, or were you far away from the girls also?

GEA: There were a couple of Anglo girls—Kathy and Nancy—who lived in a ranch near where I lived and who were my first contact with Anglo girls. They pretty much excluded me, but I sort of looked up to them because they had nice clothes; they had a horse—you know? Things like that. I was going to meet with them at the annual Mercedes livestock show, but I didn't have enough money to go. Afterwards when I told them that I hadn't been able to go, they'd completely forgotten about me. It came as such a shock to me because for a week I'd been worried about how to tell them. So I found out that I was a nonentity as far as they were concerned.

My sister was a close friend. We slept in the same bed then later in the same room for the first eighteen years of our lives.

LS: Were you close to your grandmother?

GEA: Yes. I was close to both of my grandmothers and to a "spinster" aunt—a solterna, an unmarried woman. Everybody called her "Mana" (for hermana). She was wonderful, everybody looked up to her. She owned her own house, she lived by herself, she didn't need any man. My sister and I would take turns staying with her sometimes. My sister was her favorite, but I was my grandmother's favorite. I'm pretty sure Mana was a dyke.

College

LS: So you decided to go to college?

GEA: Yes. Early on I decided to go to college. I took my entrance exams when I was a junior; I didn't even wait till I was a senior.

LS: Did many kids from your high school go to college?

GEA: No, only a few, mostly Anglos. I chose to go to a woma
university, Texas Women's University. My mother wanted to know why,
if I insisted on going to college (which she disapproved of because
college was just for whites and for males), why I couldn't go to a nearby
college, Pan-American, why I insisted on going to one 800 miles away
and twelve hours on the bus. I guess I really wanted to get away from
her. She's a very strong woman. Very dynamic. Both my parents were
very, very strong. I often think my father's death was a favor to his kids
because he was like this god, and my mother also. We wouldn't have
had a chance with two strong personalities trying to control us. They
were very controlling; they were very strict about being clean, especially
with me bleeding. The first time I ever took a bath where I could wash
my face with the same water wasn't very long ago. To clean my face
with the water my body had been in was dirty because the body was
dirty. A lot of Chicanos are like that. I don't know where white people
got this thing about dirty Chicanos. I was amazed when I found out
that my white friends didn't take a bath every day. I was shocked
because I had the stereotype that whites were clean.

LS: Was there anything positive in the institution, in this women's
college, for you?

GEA: Yes. I had written a little creative essay, a sort of journal entry,
for an English class. The teacher raved and raved and raved and got it
published in a school literary journal. It had to do with some of the
readings we'd been doing. I also brought in my background and the
culture.

It got an award. I was supposed to read it before an auditorium
full of people. But I was on scholarship, loans, and work-study and
couldn't get off work at the library. Or I didn't try to get off. I don't
know which. Someone else read it for me.

LS: Your first piece. Now this was at the beginning of your college
days?

GEA: Yes, my first year.

LS: Were there other Chicanas at Texas Women's University?

GEA: Very few. One other Chicana was a distant relative. After I was
already there we decided to be roommates. I'd had this other roommate

who was epileptic but hadn't told me about it. In the middle of one night I get up and she's having a seizure. It scared the shit out of me because she came at me and I thought she was trying to kill me. Then she fell on the floor and went into convulsions. I looked at her suitcases—she had one suitcase filled with medicine. Whenever she got mad at her boyfriend or her mother she'd not take the medicine and, as a result, go into convulsions. Later we got to be close friends, but I moved out and roomed with my cousin. She had big boobs, they hung down to her stomach. I'd never seen a naked woman other than my sister and myself until then. I don't even know if I ever saw my sister that much. My mother was very strict about us not showing our bodies.

That year, I also had my first encounters with homosexuality. You know how some dorm rooms have a connecting bath? OK. The woman across the bathroom was a friend of mine and I was supposed to go to her room one afternoon. Instead of knocking on her door I went through the bathroom to the other room—and there were two women making love!!! It freaked me out! I was so freaked out, I went [intake of breath] and I ran and ran—I ran down the hall. It was like, such a horror. It kept reoccurring—

LS: Who were these women?

GEA: Total strangers.

LS: They didn't live in the dorm? They weren't students?

GEA: They were students.

LS: But you didn't know them.

GEA: No. I guess they were just using my friend's room to make love. But to see two women fucking—I think that must have been the beginning of realizing I was queer. Because I was so horrified—you know, when you're afraid of something, you fight it? I don't know how you did it, but I totally went into denial. I wanted to deny it, rationalize it. I was like—aaahhh!!!

LS: Did you talk to anybody about it?

GEA: Yes. I told my roommate and she said, "Oh yeah. There's a lot of those here. This is a woman's school and there are a lot of those here." And I thought, "Well, maybe that's why I chose to be with women." Then I told my mother and sister, and they were horrified.

LS: I'm surprised they didn't pull you out of there.

GEA: Well, I had to leave because I couldn't afford it any more. I got out and worked for two years, then started going to Pan-American.

But that freshman year was significant for me because there was nothing but women. My teachers were women who were very nice even though they were all white. I was appalled at the games the students played with men. There was an air force base, Wichita Falls, nearby. Every weekend, three thousand of these guy—plus, we were sister college to the Aggies—would visit. Saturday night if you didn't have a boy, a man, to go out with you were considered nothing. So I was considered nothing because I never—maybe once or twice or three times—went out. The air force guy I went out with was very close friends with another guy, and I realized that he dated me for show; the two guys were really interested in each other. So the whole homosexuality thing happened in that college, both in terms of discovering that it existed and also that men were, you know. Shortly after I returned from that year at school, I found out that my cousin who lived across the street, was queer. And I have an uncle who lived nearby, and was a maricón.

LS: How did you find this out? From your family? From your mother?

GEA: No. By their appearance and mannerisms. I finally put two and two together. Then I started asking questions, and my brother said they were "de los otros," "of the others." There's a whole bunch of other names—"ass-lickers," "lambiscosos," "maricones," "mariposas," "maricas," and the most ugly word—"culeros."

LS: How does it translate?

GEA: "Cule" means "tail"; "culer" usually refers to dogs who lick other dogs in the ass and eat their shit. That's what it means.

I started talking to my cousin. I think she really was in love with me. She'd call me and stuff, and when she started getting too close I'd have my sister answer the phone and say, "Oh, she's gone." By then, I had a car (I got a car when I was a sophomore or junior in college), so my cousin would say, "But the car is parked in the back." My sister would tell her I'd borrowed my mother's or gone off with somebody else.

There was another woman, another cousin, who was queer. She lived three blocks down. But she was more like bi. My two cousins would be having little affairs. They were also primas hermanas. So it was both incest and homosexuality. When I started teaching high school, a lot of my students were lesbians and a few faggots. We'd talk about it, and they'd show me their love letters. They'd talk about when they went to camp, what they did. So I had all these little baby dykes, but I still didn't think of myself as one.

LS: Huh? These kids came out to you? Before you were out?

GEA: Yes. I was the one they confided in. A couple of them were in love with me, but I had nothing to do with men or women. This part of me—I was in pain all the time.

LS: And you were still having really terrible periods?

GEA: I had—hell—until the hysterectomy, which was two years ago. My whole life was nothing but pain. Pain. Pain. Pain.

LS: Did you ever find out exactly why you were in such pain?

GEA: Yeah. It was too much progesterone and estrogen. I was born with a hormone imbalance. But I have another theory. I have several theories, but I don't know if this interview is the right place for them. I think that when I was three months old—and I got this information from meditating—the spirit in my body left, so that I died for a little bit, and another spirit entered my body. I've been dead four times: I died for a little while when I was three months old; when I was about eight I drowned for a little while at Padre Island; and then, when I fell off the hill and broke the left side of my back, I think I was dead for a minute and a half or two minutes. But during my operation the doctor said I'd died for twenty minutes—oh wait—when was it? My heart stopped beating for twenty minutes and I stopped breathing—what did he say? I've got it all in here; I have notes and stuff. So anyway, I've died four times. And each time I'd forget the experience. So when I was in the hospital—I don't know whether it was the anesthesia or what— all the stuff came back. And then I'd repress it, because you're not supposed to remember. I think a lot of people die—their souls leave their bodies for a little while.

So anyway, the first time was when I was three months old, and the spirit that entered me was an extraterrestrial spirit, which means that it had not been in a human body before. Had never incarnated. I always think of this spirit as masculine, because he didn't like my body. He got knocked out when I fell off the hill. What's funny is that the original spirit entered me again. I got a lot of this information from psychic readers, and most of it I got from meditation and past-life regression. There were certain things I had to learn: that I had a particular destiny, a fate, that I was creating, that I had to create. The only way for me to do it was to have this other spirit in my body. I'd get certain kinds of information from this spirit. When that task was done, the original spirit came back, and I think that's the one in me now. I don't know if it's going to stay, but in a way it explains this whole feeling of alienation—and the blood—because he couldn't deal with the body. I had very intense fevers. As a young child, I had very curly hair—curlier than yours. When I was six years old the fever was so high that the roots curled; from then on my hair came out straight. When I was sixteen I had an intense fever and my hair turned white—grey. I dye it black, sometimes I henna it. I was never able to talk about any of this because it's horrible. I mean, the stuff that was going on with me is like seeing a movie or reading a science fiction book, you know?

"My Task": Making Face, Making Soul, Making Heart

LS: What does this spirit have to do with your creativity? How does it tie in?

GEA: I realized very early that I had a certain task in life: I had to reach a great number of people and the best way to do it was through art. It's almost like—god, it's crazy! In part, you were born in this world to make your heart and create your face. Your face is your personality, and your heart is your soul or spirit. Before I consciously held this philosophy, I already felt that I had to make my soul—I had to create who I was. I completely changed my fate, so that the lines on my left hand aren't like the lines on my right. They're very different. I don't have any fate lines here; I'm just creating it as I go along, but this is the fate line over here. So I felt like I had a service to perform and that it had to do with reaching people and communicating, with expressing ideas. It had to do with communicating to people—especially to those in my culture—that there's more to life than this reality. I have to remind them that we have these roots that are Indian and these roots that are Spanish. There are a lot of Indian souls inhabiting white bodies, and my other task is to remind those people that they're Indian, because their souls are Indian. You know what I'm talking about?

LS: A little.

GEA: So my task was to connect people to their reality—their spiritual, economic, material reality, to connect people to their past roots, their ancient cultures. Everybody knows all these connections, but consciously they're not aware of them.

LS: When did you find out that this is what you have to do?

GEA: I was tripping on mushrooms. (They're called "niñitos"—"the little children"—and they're also called "the flesh of the gods." The Aztecs used them for healing and ritual: when a person would come to the shaman or the curandera for healing or advice, they'd both take mushrooms and the voice of the mushroom or their inner self would tell them what was wrong.) I was tripping on mushrooms. (This was July 13, 1975; I know because I've been going through all my journals putting this book together.) So I was tripping on mushrooms and I looked in the mirror and saw my face. And I'm all eyes and nose. Behind that were other faces—it looked like the mirror was a cubist painting (because with cubism you look at something from many perspectives). So I realized that I was multiple, that I wasn't this one self—you know, the conscious self. There were other parts. (Like an iceberg: there's a part above water that you see, and then there's this whole other part under the water that you don't see. Well, looking in the mirror made me see the other part.) OK, so I realized that I was multiple. At this time I was writing the novella about Heche, el maricón, for my decadent class. I realized that this is what I was going to do: I was going to take stream-of-consciousness, but rather than just narrate an inner stream-of-consciousness I would include what was happening externally. Heche goes through things in his head and his body ritually, but it's all situated in a physical reality. Instead of a series of monologues or ideas and images, they'd be a series of visuals—like scenes in a movie.

LS: Montages—

GEA: Right. I was going to use what I'd learned in surrealism, and try to be realistic about the inner and the outer world.

LS: The juxtaposition of things that don't fit together.

GEA: Right. And magico realismo—magical realism, like in the work of Cortázar, Borges, Marquez, and others. Their thing is to be super super realistic while describing a supernatural or otherworld kind of thing. It was going to be a writing of convergence: The sexual, the mental, the emotional, the psychic, the supernatural—you know, the world of the spirits—the unconscious. I gave it a name. I called it the "Gloria Multiplex," which means "the Multiple Glorias," because I thought I was multiple. This is really bizarre because I was stoned out of my head; I said, "OK, I'm going to invent a new style." Maybe I just put together pieces of the old, but I was going to call it "Gloria Multiplex." About two or three years ago I was reading James Hillman, who's one of my favorites. (I read a lot of psychology and psychoanalysis along with occult stuff.) I was reading *Re-Visioning Psychology* and he was talking about how monotheism—the concept of the one god—is very elitist. He says that there's a plurality of things. He called it the "Gloria Duplex." But he got it from another source, from the Latin. It's the point of view of looking at things from different perspectives.

LS: It's funny you talk about cubist art also, because so much of cubism is derived from African sculpture.

GEA: Right. Well see, surrealism, magico realismo, cubism are taken from indigenous, native cultures.

So that's when I decided that my task was making face, making heart, making soul, and that it would be a way of connecting. Then my last name, Anzaldúa, is Basque. "An" means "over," or "heaven"; "zal" means "under," or "hell"; and "dua" means "the fusion of the two." So I got my task in this lifetime from my name.

LS: This was 1975.

GEA: Yes. 1975. Shortly after that I started to become a writer. Oh, the very first poem I wrote was in Indiana, in 1974. It was called "Tihueque" (Now Let Us Go). A knife was the persona, an Aztec ceremonial knife. The knife talked about its history. So my very first writing was connected to the Indian part of me. I hadn't really thought about that until I was trying to write this section in my book.

Sexuality/Spirituality/Writing

LS: How do you define the relationship between sexuality and spirituality?

GEA: I feel I'm connected to something greater than myself like during orgasm: I disappear, I'm just this great pleasurable wave, like I'm uniting with myself in a way I have not been. In this union with the other person I lose my boundaries, my sense of self. Even if it's just for a second, there's a connection between my body and this other's body, to her soul or spirit. At the moment of connection, there is no differentiation. I feel that with spirituality. How can I say this without sounding like a book? Let me back up. When I'm there being sexual, sensual, erotic, it's like all the Glorias are there; none are absent. They've all been gathered to this one point. In spirituality I feel the same way. When I'm meditating or doing any kind of spiritual thing, there's a connection with the source. Then all the Glorias are connected: Gloria who's compassionate, Gloria who's jealous, Gloria who's a freak, Gloria who's lazy. It's OK to be me. In both the sexual and the spiritual act, all the "you's" are there, and it's a tremendous amount of energy.

LS: Do you ever feel that all these different "you's" conflict with each other, in the sexual or the spiritual experience?

GEA: Yes. It has to do with concentration. Instead of being with the event itself, I think about what I'm feeling, what the other person is feeling, where my head should be, what I should do with my mouth. In the spiritual experience I wonder, "When am I going to be enlightened? When is this energy going to flow into me?" Or I think about what I have to do during the day, instead of keeping my attention on the soul's presence. It's the same kind of distraction. The trick is to get to the place where I don't think about things, where I just act. That's difficult for someone with seven air signs! I always want to control everything, which means I have to supervise and plan. I'm either in the future or the past and never in the present

LS: Do you find this happens in the writing too?

GEA: Yes, it's all part of the same thing. Last May I realized that what I do in meditation is no different than washing my face or typing on the typewriter. I was doing a meditation when the soul appeared to me in the form of a woman. (I even wrote a poem about it.) It changed my whole life around. Now, everything I do is with this soul awareness, this spirit, in the back of my mind. If I'm sitting with you doing this interview or talking with Mirtha, I no longer think about the other things I have to do. In the past, only certain acts had my total dedication. I felt that writing and teaching were my work on this planet and that nothing else mattered: I wasn't attentive to people, eating was a chore, sweeping the floor had no meaning. But now everything has meaning and is sacred—the people, the trees, you. There aren't some people who are more important than others, even though

I love some people more. Being a writer isn't more important than being a ditch digger. The definitions, categories, and restrictions society has put on these activities are wrong, not the activities themselves. A person assimilates society's definitions. The ditch digger probably feels very low in the social scale, while the writer, the artist, feels elevated in stature—not economically, but in their own self-righteous thinking.

LS: Do you ever sabotage yourself?

GEA: Yes.

LS: Why does that happen?

GEA: Initially it takes a lot of energy to gather those forces, to concentrate to do the writing, to make love, or to meditate. Before I sit down to write, I'll sweep, mop, go for a walk—anything. It's so easy when I do it—so why don't I do it more often? Why don't I fuck more often? Why don't I write and not fight the writing? Why don't I meditate and not fight the meditation? I've been doing meditation now for seven years, a meditation every night and every morning. Why do I still fight it? You asked about the contradictory Glorias? The conscious part of myself that identifies as Gloria thinks she owns it all. She thinks that's who I am. When I had those experiences with the soul and the spirit, I was bigger than that little space or that person. My consciousness extended outside that sphere. It was a spark from the divine—if you think of the divine as this huge fire and all the people in the world as these little sparks from this huge fire; we return to that fire and we go out from it when we reincarnate. But this little spark is the conscious "I."

LS: You have an image.

GEA: Yes, the ego image that wants to be top dog. It doesn't want to have masters, it doesn't want to share with anyone. So there's the conscious I's resistance: it doesn't want anything to do with the soul or the Self because it would see itself as a little clod in a big field, and *it* wants to be the big field. The other resistance is fear. To a certain extent, you're happy with Linda and I'm happy with Gloria. But there are parts of Linda you probably keep down because you don't think it would be admissible for those parts—especially the sexual parts, the parts religion and society don't permit—to rise up. We're afraid of the parts of us that are subhuman, that are like animals. We only know the consciousness part of ourselves because we don't want to think that there's this alien being in the middle of our psyche. For my whole life, I've felt like there's this alien being inside myself.

LS: And by tapping this place there's a fear. Do you think this is the fear you had when you spoke of being afraid of going mad?

GEA: Yes. I didn't know if I was imagining it, hallucinating it, or if it was real.

LS: Do you think that fear comes from the same place?

GEA: Yes. It's a fear of the "other." The movie *Alien* affected me greatly because I really identified with it. There was this serpent-like alien being, a parasite, in this man's chest. It exploded; the being rushed out—very much like my out-of-body experience. In the film, it seemed like they were taking all the things they fear and hate about themselves and projecting them onto the monster. Just like we did with blacks and like people do with queers—all the evils get projected. My sympathies were not with the people at all; they were with the alien. I think that's how the soul is: It's treated like an alien because we don't know it. It's like a serpent; it's slimy and bad. That's what they did with women's sexuality and with women. Men were the ones with the soul; they were supposed to be spiritual, and women carnal. All the evils get projected onto children, third-world people, animals, and women. So much is projected onto women: they want to "cut a man's balls," they're the "temptress," they keep a man from achieving. The same thing happens with blacks: blacks were animals, they had no intelligence, they raped, they killed—everything evil. And I think that's what people have done to the soul.

LS: I think we do it to ourselves too.

GEA: Yes. So for me it was a recognition of everything I hated and feared which was alien, other, incomprehensibly horrible because it was not "I." I remember looking at my dead father's face and realizing that he was on the other side now. He was this other thing, he wasn't human, he was dead and so in this realm of the other. To me spirituality, sexuality, and the body have been about taking back that alien other. According to society and according to Eastern philosophy and religion, I must suppress or kill a certain part of myself—the ego or sexuality. But I don't believe you have to slay the ego. I believe you have to incorporate all the pieces you've cut off, not give the ego such a limelight but give some of the other parts a limelight.

I need to accept all the pieces: the fucked-up Glorias go with the compassionate, loving Glorias; they're all me. To say I'm going to get rid of this Gloria or that Gloria is like chopping off an arm or leg. To accept this view, I also had to accept the fact that God is the Devil; they're the same person; good and evil are different parts of the same coin. Christianity did this horrible thing by polarizing God and the Devil.

LS: In this culture it's easy to polarize things because there's a desire to project negative things onto something that will absorb them—like creating all these monsters and saying that it's an "other" thing. To say it's part of the same thing means you have to accept it and love it in yourself, no matter what it is.

GEA: Today our scapegoats are the faggots, lesbians, and third-world people, but in the future it will be people from other planets or even artificial humans—androids, people born in a test tube. People will have different ways of projecting their shadows onto others. So my whole thing with spirituality has been this experience with this other alien in the body, the spirit, the writing, and the sexuality. When I was young I was one with the trees, the land, and my mother; there weren't any borders. Then I became separate, and made other people and parts of myself the other. Then I went one step beyond, into the supernatural world—the subtle world, the "other" world—and dealt with that kind of otherness. Plus the uncanny—the demon, the ghost, the evil, the apparition—become even more "other." There are different gradations of otherness. When I got so far from my feelings, my body, my soul I was—like, other other other. But then something kept snapping. I had to gather; I had to look at all these walls, divisions, gradations of being other other other, and determine where they all belonged. It was an energy of refocusing and bringing it all back together.

LS: Do you think that's why you had to write?

GEA: Exactly. Writing saved my life. It saved my sanity. I could get a handle on the things happening to me by writing them down, rearranging them, and getting a different perspective.

First Turning Point: Teaching (and) Chicano Culture

LS: OK. Let's shift here and get back to the chronology. I want to know about the turning point around 1965. You coming into contact with—

41

GEA: Chicano culture—

LS: —in writing. When you were in school you were studying to be a teacher?

GEA: Yes. I had all these programs—early childhood development, special education, and secondary, English, art, and education.

LS: You were really taking on the world.

GEA: And I was working full time, and Saturdays and Sundays I still worked in the fields. I don't know how I did it! I graduated from college in '69. During the whole time I was just trying to survive. To me, the turning point was when I started teaching because I usually learn the most when I teach—which is why I love to teach creative writing. So I started teaching these little kids—five year olds—bilingual. I was teaching them Spanish and English—little songs. I started looking into the culture, what I could get from the culture. Because the whole school was white, the curriculum was white. It was all in English.

LS: This was the late '60s?

GEA: This was 1969.

LS: And you'd already learned a lot about Chicanos prior to that?

GEA: Yes. Around '65, '66, but not that much. In college I picked up this book, *Yo Soy Joaquin*, by Corky Gonzalez, a Chicano. It was a long narrative poem about the history of Chicano people, and he took it down to the roots. Then I started reading everything I could get my hands on.

LS: Did you find this book in a college course?

GEA: No. I love bookstores, and I was in one reading about the farmworkers. (I knew I wanted to help because I myself had been a farmworker; I wanted to become a teacher so I could teach migrants, teach farmworkers.) So I was reading about César Chávez. But this reading had nothing to do with formal school. It just happened that the bookstore had this book. I sort of did a return to the culture because when I was little, to be Mexican was very bad so everybody wanted to be white. Anything Mexican was put down—the food, the traditional stuff, the heritage. If you were Mexican from the other side, you were like a mojado or a bracero, and Chicanos really looked down on Mexicans.

LS: And you had nothing positive in school.

GEA: No. If you were caught speaking Spanish on the school grounds you were punished—physically punished, spanked or hit with a ruler. They couldn't understand Spanish and we couldn't understand English because we weren't around English-speaking kids. The whole culture was put down. The Chicano movement was a revelation to me because here was a part of myself I could finally accept; it was OK to be Mexican. The movement was one of two turning points.

But I didn't really delve into Chicano culture until I started teaching. When I started teaching freshman in high school, and I team taught with this woman—that's when I did all the research into the literature. I got stories and plays; I did background on Chicano writing. I wrote to this guy named Amado Muro. I wrote to him and asked him if it was OK if my class adapted his story into a play. I later found out that he was a white man who had taken his Chicana wife's name. He wrote under her last name, he wrote about Chicanas and Mexicans.

LS: Did he ever write back to you?

GEA: Yes, and my class did the play. So it was when I started teaching high school that I started using the material. I'd make copies of parts of *Yo Soy Joaquin*. It's a little skinny book, so I'd copy parts of it every day and use it in school.

LS: How did your students feel?

GEA: They were really happy. They could write about their own experience. They didn't have to write from the point of view of being white. So they could write about the stories that Tía so-and-so had told them. They could write about the time they saw this ghost or that. You know, they didn't have to write about things that weren't part of the culture.

LS: Were there other Chicana teachers, other Chicanos?

GEA: The woman I was team teaching with was Chicana. See, the reason I ended up teaching preschool and the mentally retarded was that they wouldn't allow me to teach in high school because I was Mexican. I kept going to the superintendent's office and saying, "Look. I have a secondary degree; my grades—" They kept saying there wasn't an opening, but finally, there was an opening, and I started. At the same time I started, this other woman, Cynthia, started. Around this time they opened high school teaching to Chicanos. But before that, Chicanos only taught elementary and whites taught the upper classes.

LS: Where were you doing this—around where you grew up, or around where you went to college?

GEA: Where I grew up. I was driving thirty miles to teach. I taught at the San Juan elementary. San Juan, Alamo—wait. There was another city in there—the Independent school district—Pharr Farr San Juan Alamo Independent School District. I taught there for five years.

LS: You went to high school to teach after five years in the elementary school?

GEA: No. I taught preschool for a year, and I loved those little kids. Then I taught the mentally retarded and emotionally disturbed kids for a year and a half. That was very hard on me. I had six- and seven-year-olds. They were disturbed, retarded, but their IQs weren't that low. I couldn't take it; it was very painful. I had one kid named Sergio who had about fourteen brothers and sisters, and the fourteen brothers and sisters, the father, and the mother took turns beating him. I couldn't do it. I was the only teacher and had the same kids the second year. I started teaching high school mostly to get away from that kind of horror.

LS: Now we're in the very early '70s? What was going on for you in your classroom that put you in some kind of a social context? There was a whole lot of stuff going on in this country, in the late '60s and '70s—with Vietnam, with the Chicano movement emerging. How do you fit into what was going on?

GEA: Well, my brother was wounded in Vietnam, and he came back half dead and unrecognizable. He's like six feet two and weighs about 200 pounds, but when we saw him he weighed only 87 pounds. I was the only one he could communicate with because everybody had an idealized version of war, so he'd tell me all these horrible things that had happened when he was fighting in the front lines for a year. Just before he was shipped home—because he'd served his year—everyone in his platoon was killed except him and his captain. He ended up in the bottom of a foxhole. The next morning when they found him, he was drowning in the blood of all these other bodies, which is what saved him. So I was very invested in the antiwar movement. And I'd been a migrant worker and a farmworker, so I was invested in the farmworkers' movement. I think I was more concerned with the migrants and the Chicano movement than with the antiwar movement. I was going to MAYO [Mexican-American Youth Organization]; I was going to political meetings around the Chicano movement. I was also very disenchanted with it because it was all the guys. So when I met up with the feminist movement, I was ready for it.

Second Turning Point: Entering the Feminist Movement

LS: All right. Let's tune in to that a little bit. How does that fit in? Where does it fit in?

GEA: It started when I went to Indiana. Every year, two teachers from every state would be selected to follow the migrant workers. I was selected, and I chose Indiana—I don't know why I chose that state. I was director, my job was to do in-service and be the liaison between the migrant camps and the school officials, to help the children in the migrant camps. I was also bilingual consultant.

LS: In the public schools?

GEA: Yes. My job was to go around to all the schools and give talks on curriculum and background—the teachers were totally ignorant—and see that the money was spent properly.

LS: There were a lot of migrants in Indiana?

GEA: Yes. They did all the crops. Some would stay for a week, some for six weeks, and some for two or three months. So that's where I first started getting a hint of feminism, because my office was the northwestern regional service center, which was an office of consultants. In '74 I quit and moved to Austin to go to graduate school.

LS: You went back?

GEA: Yes, and I met this fairy faggot named Randy.

LS: Randy . . . Isn't he in a story?

GEA: Yes. He and I became best friends. He encouraged me to go to a lesbian meeting at WomanSpace. So I went.

LS: So he probably knew you were a dyke all along—

GEA: Oh yeah. Yeah, he did. I started going to WomanSpace regularly; it was sort of like a reading group. We read Marge Piercy and others. Randy was a feminist; we'd go to a bookstore and he'd point out books to buy. "Buy Shulamith's *The Dialectic of Sex*." He loaned me a book about Pierre Louÿs—have you ever heard of him? He's a French writer who writes about lesbians. And he had me read Monique Wittig. He'd just point and I'd buy.

LS: Why did you go back to Austin?

GEA: I got my master's there. I forgot to tell you about that part. While I was teaching at the high school, in the summertime I'd go and work on my master's. That's where I first met this woman. She was this tall skinny woman, and I met her in one of my summer classes. In '69, '70, and '71 we were like best friends. We did everything together. She didn't have a man, and I never dated. I could feel stuff between us—like she was into me. I wasn't that attracted to her, but I wanted to talk about it, so I told her one time, "Why don't we talk about this thing?" She said, "What thing?" And I finally said, "lesbian feelings." She turned around, walked out, and I never saw her again. Well, I saw her once more. She left school a week before it ended.

LS: You blew her off?

GEA: I called her at her home when I got to the valley. Her sister answered, and I could hear at the other end of the phone her sister saying, "It's Gloria blah blah blah"—you know, because we used to call each other in between the summers. I heard her yell, "Tell her I'm not here." I waited and later wrote her a letter. She never answered. So then I called her again, and her mother answered and said "She doesn't live here anymore." Which was nonsense. This woman was ten or fifteen years older than I was; she'd always lived with her mother. She wore her hair up in a little bun.

LS: Classic.

GEA: I wrote her a third letter. I saw her one last time, at an in-service day for high school teachers, where everyone from all the different schools goes to one school. I walked into the auditorium to hear the keynote speaker. There weren't many people in the auditorium and she was sitting alone, near the front. As I was walking up the aisle I saw her and called her name. I started walking towards her because I wanted to sit by her, but she got up and walked to the other end of the aisle, out the door, and I never saw her again.

LS: Wow. Why was it easy for you to say, "Let's talk about these lesbian feelings"? Usually there's a stigma attached to talking about lesbianism; it's not easy to talk about.

GEA: I've never had that problem. That's why my cousin and the kids in high school would come and talk to me. Being a lesbian has never been an issue for me. What has been an issue is sexuality— of whatever kind.

LS: OK. We'll talk about that later. Now, let's go back to feminism and this turning point in your life. This is the mid '70s.

GEA: Right.

LS: Was WomanSpace a campus group?

GEA: WomanSpace was an outside-of-campus space. We had our meetings over at the Y. But most of the women who went there were students.

LS: Were they mostly white? Were there Chicanas?

GEA: I forgot to tell you the other part of it. It was like I had two affinities. I had these white women, feminists, lesbians—

LS: In WomanSpace?

GEA: In WomanSpace where the consciousness-raising meetings took place and on campus. At the same time I was involved with Chicanos and had some Chicano friends. Mostly they were faggots. There was this guy, a drag queen, and there was my next-door neighbor who was straight, but—you know. There were people who lived around me in the apartment complex. There were very few Chicanas in school, especially in graduate school. There was only one other Chicana in comp. lit., Mary Margaret Navar, who years later translated one of my poems. I didn't even know she was in the same program until I saw her in D.C. and she said, "Oh hi! I'm your translator."
  In '75 I met a woman who called herself bisexual and I met one of the first white lesbian friends I had. She had 2-inch hair under her armpits, and that shocked me. I met most of these people through

Randy. My roommate for two semesters was a Chicana lesbian, and her lover. I was around gay people. I just didn't have a sexuality. I was like autoerotic. I wasn't fucking men; I wasn't fucking women. But I started thinking of myself as a lesbian. The consciousness-raising gatherings were really good for me because they made me talk out. These lesbians were all saying, "Oh no. The Chicanas are oppressed," and defining Chicana oppression to me. But I was right there and I said, "Why don't you ask me? I'm right here." I started speaking out and being an active participant rather than just sitting on the sidelines listening to other people talk.

LS: So you have the Chicano movement, with men, and the feminist movement, with lesbians: Were you trying to make links between these different parts of your life? Were you trying to bring them together?

GEA: Yes. I was thinking about connections, and writing was perfectly in the center.

LS: Good. That's what I want to hear about.

The "Path of Writing"

GEA: I've always been aware of this path that I have—the path of writing. "Tlapalli" means "the black and red ink"—the path of the black and red ink is my path. "Black" means writing, and "red" means wisdom. Both the red and the black symbolize knowledge of things that are really difficult to understand and also knowledge of other realities, like the world of the spirits, the world of the body, the world of the unconscious. Even then I was living life so that I could write about it. I became involved with spirituality. I went to some lectures given by a Buddhist. I started doing I Ching, the Tarot, and psychic readings. The writing was the hub, and all these other things were the spokes of the wheel.

LS: When did writing make that connection? When did you put writing in the center like that?

GEA: In 1974 in South Bend, Indiana, when I wrote my first poem; I wrote the first story. I started the novel.

LS: How did that happen?

GEA: I was working in the northern regional service center which housed all the consultants. There was a library there. So I went into the library and found this book on Nahuatl poetry and the history of the Aztecs. I found what they call a "tolteca." "Tolteca" means "artists,"—not just people who make pottery or people who make verses but an artist in all the realms. And I wanted to be a complete tolteca.

LS: So you wrote a poem.

GEA: I wrote a poem about the obsidian sacrificial knife. I also wrote a song, "The City Circuit Song." It was about my traveling, I was on the road three days out of the week. I was reading *Seth Speaks*. I don't know if you've read *Seth Speaks*. It's by Jane Roberts. She's a medium, and Seth's voice speaks through her, the voice of a future self. He talks about the history of the earth, biology, chemistry, psychology, race, sexuality—everything. I wrote a poem about Seth.

I was really quite into the occult. I wrote a poem—I think it was called "Hummingbird"—about being Azteca, being this woman of two cultures, sort of like sitting on this wall, on this fence and putting roots into both the white culture—not only the white Spanish culture but the white Anglo I grew up with—and also into the india.

Being in Indiana really helped me because I went to Notre Dame and took a course in philosophy. I met this man—what was his name— Julio Samora? He was a writer of history. And I met his wife, who worked with the Headstart program. I also met several other Chicanos. So my stay in Indiana was like the cementing of the interest in the Chicano that I'd had before. But here I was a participant. I was involved in AMOS, an organization of migrants; I was involved with the state department; and I was involved with different HeadStart programs in the city and with anything that had to do with school. The groups were very political, much more political than the groups in Texas because they were getting a lot of shit.

LS: OK. Now let's connect writing back to when you were in Austin. You said that writing was at the center of everything and that this was when you were finding out about feminism, lesbianism, and being gay. What did you write then?

GEA: I guess the beginnings of the story you saw in *Conditions*.

LS: "El Paisano"?

GEA: —the beginnings—just the notes. The first year in Austin I took

49

a writing class, and wrote a short story called "The Funeral of Sabas Q," based on autobiographical stuff from my father's funeral. I took a writing course every semester because if nothing else, that course would force me to write. School is such a heavy thing. There were no women teaching writing. There was a man there, Michael Newshaw, a sort of popular writer—on the best-seller list and shit. He was very sexist, racist, homophobic, and didn't like science fiction or anything like that. But I got some technique from him. So I took a class with him. There was a British poet, I don't remember his name. And there was another man named David Olie, from Oklahoma.

LS: How did you get technique from this man who was against everything you believed in?

GEA: I'd sit in class and say, "OK. This man is going to insult everything I believe in. I'm going to ignore that and I'm going to see how he deals with characters, setting, dialogue, mood."

LS: You were able to do that?

GEA: I was able to do that. Maybe it's the Libra in me. I also I took an independent study with him. He'd always give me As. I think I took three courses with him, and I only had to see him twice a semester. All he did was give me the deadlines. So that was great.

At the same time I was writing, I was also studying surrealism, avant garde literatures, and Spanish. I was reading Cortázar, Borges, García Lorca, and Gabriella Mistral. It was wonderful because this whole world of Spanish literature opened up to me. I was doing Chicano literature and feminist literature, all the literatures I loved the most. There was no such program; I invented it and talked them into letting me do it.

LS: OK. Feminism: What did you draw on? What strengths did you get from feminism?

GEA: I got a lot from Judy Grahn's *A Woman Is Talking to Death*. Marge Piercy's *Small Changes* made a great impression on me. Then the theoretical stuff. I read Ti Grace Atkinson, Sheila Rowbotham. Along with feminism I was reading feminist psychology like Esther Harding's *Women's Mysteries* and Mary Daly. I was combining everything. I was getting Chicano feminism in the flesh and white feminism through books. The only problem was that Chicana feminists were straight, and that drove me into white feminism because most of the women in WomanSpace, the group I mentioned earlier, were lesbians. I was being pulled in different directions.

LS: Was there one turning point where things pulled together for you around women and feminism? Or were you just putting all these pieces together?

GEA: I think I was trying to pull it together. They came a little bit together when I met the Chicana lesbian I lived with. But all of these things came together when I left Austin in '77 and went to San Francisco.

LS: What about class issues?

GEA: Oh yeah. Interestingly enough, the class stuff came up between me and a man lover I'd had years before. He was from Peru, and he put down my Spanish; he said that Chicanos were corrupting the Spanish language. He was upper middle class; his father was in an embassy position. I always knew when I was little that Chicanos were poor and lower class, and the whites were upper class and stuff. But it didn't dawn on me that within my own people there were classes until I met this guy who was so up there. When I was in school the class issue was very, very strong because there were 47,000 students. Out of the 47,000 students, 1,846 were Chicanos. Out of that number, there were 143 in graduate school, and 60 out of the 143 were women. OK. Austin is a very split city. It's got a large population of Chicanos, but they live on their side of the river. (This is the river, not the tracks.) Very few went to the university; very few were in this part of the city. So all the while I'm there, all the teachers and professors are white, middle class. I had one professor, James Sledd, who encouraged me, and he was a rebel. He was like the outcast in the English department. He was the one who got me started to write about my experiences. That's when I first started articulating El Mundo Zurdo, in his class.

LS: Were you calling yourself a writer then? Did you think of yourself as a writer?

GEA: In my journal I've called myself a writer since '74. But when people would ask me I was very self-conscious about not having published very much. (I'd published maybe seven poems.) So I'd just say, "I write." There was a Chicano writer, Alurista, teaching at the university. I'd go to some of his things.

51

In '76 I started working for *Tejidos*, a Chicano literary magazine. I met these people in 1975, from *Tejidos*, and I became friends with a woman who's a dyke; I know she is. She didn't know she was but she's such a dyke. We started hanging out together, and I started helping with the magazine; I'd do proofreading, publicity, and correspondence. So that was my connection with the literary stuff. I mostly wanted to be there because I'd read the manuscripts coming in. So very early on I got to read women's things—Chicanas'. I forgot that part; that was a very interesting part.

Third Turning Point: Becoming a Full-Time Writer

LS: Was there a turning point for you when you stopped saying you were someone who wrote, and someone who wanted to publish?

GEA: Yes. The turning point was when I gave up my university teaching job as a lecturer, left the Ph.D. program (I was A.B.D.), went to California, and just survived on temporary work. I was a full-time writer. I've been a full-time, self-employed writer since '77.

LS: Bravo. That's when you left Austin?

GEA: Yes. I had all this training and degrees, and I gave it all up. I don't know if people have to give it all up for writing, but I had to. After that I started calling myself a writer.

LS: Why San Francisco?

GEA: When I was real little, I saw my future, and I saw all these cities where I was going to live; the vision gave me the approximate years: Indiana first, then Austin, then San Francisco for three years. I ended up staying in San Francisco for three and a half. Then New York for about two years; I think that's going to be shorter. I was going to be in Italy and in Mexico, but that got switched around: I'm going to Mexico first, then Italy. India, South America. I had a sense of my destiny very early.

LS: So when you went to San Francisco, you went calling yourself a writer. Making that move. What experiences did you have publishing? You said you felt self-conscious. You'd published *only* seven poems. Where did you try to publish, during this time?

GEA: One was published in the Pan-American University magazine.

Pan-American was where I got my B.A. Several were published in *Tejidos*. Those were the only two places I submitted.

LS: You didn't send anywhere else? Why?

GEA: I wasn't ready. I didn't send them out when I didn't think they'd be accepted by a particular magazine. I usually have intuitions about when and what to send out My intuition has not been working so much now because I got a rejection—my second rejection—the other day. Ohhhh.

LS: So "not ready" is based on intuition?

GEA: If I listen to my inner voice I know when a particular magazine wants something and I know whether they'll publish it or not. Sometimes I get excited or greedy and I send something out. Like, I sent *Sinister Wisdom* a long poem called "Basque Witches." I knew that wasn't their kind of stuff, but Mirtha said, "Yeah, this is the best poem you've ever done. Send it. Send it, they'll be crazy if they don't take it." But Adrienne Rich thought it was too idealistic. I always know, I always have a hint. If I don't have it, I use my coins. I used to have divination rocks. Or I meditate and the answer comes. My friends have been wanting me to publish this manuscript of poems, *Tres lenguas del fuego*, that the Santa Teresa poem is from. I'm not ready, and people aren't ready. Maybe in four years. I have an idea, like I know *La serpiente* is going to be published in '84.* Andrea is probably going to take another three or four years after that. You know what I mean? I have a sense as to when people are going to be receptive to a particular work.

LS: When you say "people," where do you think of publishing? You sent something to the university where you went to school. And to the Chicano magazine.

Another Turning Point: Teaching "La Mujer Chicana"

GEA: Sí. The first things I sent out were to Chicanas and Chicanos. I started feeling out Chicanos when I became a lesbian. They weren't ready for that kind of thing. The only group I thought receptive to my work was the feminist community.

---

* *La serpiente que se come su cola* was never published. It functioned as what Gloria calls a "first draft" or a "generic autobiography." Portions of *La serpiente* made their way into *Borderlands* and *La Prieta*. [ALK]

LS: Why?

GEA: In the feminist community, more parts of me are allowed. It allows me to be Chicana, to be queer, to be spiritual. The Chicano community does not accept its queers. You should see the funny looks I get when I speak to Chicano audiences. The schools don't want me. Texas, right now, where I'm going to do a talk, I'm having a lot of trouble getting support. I used to teach "The Mujer Chicana" at UT Austin. They banned that course a few years after I left because they said it was divisive of men and women in the Chicano movement. OK. Right now I'm asking them two hundred dollars to pay part of my transportation, so I can come and talk; I'm getting other funds from other organizations. *This Bridge* is being used in four classes at the university. They're using it in the Chicano information center, but this guy, Rudy de la Garca, won't endorse me. I used to teach there. I forgot to tell you, teaching "The Mujer Chicana" was another turning point for me.

LS: That was when? Mid-'70s?

GEA: No. See, I had a bunch of turning points. Meeting Randy was a transformation. Then, tripping on acid and mushrooms.

LS: Having a vision—

GEA: —was a turning point. My work with *Tejidos*, and my teaching. Then La Mujer Chicana in '76.

LS: You were a graduate student, working on your doctorate, and you developed this course?

GEA: I didn't develop the course. Inés Tovar Hernández, another Chicana, had developed it. She taught it one semester; I took her class and taught it the next semester. I also taught "Chicanos and Their Culture." So it was a Chicana/feminist class. I changed the course a bit and added a new element—homosexuality—which was sort of radical at this time and in this state. So that was a turning point, because it connected me to my culture and to being queer, to the writing, and to the feminism. It's so strange. I haven't written explicitly about that in the serpiento autobiography.

LS: Now you have something to think about. You went to San Francisco in 1977.

GEA: After leaving Austin, I cried for 20 miles.

LS: And then you stopped crying.

GEA: Yes. Yes.

LS: What happened with your writing in San Francisco? What I'm thinking about is the introduction to *This Bridge* and you going to Merlin Stone's retreat, and the decision somewhere in there to work on *This Bridge Called My Back*. Was it a culmination of a lot of different experiences?

GEA: Yes. The decision to do *This Bridge* started when I was teaching La Mujer Chicana; I realized that we needed this kind of book. I had to scramble everywhere—magazines, newspapers—for material to teach. There was a strong Chicano movement going on in the 1900s, 1915, 1930. But it's all in little bitty tabloids and newspapers. It's not documented by the dominant society. In that Chicana class, I also taught black and white, which I wasn't supposed to do. But I always went for integrating. I've never been a separatist, along any kind of line, which has made it easier for me to get along with white people, and upper-class people. So I went to California, to the gay mecca. Because I was going to be a writer. I was going to be around an artistic community, and I was going to be bohemian. [Laughter]

LS: Finally.

GEA: Yes. I found this commune of fifteen people after about two weeks of staying in this motel where in the middle of the night all these prostitutes were coming in with their tricks, and drug addicts were banging on the door. I had to barricade the door in fear of my life; it was very traumatic. So then I went into this commune: In the commune were one black man, a Chinese guy, two white lesbians, two bisexuals, and a couple of faggots. It was a mixed class and race group but mostly white and straight. And I started writing *Tres lenguas del fuego*. I went to several workshops in the city. One was called Cloud House, a hippie-, faggot-type place. I went to Small Press Traffic, which was the best thing I ever did. There I met a gay man named Bob Gluck. I took his writing workshop, and he gave me the first reading in the city. This black woman, Gabriel Danielle, and I were in his class. (Danielle is into the spirits, by the way.) With her I did my first reading in San Francisco. And people liked it. So I was supporting myself by being a technical writer for the University of California, UC Med Center. It was awful. I was also doing temporary jobs with Bell Telephone and insurance companies. I'd work three months, and then quit and write three months. I couldn't both work and write; I'd come home really tired. So then I thought, "Well, maybe I'll get a temporary job," so I got a temporary job with a resistance group. I was there for twenty hours a week. I was their office person, and I did everything: I put out a newsletter, answered the phone, did errands, and did the bookkeeping. That enabled me to write because I'd just do four or five hours a day and I had four days off. I called myself a writer. As soon as I hit California, I called myself a writer.

LS: Did you publish anything else out there? Did you work more with feminists out there?

GEA: Yes. I started attending the Feminist Writers Guild meetings.

LS: Ah. The infamous Feminist Writers Guild. That group of white women, that's what it sounds like.

GEA: Yes. And that's where I met Cherríe—at Old Wives, one of my favorite bookstores. I heard Cherríe talk; her name was Cherrie Lawrence then. After the meeting I went up to her and said, "You're a Chicana, aren't you?" She was really surprised because nobody had ever said that to her. And I said, "Yeah. It's the way you say your e's, i's, and a's. I can spot a Chicana a mile away." I organized a reading and asked her and some other people to read. I became a member of the Feminist Writers Guild. I was on the local steering committee, and then they elected me to the national steering committee. I came to New York in '78. I was on a radio show, I went to a warehouse where readings were taking place and I read. We'd go to all these tables, and there was Ellen Marie Bissert, and 13th Moon, and Jan Clausen. Of them all, Jan Clausen was the friendliest, so I stopped and talked to her. I told her about going to Merlin Stone's workshop and all the shit that came down, and about the book I'd started. Cherríe had not yet joined me in the book, so I asked Jan if she could put an ad in *Conditions* about the book, and she solicited material for me. Later I got a soliciting letter from Irena Klepfisz who was a member of *Conditions*. I sent her and Jan "Holy Relics," and it got published the following year.

LS: In *Conditions 6*, right?

GEA: They also printed my soliciting letter at that time. I was also putting together a third-world women's directory with Merlin Stone.

It listed the names of third-world women and what they could contribute—talks, workshops, areas of expertise. When people organizing readings and conferences said, "Well, we don't know any third-world women," we'd hand them the directory.

LS: OK. Now back up for a minute. Tell me about your experience as a Chicana lesbian in the Feminist Writers Guild.

GEA: It was awful. Cherríe and I were the only third-world women.

LS: No black women?

GEA: Not at that time. Maybe later. But I wanted to connect my chicanismo with writing and feminism and lesbianism. And that was the only group where I thought I could do it—

LS: —and you couldn't.

GEA: No.

LS: How did you two deal with the racism there? Was there homophobia also?

GEA: No, because almost everybody on the committee was gay. It was another turning point for me, I met Cherríe, Leslie, Abigail—I met all these lesbians who became very good friends. It also gave me access to the national stuff, not just the local. The racism was veiled, but the classism was overt and really got to me. We'd have our meetings in different people's houses. A lot of times we met at my house, because it was a commune with a lot of common space. But some of the people whose houses we went to were upper middle class. You know, the furniture, the bathroom, and everything. They didn't want to talk about the oppression of third-world women because that would be ranking oppressions, after all, and there were other kinds of oppression—like psychological. Kim Chernin and Susan Griffin were part of the Guild. Cherríe and I couldn't talk about being third world and being oppressed. They were interested in our being third world, but they weren't interested in anything about the oppression, or in being asked, "When are you going to deal with your racist shit?" But Cherríe and I would bring it up. Cherríe was more vocal than I was. She had very recently begun to identify as third world, rather than as white, and had begun to find her Chicana roots. So she was much more adamant, much more aggressive in calling people on their shit. Whereas I'd had a lifetime of it. But for her it was—not new—because she had grown up in L.A. with Chicanos. You know what I'm talking about? Her father was white, and so she could pass. Now she was identifying as Chicana, and all these injustices were really a shock to her.

LS: She had a different kind of anger, also.

GEA: Yes. A different kind of anger. None of what was happening was new; I was tired of fighting it, and I had to see whether my speaking was going to make a difference. If it didn't, I wasn't going to waste my energy—because I'd gone through that in the Chicano movement, at WomanSpace in Austin, at the Chicano Studies Department, and in Indiana. My whole life was like ramming my head against this wall. After a while you figure out where the dents are, the holes where the breaks are. And that's where you ram, but you can't do it constantly. (By the way, Cherríe was the one responsible for the Feminist Writers Guild Constitution. She's a very hard worker; she practically wrote the whole thing herself.)

LS: So did things get better at the Guild, or did you decide to leave?

GEA: Things got bad. I finished my term of office—I had two terms of office, the local and the national. She had only the local, and hers got done first. I could hardly wait until mine was done because the feminists coming in weren't like the ones we had started out with. It was like starting from zero. From scratch again because all the work we had done—

LS: It was like beating your head against the wall again?

GEA: Right. All the women we'd been interacting with had left or gone. Those in the new group were all upper middle class, conservative, and more straight than lesbian. The whole makeup of the guild changed.

LS: So you left.

GEA: Yes.

This Bridge

LS: Where was *This Bridge* in its genesis? Had you started working on it? And how did that decision come after the Merlin Stone workshop? Had you thought about it for a long time during the Guild years?

GEA: In February 1979 I went to a Merlin Stone workshop. Two days after I got home I did the soliciting letter, and I got feedback from Merlin, Cherríe, Randy, and others. But most of the letter stayed the way I had written it. OK. Some time goes by—a few months—and I'm getting my shit together, compiling this list. Because who am I going to send the call for contributors out to if there's not this list? When the letter was going to be printed and mailed out, I went to where Cherríe worked as a waitress and I said, "Cherríe, this is your last chance." I'd talked to her before about doing the book with me, but she wasn't ready. I told her it would open up this whole thing, with the race. I said, "This book, if we do it, is going to change your life; it's going to change my life." That night she decided that she wanted to be coeditor, so at the end of the call for papers we put in her name and address, along with mine.

LS: Now, the vision for this book began years earlier?

GEA: As I mentioned, it began when I was trying to collate material for La Mujer Chicana course, and I thought, "Wow, if somebody had a book like this, then I wouldn't have to do all this work." So the idea started there, but it didn't really gel until I talked with Merlin. She's the one who said, "You can do that," because I never thought I could.

LS: OK. Your letters went out, and the soliciting letter appeared in *Conditions*?

GEA: Yes. I mailed out tons of them.

LS: The leads you got from women all over?

GEA: To every woman's organization in the U.S., every women's studies program in the U.S., every third-world organization that I could get a name and address for, plus all the third-world women my friends and I knew. And it came out in the Feminist Writers Guild newsletter and in *Conditions*. I posted it everywhere. The first manuscript I got was from a Chicana; we had to reject it because it wasn't that good. Then a couple more came from Chicanas. We wanted stuff that really engaged, but most of the manuscripts we got in the beginning were already written for other purposes.

Audience and Voice

LS: Where do you fit now in a writing community—as a feminist, as a third-world woman, as a Chicana? Do you see yourself in a larger writing community? Do you think of yourself as being very alone in your writing?

GEA: No.

LS: Especially after editing this book.

GEA: I've always felt that my first audience was Chicanos and Chicanas. But I always felt that I was going to write for a lot of different people. I never even felt that I was just going to write for people in this country. How's that for an ego?

LS: No. Visions are important.

GEA: I've always had a planetary vision, not just a regional or even a national one. That sounds a little corny.

LS: When you think of that vision being so broad, do you think about what you have to do to reach such a diverse audience? Does it affect your voice as a writer?

GEA: No. I think I have to particularize rather than expand my voice.

LS: How do you do that?

GEA: Well, by writing about what I know, which is Chicano culture. I particularize by writing about women, by writing about being queer, by writing about the farm and the ranch. By writing very concretely about particulars I can reach a large audience. Does that sound paradoxical?

LS: No. Do you ever close your eyes and think of who you see as an audience?

GEA: Yes. The audience I see will never read my books. My mother. My sister has read a little. My brother—I think I was writing for them. I also see Cherríe and Mirtha and Randy and Christine—my friends. But my first audience was not my mother and not my friends. My first audience was these ancient, very poetic people—the Toltecs, the Aztecs who were writing poetry. Their whole civilization is based on metaphors, on symbols and poetry. My first audience was the occult, the spiritual. Like I was writing for these people, for these spirits that aren't here physically. You know what I mean? It's really weird.

LS: What kind of voice does that give you as a woman? Can you talk about your voice in writing? Does it change depending on what you write?

GEA: Yes. I have many voices. But I think the voice I most treasure is this little voice I had when I was little, which I call Gloria Gaurita; she was my little child-self. She was repressed and never got a chance to be a child. She had to be adult. I associate creativity and imagination with her. She's tender, open and vulnerable. I think that's my main voice. And then I have these other voices. You know, Gloria the lesbian, Gloria the feminist, Gloria the person interested in philosophy, psychology, psychic phenomena.

LS: When do your different voices come out? Do they come out for the different kinds of writing you do? For an introduction to an anthology, is it a different voice? Is it different in a novel? Is it different in poetry?

GEA: No. I try to let them all come out. In writing Andrea, in the story "El Paisano Is a Bird of Good Omen," I wanted all of those to be there: the feminism, the lesbianism, the spiritual person, the deep roots to the culture, other worlds. I try to let all the voices speak there.

Publishing and "El Mundo Zurdo"

LS: Where do you want to publish?

GEA: I'd like to publish with Kitchen Table Press, the third-world women's press. I'm going to send them a letter about *La serpiente* and see if they want to look at it. I think of publishing with Chicanos, which is probably an impossibility, or it will be an impossibility for a long time. The "Dear Women of Color" letter has been published in a Dutch anthology, and it's going to be published in England in another book. Cherríe and I have started talking about translating *Bridge* into Spanish. Eventually, I'd like to be published internationally. I think it will happen because my whole life has been an apprenticeship and it probably always will be. I work every day on my writing. It's not a sideline; I'm not a Sunday writer. Everything I've done my whole life has been towards this. A lot of times I have to choose between getting involved in relationships or the writing. And the writing—it's like I'm married to the writing. The writing is my lover. I call her la Musa Bruja. I wrote a poem about that—"The Muse Witch." She's a very jealous and possessive lover. I'm Libra, the double 6, which is the lover, so I need people. I love to be with people. I love to talk; I love to give readings; I love to interact. But the writing act is a solitary act. So this pull has always been one of my conflicts. I've gotten to the point where I think

I've done enough of my work—of being an apprentice writer, of gathering the knowledge and the experience, of reading and observing—in this first half of my life. So I'll be able to devote more of this second half of my life to interacting with people. But I feel this compulsion from the writing. Everything I see, everything I read; it's like—where's this going to fit into the writing? It's this all-consuming obsession and passion. And I hate it sometimes; I'll curse la Musa Bruja. I feel like she's my lover and I can't take her home.

LS: Do you think about trying to publish in larger presses, in presses that can publish more copies, that do greater publicity? Do you ever think of reaching a greater audience through that medium, rather than through Kitchen Table or Persephone?

GEA: No. I think it's a myth that larger presses always publish more copies and reach a wider audience. *Bridge* has sold about eighteen thousand copies, but if a major press had handled it, it wouldn't have gotten out, and we wouldn't have gotten as much of the royalties. The big publishers sit on a book for two years; then they remainder it, or it rots—after it's out, it rots in the warehouses. Very few of the books they print get out. Most of the books are tax write-offs. It's a big business, often a swindle. Persephone did much better by the book than any of those publishers. The only thing is prestige. I was talking to Kenneth Pritchard—he has this book about fairy fathering, faggot fathering—and I suggested that he try some small publishers. He said, "Oh well, my agent this and my agent that," and talked about Robin Morgan's book published by Doubleday and all that. But unless you're Adrienne Rich or Robin Morgan, your book is going to sit in the warehouse. Forever and ever and ever. I mean, they may do a big promotional thing in the beginning and then—you should talk to Cherríe and other people who know more about it.

LS: Well, do you think about the prestige? There's a conflict with a lot of feminist writers about wanting to be reviewed in the Sunday *Times*, wanting that kind of prestige. Jan Clausen writes about it in *A Movement of Poets*, when she talked about how a lot of feminist publishing is separatist, in the sense that it's in the feminist community and doesn't go much beyond that. So when we talk about wanting to reach a large audience, is that a contradiction?

GEA: No. Because I think that Kitchen Table probably wants to reach a large audience. You can be a small press, feminist, and still do that.

I've never wanted to publish with a mainstream publisher. I don't know why. I wanted Persephone to distribute *Bridge* to B. Dalton, to drugstores, you know. But see, my other vision is El Mundo Zurdo. It started out as a place for people to come and do their writing, like a retreat. (It was going to be in Italy, but now I think it's going to be in Oaxaca. And I'm going to try and get over there this July.) Along with the retreat is a publishing house that would publish not just third world, but white. Not just lesbians and faggots, but straight. A press that's not separatist in any way. But I don't know when that's going to become a reality because right now I feel that part of my job is not to organize and not to set up a publishing company. In San Francisco I started an El Mundo Zurdo reading series and an El Mundo Zurdo creative writing workshop that I did for about a year. Right now, my energy has to go into the writing. I don't know about the future. But several women have said they're interested in setting up El Mundo Zurdo Press. And one person said they were interested in setting up a magazine.

Writing the Body, Becoming a Mouth

LS: Let me shift to one other area we haven't talked so much about. You talked about feeling different as a child, being outsider and other. What about within the feminist community? What differences are there for you as a writer?

GEA: They ignore the body. It's like they're from the neck on up. Even though it's about lesbian sexuality, it's like they don't have any words. No vocabulary. They don't describe the movements of the body. I don't know of anyone who writes through the body. I want to write from the body; that's why we're in a body.

LS: I'm trying to think if there's anyone who writes from the body. I'm trying to think of something that moved me. Can you think of anything?

GEA: No. Some of the S/M people try it, but I don't know if they're succeeding. Monique Wittig does it, but in a very abstract, detached way—it's almost like looking at a movie rather than being in a movie.

LS: Absolutely. She's doing very important work. But that whole French feminist tradition is so kind of linguistically, theoretically removed. I have a real hard time reading it.

GEA: I have a symbol for the body, for sexuality, for female—the feathered serpent. According to the Olmecs, the earth was a serpent, and the Aztecs have serpents everywhere. The serpent lives in the underground, and is connected with the earth. The birds are connected with the sky, so with the feathers I'm joining the upper realm and the lower realm.

LS: So that's a goal for you, to merge—

GEA: An integration. And the body is the bridge. That's what I haven't seen. People don't deal with the body, and yet they don't deal with the spirit. They deal with the head. The mind. You know what I mean? What I'd like to do is talk from the body and also from these other realms. But people don't do that. I have yet to read anything about lesbian sexuality, about how lesbians feel about their bodies. There's nothing. People don't talk about—

LS: I think it will come from lesbians before it comes from straight women. Just because the contradiction of straight feminism, sexually, is a difficult contradiction.

GEA: Sí. So for me the serpent is a symbol of female sexuality, of all that's repressed. I also feel as a writer that I'm just a mouth, that my body is the medium for the words. It's like—this is my belly, and it's a cauldron. Everything goes in there: what I felt, what I saw, what I read, what happened to me. It's like putting all the ingredients for a soup in your belly, and the whole thing cooks. When it's just right, out comes the poem or the idea or the image or whatever. So this is the vehicle for the word. A lot of times I feel like I'm just a mouth, and these things pass through my body and come out of my mouth, or through my hand.

LS: Why? For reasons outside yourself or within?

GEA: I think I chose that kind of task. To communicate. When you communicate you're just a vehicle, just a mouth.

LS: You talked about lots of reasons for writing in "Speaking in Tongues," the letter to women of color: to compensate for the real world, to order the world, to become intimate with yourself, to self-discover, to dispel the myths that you're mad, to find self-worth, to write the unmentionables, and to show that you can and that you will write, the act of doing it.

64

GEA: Right. And it's making my soul, creating myself as I go along. Discovering myself. It's the same thing as creating myself.

LS: Why did you write "Speaking in Tongues" in the form of a letter?

GEA: Because of the deadline. It was a poem. It was going to be this poem, but we had this deadline. And with a poem, you have to work more with the language. You have to let it sit and gestate more because every word has to count. You can get away with things in prose. I tend to treat prose the way I treat poetry; that's why it takes me so long to write anything. But the form of a letter made it more intimate. It was like I was sitting across the table from someone.

LS: That's the whole notion of audience. The choosing of a letter was really important for you because you really had a very clear audience. You were writing to third-world women.

GEA: But I also felt that the letter was very impersonal. Particular, but impersonal. By impersonal, I mean that it didn't come from me, that I was just this channel. This mouth. I don't know if that sounds strange to you. If I'd sat down to write a letter, I would have addressed it to Cherríe or somebody I know who's a writer. And it would have been—I don't know. I don't know. It just felt to me when I was writing that letter that I was speaking for more than myself. You know what I mean? I've never felt that way about writing anything else.

LS: Earlier, when we started talking about sexuality, about differences in the feminist community, you stated that women aren't able to write about sexuality.

GEA: Not even talking about it. They might talk about it to their lover, but they don't even talk about it to their friends. It's like you and I could sit and talk about a political meeting we went to or something, but— we're strangers; we can't sit and talk about last night, fucking so and so, and what that meant.

LS: Has the writing that's been published—the S/M stuff that's just come out and the whole forum for talking about sexuality in women's newspapers—been a positive step? Is sexuality opening up?

GEA: Yes. I think it's a very positive step—whether you believe in S/M or not—because it says, "Here is another way of being lesbian. There are other ways." But the conservative feminists—or whatever they're called—I think they have this book of rules about how to be a lesbian. My sympathy with the S/M people is the freedom of speech, because we were denied that. There was white feminism, and they'd define what being Chicana, being black, or whatever meant. That's what they're doing with sexuality. Anything that opens sexuality up, liberates something in me. For someone to be able to say what their fantasies are—if those fantasies have to do with dogs or whipping or their father or whatever—it opens things up. It allows me to write my fantasies. It allows me to communicate my fantasies, which are equally taboo, or whatever.

LS: Were you able to open up more, to talk about sexuality after your hysterectomy? After you weren't in such pain?

GEA: Yes. That was one of the transformations. It was like everything coming to a head: All the pain, all the secrecy, all the things I'd repressed about my body. I saw it as a lesson; the body has to speak, and if it can't speak through any other way—to make you sit up and take notice—it makes you sick, so you have some time on your hands. That's how I felt when I was in the hospital. I had repressed parts that had stagnated, gotten poisonous, and formed these tumors, and it was a turning point for me. I called it "the woman I kept locked up in the basement." It was "Gloria with feelings"; some of the feelings were very politically incorrect. One feeling was that I was in love with my friend, Randy, who's a faggot. He was also in love with me, and we couldn't deal. The sexual part of it was nothing; it was that when you connect with a person on an emotional, spiritual, mental, psychic level, you want to connect physically too. But that was very bad, to do that. In my eyes, in his eyes, in the eyes of the world. I'd already faced that— you know, two women, and here it was—with this man. The operation and the near death just brought it all up. It was like I couldn't keep this woman locked up in the basement any more. I feel like the whole planet is going through that: the woman inside us and inside men is rebelling. She's got to come up for air, and I think that's why the feminist movement is so strong, because that's part of women's struggle to be liberated and allowed to share the world. Like I told you about religion, where the feminine principle doesn't even exist. It's the same way in the society. So there's this whole return of the feminine. And that happened physically to me in the hospital. It was like my body was acting out all these things—the suppression of women for two thousand years or whatever. I took what happened to me very concretely and also very metaphorically. I had a rage that I'd buried, an anger. I was very angry—

at society, at white people, at my mother, at my father for dying and leaving my mother. My mother was twenty-eight when he died, and she wasn't supposed to have a sexual life, to fuck. When your husband dies, you're faithful to him until you're dead. The depression—I'd been depressed for many years and didn't even know it!!!

LS: This was all two years ago?

GEA: Yeah. And I'm just now dealing with it in this book I'm writing. I call it *The Death Rites Passage.** The rites of passage were all my turning points, from the time I was born until two years ago.

LS: I'm interested in differences within third-world writing communities. Do you feel close to other third-world writers who are different than you?

GEA: First I was connected with the Chicanas; I was connected with the Nahuatl writing. I read a lot of Nahuatl poetry, and then I got connected with the Native Americans, and then the black and the Asian American. Right now I'm more interested in connecting with Latina writers. Cherríe and Mirtha and I started this Latina writers support group, and even among Latinas—I've found there are more differences between me and Latinas of different countries than there are between me and Native Americans. Or U.S. black women. I don't know, it's really weird. Maybe it has to do with class.

LS: So you're just learning about it now. I mean, we learn every day.

GEA: Yeah. But I feel there's something very similar in a black woman writing about her grandmother, an Indian woman writing about her grandmother, and me writing about my grandmother. Sometimes it's more similar to me than someone from Argentina or Brazil writing about their grandmother. It could be because we're here in this country.

LS: I have just one or two other odds and ends. Do you ever want to teach anymore?

GEA: In San Francisco I taught women's studies. Cherríe and I were both teaching there as part-time lecturers. I made up my mind when I moved to California that whatever teaching I did would be writing. Nothing else. So I taught feminist journal writing. Since then I've taught

---

* This title later became *La Prieta, The Dark One.* [GEA]

the El Mundo Zurdo creative writing workshops in San Francisco. I've carried them over here, but I call them "speaking in tongues." I'm going to start one in January. The only thing I want to teach is what I want to learn, which is writing. In the writing I incorporate visualization, meditation, concentration—all the magical things.

LS: These are all part of these workshops?

GEA: Yes. Everything goes into the workshop. Whatever I'm interested in—psychology, the body, doing rituals—all goes into the workshop. I always start the workshop with a ritual. I always ground people: we always meditate before we write, and I show them tools for how to connect with their inner self. I'm trying to integrate everything: what I know about Chicano literature, third-world literature, psychology, how the body functions, the brain waves—it all goes into the workshops. I don't ever want to teach in a university, unless it's a special class, and only one. Because universities can really subvert you.

LS: Yeah. I know that! I'd like to ask two more things: Is there anything else you want to say, that you can think about—not connected to anything? And, do you think that what we just did is useful to you as a writer?

GEA: Yes. I can start with the last one. The work I'm writing now is about turning points in my life, *La serpiente que se come su cola*, and there are some commonplace things that I entirely left out—like teaching La Mujer Chicana and a lot of that stuff about Chicanos. (I don't know why, maybe because it's so much a part of my life.)

LS: I see that you have some notes, so if there's something else you want to say that we haven't covered . . .

Other Influences

GEA: For me, a symbol for integration is the heart beating. You have your heart; it beats. Then you have a heart over here—the sexual heart, when you have an orgasm. When you meditate you set off a third heart. When you can get the three synchronized it's wonderful. It's like pure ecstasy. OK. So the first I knew of a heart beating was at my mother's breast, through the heart, through the breast; it's like the physical heart and has to do with the body, sexuality. Then, there's the feeling heart, and then the spiritual. I use those three as a symbol. There may even be a fourth heart; I don't know. Can you think of a fourth heart? There could be the beat, the rhythm of the universe.

LS: Outside, as opposed to inside?

GEA: Right. And that connects with this one. When I meditate sometimes I can synchronize the three; that's why I love to meditate.

LS: Do you make those things happen in writing, or is that what you want to do?

GEA: That's what I want to do in the writing. Sometimes I have a sexual heart, but not the other two. The most difficult one is the spiritual. It took me years and years of meditating to be able to do it. Once you do it, it's so easy, but then you don't want to do it. It's like writing: You love it, but it's so hard to get yourself to sit down and do it.

LS: And then it feels good again.

GEA: Yes.

LS: But when you're away from it, it's hard to get back to it, when there's distractions. You sometimes forget how it feels.

GEA: One of the things I didn't talk about at all is the next eighteen years, the present age cycle that the earth is on, is ending.

LS: In 2011 or something?

GEA: Well, according to the Mayan calendar, it's 2011, December 24th. According to the Aztec calendar it's August 16, 1987. A friend of mine figured it out on a computer; she has it down to—I don't know—the year 2003 or something. But anyway, what's very important about these next eighteen years is that the past is going to come together with the present and the future. So all the stuff I'm talking about—the ancient roots of the psyche of the americana, or the psyche of the black person, or the white person, or whatever—is surging up to the top. At the same time I feel all these little earthquakes in my body, like with illness and dying and stuff; I think that people as a whole on the planet are going to be feeling those things, or are already feeling those things. I'm just—we're just litmus paper of what's going on in the universe. It's very important in my writing that I talk about the next eighteen years. And part of Andrea—what you read is the past, and then I have the present, and then the future. The present is all this stuff that's going on—revolution, earth changes, the political upheaval, the norms, changing values, religion. The future part is looking back at that transition from the Piscean age to the Aquarian age, from el mundo quinto sol, the fifth world sun, to the sixth world sun. So part of it is very visionary in terms of looking to the future. I'd so been concentrating on the roots and the past that I forgot to mention that. Sometimes I overdo the looking forward, and not—you know?

LS: So that's going to be in this book also?

GEA: Yes. I have a section called "Five Movements," which is the Aztecs' name for this age. Olin, this is the fifth movement, and according to the Aztecs it's going to end through earthquake and fire. So you can see the enormity of the task. And I get very impatient because it's so slo–o–o–o–w. I mean you write a page, then you revise it and revise it again and again.

2

···

Within the Crossroads

Lesbian/Feminist/Spiritual Development
An Interview with Christine Weiland (1983)

···

(1998–1999)

ALK: In this interview, as in the previous interview with Linda Smuckler, you describe your earliest remembered spiritual experience as a type of self-multiplication or self-extension that occurred when you reached for a piece of fruit. Can you elaborate on this experience? In what ways is it relevant to your life today?

GEA: There are certain cultural assumptions, injunctions, teachings that didn't take with me. One of them concerned the physical body's limitations. When I reached for that fruit, somehow or other my arm got longer and I noticed concentric selves like sheaths, one within the other within the other. But I realized that I wasn't supposed to be able to extend my arm beyond what I'm physically capable of doing, that I shouldn't have been able to reach that high. This also has to do with the first time I touched myself, masturbated, which I also knew I shouldn't do. (I wrote a story, "El segundo corazón/The Second Heart," about it.) I have this part of myself that's stubborn and wants to keep doing something; if I have to hide to continue doing it, I will. So I kept on entertaining spiritual experiences and I kept on masturbating.

At the time I had no way of explaining this experience, but later as an adult I started putting together its significance, its meaning. I came up with the idea that the body doesn't stop at the skin, that it extends— I don't know how far, maybe it could extend down to San Francisco, maybe to the moon. But we limit the body, we shrink it. It has to do

71

with belief. People who can experience things from a distance *believe* that they can, like shamans who travel great distances; their souls leave their bodies and suddenly they're across the ocean. You can teach yourself how to do this through certain practices and techniques. I've only been able to feel that my soul has left my body when I dream or when I've had out-of-body experiences, which have always resulted from some kind of shock—something traumatic, unexpected, something unplanned for—not through willed intention and self-discipline. So anyway, here's this child who could extend her body, but was it a physical body or was it some kind of invisible body that she elongated?

ALK: Somehow or other you got the fruit, right? Did you think someone else brought the fruit to you? Did you get the fruit by literally extending your hand? Or did it occur on a spiritual level?

GEA: Yes, I got the fruit. No one else brought it to me and it's not that my muscles and bones grew, became elongated. There's an invisible body, your soul, that can leave the physical body and actually manipulate by remote. It would be wonderful if I could believe that if I wanted to be five eleven, I could just elongate my body and become that tall! But human beings have made a contract about what's possible, and one of these contracts concerns the belief about bodily limitations.

I believe that humankind is coming to a point where there's going to be a huge metamorphosis and our physical bodies—or maybe it's our invisible bodies—are going to change. I'm revising a story titled "Puddles" where la Prieta turns into a lizard-woman; she has a lizard skin and her sense of smell changes. It happens in nature. Look at the difference between a butterfly and its larval state. Or look at salamanders: Some are terrestrial and become aquatic and some regenerate, they change their form. (I'm also writing an axolotl story.) I think humanity is going to take an evolutionary leap and things are going to be different.

ALK: In this interview you claim that spirituality is a tool of the oppressed, the "only weapon and means of protection oppressed people have. Changes in society come only after that." How have your views on the political efficacy of spirituality changed in the seventeen or so years since this interview?

GEA: My views have become more solid. When you're going through a lot of emotional pain and don't have anyone to support or help you,

you're thrown back onto your own resources. You kind of surrender to the will of universal consciousness, to God. Or you say, "I need help; I have to make changes in my life." You have to commit yourself through intention, so prayer is really good for that. I had some horrendous experiences where I was totally isolated and totally alone. (Some of the poems in *Borderlands*, like "Antigua, Mi Diosa" are about this.) I had to find sustenance somewhere. I needed a connection with something outside myself that could sustain me but I was really fighting it. I didn't want to accept la diosa, that spiritual help—or maybe it's imaginal help, as it all takes place in the imagination. So when a woman or a group of women or men or a whole race has been oppressed historically, over and over, they have to create some means of support and sustenance in order to survive.

ALK: A lot of people would agree with you but would argue that this spiritual survival become a form of escapism which maintains the status quo: "Things will be better in the future, but we can't change the fact that we're oppressed now." For you, however, spirituality is very political.

GEA: When beliefs become institutionalized (like certain aspects of la Virgen de Guadalupe), they becomes an opiate for the people. But if you maintain a connection that doesn't have all these institutional trappings, it's political. This is one of the reasons I'm so weary of political, religious, and academic institutions: They come with agendas and trappings which lull you into not challenging things.

ALK: You're saying that spirituality can be a force and energy for bringing about change?

GEA: Yes! I don't even know if "spirituality" is the right term because it's been so misused.

ALK: What would you use instead?

GEA: I've been trying to think of another term. I keeping coming back to Mexican indigenous terms to see if I can appropriate cultural figures or words and apply them to the twenty-first-century experience, but I haven't come up with anything yet. I know it has something to do with the imagination, the inner life, but the terms that I come up with don't work. It's like the problem with the word "gay": if you use "gay" to describe medieval homosexual activity, you're transferring from one age to another. You have to somehow reformulate it. Likewise with "spirituality."

ALK: Let me know when you find a new word! Your view of good and evil in this interview is very nondualistic: You state that you've always believed "God and the devil are the same person, that evil and good are the same." Do you still hold this belief? If so, could you apply it to the manifestations of evil that confront us—in everything from racism/sexism/homophobia we experience today to the decimation of indigenous American peoples to the Holocaust?

GEA: Yes. It's a very real paradox. We live in physical reality in order to experience certain things. Often people don't try to make order out of the chaos, turmoil, oppression, and pain in their lives. Left to ourselves, we don't want to deal with any of that—right? But say you have a chronic disease which some day will give you an aneurism or a heart attack. That adversity forces you to try to give significance to the negative experience and the doubts, confusion, and ambiguity. We cocreate our experiences and the things around us. The things which have happened to me—the diabetes, the near-death experience on the operation table, the racism, the homophobia, the sexism that comes with being a brown girl living in ranch country—forced me to mine some kind of meaning from these events, experiences, feelings, thoughts. That's how we make our soul, how we evolve as humans. Sometimes we can evolve through the good things—through the connections, the love, the empathy, the joy, the enthusiasm. But the good experiences don't force us to search for meaning. I've been mugged twice. I spent a lot of time figuring out why this happened to me: Did I provoke it? Should I have been out on the street? I don't scrutinize a happy experience as much. I don't dwell on it, I don't do the soul work that I need to do as a writer. I'm not saying that Jews created the Holocaust or that the woman who's been raped has created that experience for herself, because she doesn't. We don't do it individually. We don't even do it as a human species, we do it as all life. We do it in conjunction with the creative life force. Does that make sense to you?

ALK: Yes. From one perspective events can very clearly seem evil, but from a much different perspective they're actually a part of a larger evolutionary process.

GEA: Look at my experience with diabetes: it's not just about my immune system killing off the beta cells so that my body no longer secretes insulin. It's not the cells; it's not about one antibody configuration of cells killing off another configuration. It's the whole person, every system in the body. Every biological system, every emotional system, every soul system. Similarly, it's not just about the individual person; there's something greater. I really do believe that we have to create our souls, we have to keep evolving as souls, as minds, as bodies—on all the different planes. If it takes adversity to force us to learn, to do, to create souls, to evolve, then we're going to get adversity. Right now, we learn through adverse experiences. Maybe in the future it won't be this way and maybe some people can learn through their dreams. If I had a choice of being raped in this reality or in the dream world, I'd rather be raped in the dream because it's a different plane, a different signification system; it's not flesh and blood. At least I don't think it is. If I've come into this life as a Chicana born of Amalia and Urbano who were farmers and ranchers of campesino working class, and I wanted to go through certain experiences and build my soul up in certain ways, then it seems to me that if I'm part of this greater universal soul I would know exactly what sort of things I needed to deal with in this life. If I needed to deal with depression or with being too prideful or with greed, then I'd suffer these experiences until I learned to detach enough to get perspective, to give it meaning. I believe that the universe is a text which we cocreate. But when you're in flesh and blood—when you don't have that distance—when you're in the midst of that pain—you can't see anything but its immediacy and so this enemy becomes all powerful; there are no redeeming qualities. But by stepping back and asking "OK. What's my responsibility in this? What part did I play? What's the meaning?" you get into symbolic and archetypal patterns.

ALK: So you're talking about a way of attaining agency. When you view good and evil dualistically, the negative events have tremendous power over you. By shifting your perspective you acquire power to bring about change.

GEA: It would be ineffective for me to look at white people or men with hatred and see them as the enemy. It would not serve me and it would not serve them.

ALK: And this perspective empowers you.

GEA: Yes, and it often changes the other people as well; they begin acting differently. I've been with people whose racism continued no matter what anybody did, but I've also been with racist people who, when I didn't reciprocate in hate, changed their behavior toward me. At least for that moment, they changed. Those too entrenched in their patterns keep repeating them. I know this sounds kind of Pollyanna, but I really think that when someone does you wrong you have to forgive them; you have to let go and get on with your life.

ALK: I've realized that recently; it's very true. Otherwise, you're enslaved to your own anger.

GEA: It takes your energy and whatever takes your energy and attention enthralls you, enslaves you. If you dwell on this person who did you wrong, you're giving them energy which you could be using in more positive ways.

ALK: In this interview you assert your belief in an underlying/ overarching commonality that goes beyond human beings to include everything. You suggest that if we all recognized our commonality "there'd be no more violence" because we'd realize that harming someone else harms ourselves. Doesn't this belief in a cosmic universal energy/force contradict your use of labels? And if not, why not? (I'm playing devil's advocate here!)

GEA: No. We need to be able to switch between looking at differ-ences and looking at commonalities. I don't think one is superior to the other; we just need some kind of negotiation or balance. Have you seen drawings that seem to represent two very different things— like the picture of a vase that when examined from a different per-spective seems to be the profile of two human faces? It depends on your perception, what you focus on. During the last few centuries— or maybe even longer—people have focused on differences, on the stranger. Difference is threatening to the perceiver. From the begin-ning of time to the present, all the wars, ethnic conflicts, class con-flicts, and so on are based on the belief that people who are different from you may harm you. What I want to do is blink my eyes and see the other from a different perspective, focusing on what we have in common with a rock, a tree, a bird, a black person, a Jewish person, a gay person. Look at the commonalities: We have a consciousness, we have a soul.

ALK: I believe that to get beyond racism we need to get beyond the idea of "race." As long as we use labels we'll create unnecessary divisions among people.

GEA: I use labels because we haven't gotten beyond race or class or other differences yet. When I don't assert certain aspects of my identity like the spiritual part or my queerness, they get overlooked and I'm diminished. When we come to a time when I don't have to say, "Look, I'm a dyke," or "I'm spiritual," or "I'm intellectual," I'll stop using labels. That's what I want to work towards. But until we come to that time, if you lay your body down and don't declare certain facets of yourself, they get stepped on.

But we do need to start talking about a time when labels won't be necessary. The idea of getting beyond race comes first and then people open up to it. They begin saying, "Yeah, I could act this way," and then several decades later maybe it becomes a cultural fact, a part of consensual reality. But you're right, the idea of race has to change. I think we can invent other categories, rather than race, but we'll always have categories because our languages demand it and because as humans we're such a diverse species. We have to redo the old categories or we need to create new ones as we go along.

ALK: I'm fascinated by your concept of a "yoga of the body." Do you still have this concept? If so, in what ways has it developed since this 1983 conversation?

GEA: "Yoga of the body" has to do with flexibility and fluidity—going beyond physical boundaries. It has to do with extending beyond limitations. Yoga is the ability to move your body in a flexible kind of way. You have these stretching exercises, you curl your legs a certain way, you work in conjunction with the breathing. (In my younger days I did Kundalini yoga.) We need that kind of flexibility when we work with the imagination and with our minds and feelings. We need a yoga of the body which includes the mind, the spirit, the imagination, the soul. If you're an artist, creativity is a yoga of the mind, of the imagination. Everything that writers do—whether it's fiction or images—has to go through the body. Readers are also affected physically. Every word you read hits you physiologically—your blood pressure changes, your heartbeat changes; your cells, your bones, your muscle are moved by a beautiful poem, a tragic episode. So that's the kind of yoga that I want: a yoga filtered through the body and through the imagination, the emotions, the spirit, and the soul.

"Within the Crossroads: Lesbian/Feminist/Spiritual Development"
An Interview with Christine Weiland (1983)

Early Life

CW: You said you were born when you mother was sixteen. Did your mother plan on having you at that time?

GEA: No. I was conceived before the marriage ceremony and was born a month or something like that before I was supposed to be, and I think she had some guilt about it.

CW: When you were born it was pretty obvious to everyone that you were early. How did your mother feel about it?

GEA: Well, I don't know if it was very obvious to everyone (there's not that much difference between nine and eight months), but I think it was obvious to my mother, my father, and the immediate family. They knew. I think my mother felt OK until I was three months old and blood started appearing on my diaper; I began having a period. She probably thought, "What did I do wrong? . . . Oh, it's the result of a sin." My mother has a pretty healthy attitude towards sex, except that she's adopted all the standard ideas—that it's dirty, that all men want is your body. But otherwise, she has a much healthier attitude towards it than most people in South Texas.

CW: Do you know how your father felt about your mother being pregnant?

GEA: He was in love with her from the time she was eight years old. He was the school bus driver when my mother was eight. (When he was in school, he was also the bus driver.) He was six years older than my mother. He wanted her and was already madly in love with her. He knew that she was going to be his wife. My mother wouldn't have anything to do with him. At eight she didn't like boys. I don't know how he felt about my birth. I think he felt that I was a special child. I always felt he treated me like I was special because I had this handicap—I bled. Technically, I was menstruating and able to bear a child, even though I was so young. I mean, there was something special and something freaky about it, but my mother felt the freakiness more that my father. I think he was in awe of this event.

CW: You mean of your having a period so young?

GEA: Yes. He was always with me in my head, in my consciousness. He stayed away from me but it was like he was always there, watching me. His presence was always with me, so when I was little I felt this intense sexuality towards my father; I don't know whether I picked it up from him or he from me. Or I could have mistaken this connection, this spiritual connection, for sexuality. As a child I knew there was an energy between us. I also felt it with my mother but we weren't supposed to touch her because my sister and I were girls. It was OK for my brothers to be intimate and touch her, but we weren't supposed to. However it was OK for the male parent to touch the female child and play with her, and my father did that until a certain age.

CW: Do you remember what age?

GEA: I think it was when I was five or six because around then my breasts started growing. That's when I realized I was really strange, really different from everyone else. It's just real strange—the relationship I've had and still do have with my father though he's dead. I still feel his presence strongly.

CW: What kind of person was your father?

GEA: My father was strong, a leader in the community. He adored his father, who was a womanizer and had mistresses, four different houses he visited. He was married to my grandmother but he also had these other "wives." He'd take my father and his second son, David, with him, and they'd play with his other children. It was a real close family thing except that it excluded my grandmother. It was just my father and the children of the other women. His father died early of a heart attack, just like my father died early of a heart attack. His father's death was a great shock. There were nine in his family and he became the head of the household. He began supporting them at the age of twelve.

My father was not as talkative as my Uncle David, and not as loving—my Uncle David was always touching and kissing and hugging. I had that connection with him, that physical connection with my uncle that I didn't have with my father. My father was afraid to touch me. After I was six he'd only touch my head.

CW: So you were cut off from touching anyone, because you couldn't touch your mother and—

GEA: I couldn't touch my father. I knew—very early—that there were a lot of these incestuous feelings between myself and my father which I may have transferred to my brother around the age of ten or twelve, or maybe even earlier than that because it was so incorrect to have those kinds of feelings about your father The sexual feelings were very strong in the whole family, between me and my sister. Maybe more on my sister's part than on mine. There was never any of that with my brother. I had daughter-father fantasies but I didn't put my face or his on the fantasy. There was just any father, any daughter. They were all heterosexual fantasies until I discovered that there was another sexual way of being. Then I started experimenting, creating sexual fantasies with women—or with men and women. But I had sexual fantasies about father-daughter, sister-brother, woman-dog, woman-wolf, woman-jaguar, woman-tiger, or woman-panther. It was usually a cat- or a dog-type animal.

CW: Do you remember any of the fantasies specifically?

GEA: Yes. In the father-daughter fantasies there was a lot of physical contact between the father and the daughter, like bathing and disrobing from a very early age, from the time the child was a baby. And then three years old, five years old. Most of the erotic fantasies had to do with touching, kissing, and holding, with the girl child feeling pleasure. Then gradually as she got older, very gently—it wasn't like a rape— very gently the father kissing the body, licking the body, touching the breasts, and as she got older, going down on her. As she got older, she would touch him and play with his penis, put it in her mouth. When I was younger most of the fantasies never got to the point of intercourse. When I got older, the fantasies became more graphic and more sexual. Then it was strangers. It wasn't father-daughter but just any woman, any man. The animal fantasies were because I lived on a farm and observed animals copulating. In my animal fantasies I was outside in the jungle or on the grass or on top of a hill. The panther was usually a pet. In the fantasies it was OK for me to see that it was happening to me. I'd be playing with the animal and then getting fucked. Usually I'd be on my stomach and the animal would be pretty large, a large dog or panther. Later, when I found out about homosexuality, sometimes the animal would be a she-lion or a she-panther. It wasn't always a male.

CW: Did you talk to other people about it, or was it something you kept to yourself?

GEA: It was something I kept to myself. I've always been pretty much of a loudmouth; it's hard for me to hold secrets. I might have started telling people, and they probably shut me up. My mother says I'm shameless because to me, nothing is private. Maybe that's why I became a writer. My sexual life, my fantasy life, my spiritual life are unveiled, divulged. If there's a veil, it's for myself, but once I realize something, then the whole world can know it. I didn't start talking about my fantasies until I met Randy. I had a few women friends with whom I tried to talk about these things, but women aren't as eager to talk about their sex lives as men are. Especially faggots. So it was fine talking about fantasies and my different sexual experiences with Randy.

CW: After you were born, did your parents plan the other children or were they surprises?

GEA: My mother had a diaphragm, I remember that. We lived on a ranch, miles away from anything. The only kind of planned parenthood people had was that the man wouldn't ejaculate into the vagina. Women took certain herbs if they didn't want to get pregnant and they'd go see a curandera. I don't think my mother ever bothered with that. She wanted to have children but she didn't want to have me. I came too early. Once I came, though, it was OK for her to have the others. She wanted to do it early and had all of us before she was twenty—a child every fifteen months. So it's like we grew up together. She stopped having children after my father watched my little brother's birth. The doctors didn't allow fathers to watch the childbirth, but my father insisted. He watched and found it horrendous. He didn't want my mother to go through that painful process again. He thought she would die. I mean, my mother was very healthy; she probably could have had another four kids, but to him that experience—! And then having helped animals on the farm giving birth. So he had her tubes tied. He said, "No more children. Four is enough." So that was it.

CW: She didn't have anything to say about it? It was your father's decision? You said, "He had her tubes tied."

GEA: Yes, he insisted. But he couldn't get away with anything if my mother didn't want it. She had a strong voice in the household and stood up to my father. I think my father was weak only to her. I guess the Pisces predominated in him with his relationship to my mother because she could do pretty much what she pleased. There were certain points where she put her foot down. He probably listened to her more than she listened to him. My family is very atypical because in other families it's not that way. My mother kept the money. But my father loved her so much he couldn't see her go through this pain again, and I think she was ready; four was enough.

My parents were very loving and intimate towards each other. They would always be fighting and arguing. And very intimate; they fucked a lot. It was very sexual. I don't know where my mother got this thing about women being subservient to men because she never was—not to her brothers, not to her father, not to my father. But she paid lip service.

CW: Did she find the birth process horrendous?

GEA: No. I think she thought that's just the way it was. It probably would have been less painful had it been natural childbirth, but she was proud that we were born in the hospital and the clinic, whereas most of the other kids were born through a midwife which, I think, would have been better.

CW: But she thought it was better for the child to be born in a hospital?

GEA: Well, my father thought it was safer in case anything came up. I think my mother got over her fear after I was born, her fear of dying or whatever fears women have when they're having a child for the first time. I've never had a child, but I'm sure there's a basic fear that something is going to go wrong: you're going to bleed to death; you're going to die; the kid is going to be born abnormal, dead, or a monster, or something.

CW: Has your mother talked about those fears?

GEA: Only if I ask her point blank. Mostly she says she doesn't remember, it's been so long. She and I can talk intimately. She's like me—a big mouth. I mean, she told me about my father having intercourse with her and how she felt about it. I don't know if I've ever asked her how she felt about the birth. I've asked her things because I'm writing an autobiography and there were certain things I want to know that only she can tell me. I ask when my sister's not around because my sister will think, "Oh, well, she wants it for her book."

CW: Did your parents have a preference in the sex of the children? When they found out that your mother was pregnant the first time, did either of them desire to have a male or a female child?

GEA: I think that they wanted some boys and some girls, but I don't know if they wanted them in any kind of order. I always felt like my mother would have wanted me to be a boy. I think with my father it was OK—as the firstborn. There was, and still is, a strong preference for males in my culture and in my family—which doesn't mean my mother doesn't love me and my sister as much, just differently. It means that there are certain things we're supposed to be and do as women. Our role is to wait on our brothers. That was the first thing I rebelled against: ironing their shirts, fixing them dinner, and serving them food. I love to serve people and make food, and I'll do it for friends, whether male or female, but to have it imposed on me—!! My brothers are intuitive. They're very atypical and have a very strong feminine aspect to them, especially my brother, Nune.

CW: How is Nune atypical?

GEA: He had to fight his feelings, to become strong and not cry inside. I don't mean physical, real tears; he had to grow a thick skin and become less sensitive to the world—because he was born male. My brothers, it's almost like they had to work hard at their masculinity because they had so much of the other. If the pressures hadn't been on them they both probably would have wanted women's things. I had to grow a thick skin for the same reasons: to not get hurt, to not be so sensitive to the world. But I didn't have to live up to a macho image. I had a knack for male activities: I'd fix things and fool around with machines. But I also did female work like knitting, crochet, and leathercraft. I did both traditional women's and men's work. For me one wasn't better than the other. My sister didn't do men's work. She has no knack for things like putting up curtains or plugging in a TV; you have to do it for her. She has so much energy in her body that she gets shocked. Sometimes when I touch a doorknob I get shocked too.

CW: Were you encouraged or discouraged in doing any of the various activities you did?

GEA: I was discouraged from the male acts, but I've always been real stubborn and I'd just go ahead and do them. I got away from punishment by saying "Oh, sure" but still doing what I wanted to do. When something got under my skin, I'd stand up and protest: I'd yell and scream and get punished. That was fine, but things didn't seem to get under my skin very often. I mean, if my mother was yelling and screaming that I should do this and that I should do that.

CW: What kind of things specifically would she say you should or shouldn't do?

GEA: Clean the cupboards, clean the house, iron the clothes, wash, grind the corn, can tomatoes, can corn. Those are the kinds of things I should do. I shouldn't go out, get dirty, jump across ditches, shoot the twenty-two, go hunting snakes, but it was OK for me to mow the lawn, learn how to drive a tractor, and do that kind of work. My brothers wouldn't help around the house, so I had to do the men's work outside—pruning, cutting, watering, putting up the clothesline, fixing the roof, digging holes for the trash. (We buried the tin cans and burned the paper.) It was OK for me to do these male tasks because it helped my mother.

My brothers didn't do work around the house, but they didn't get away with stuff. My father punished them whenever they disobeyed. They were always fighting (they still are). He'd make them kneel in or by the closet for a certain length of time. He might have struck them a couple of times, and my mother struck them on their bottoms with her hand—but never with a belt or a stick or anything. My mother would yell and scream at my sister and me, but my father didn't even have to raise his voice for us to obey. He was that kind of person. But I never got spanked by either parent. They were so strong, Christine; they had such strong personalities.

As I grew older I put out that I was book smart but not smart at anything else. But I was very cunning in another way. I always knew how to do any task in the shortest amount of time with the fewest number of movements. Like picking cotton: I'd figure out a way to move my hands fast and to position the opening of the sack properly in a special way so that I could pick my hundred pounds or whatever and then go home to read. With the hoes, I'd make sure that my back was straight, that when I lifted the hoe and put it down I wouldn't strain my back. I figured out these kinds of things with my body that people who'd been working in fields for generations hadn't figured out. So when I became an adolescent, the role I played was that I lacked common sense, was absentminded, forgetful, didn't know about relationships. It was all a mask. But when I was little there was no mask; everybody knew I was real sharp. My sister was so dumb, she'd always get punished. I mean, if you know that if you say "no" you're going to get punished, but you keep doing it a million times, don't you learn?

CW: So you'd deal with that by just saying "OK" and then not doing it anyway?

GEA: I'd deal with it in a variety of ways. Sometimes I'd say that I'd do it later, a postponement. Or I'd just say, very calmly, "I'm not going to do it." My mother didn't know how to handle me. Out of all her children, she says, I've been the most disobedient and given her the most trouble; I've been the rebel, the black sheep, everything. But I haven't, I've just been myself. When I felt very strongly that I wasn't going to do something, I'd just say it.

CW: How did she react?

GEA: It would infuriate her. She'd give up in disgust or she'd say, "I'm going to let your father deal with you," or she'd yell at me. If I didn't want her to get upset, I'd be very vague. I tried not to upset her too much, she had four of us to deal with. I love my mother, I always tried to make things easy for her. I bought her stuff, I made sure she didn't work too hard and even if I hated washing dishes all the time, I'd help. I looked after her. When we cooked, I made sure she got good food instead of my brothers always getting it. She was like a prima donna to me. You know, we were poor; we were working all the time. I felt very close to my mother. She's also Libra. Her birthday is October 4th, about eight days away from mine. When I was young, a lot of my manipulation was done to help her. I really got into hating her when I was an adolescent. I wanted to hurt her, stick the dagger in her back. There was this love-hate between us, but I think a lot of it had to do with sexuality and being at the age when you want to establish an independent life of your own—fourteen, fifteen, sixteen. For me, I think it was earlier.

CW: Why did you want to take care of your mother at such a young age?

GEA: I've always been that kind of person, and I did the same thing with my sister and brothers. If I love someone, I don't want them to be upset or to suffer. Part of my problem was—and to some extent still is—not telling people certain home truths because it hurts them. If I see someone very vulnerable, I won't confront them. I've learned to be very diplomatic and say things in ways that don't hurt people. Don't you agree that I usually say things in a way that doesn't hurt them a lot?

CW: Yes.

GEA: I don't know. I just have a lot of love for people, and a lot of love for my sister, my brothers, and my parents. It wasn't because I was protecting my mother more than I was protecting the others. She had a heavier burden, and she was also the person I interacted with the most because the mother rears the child. She was the one laying down the way we should be and what we should do—the traditional, cultural thing. Up until I was eight or thirteen I was my mother's little kid and I did a lot of the tasks that would take weight off of her, like shopping and cooking. When I was in high school, I took homemaking classes. The teacher would come to the house and see my menus and the cakes and breads and stuff. Then at one point I gave it up; I just didn't do it anymore. My sister always says that I never cooked, but my mother remembers. Everybody in the family was angry that I had stopped being this kind of person.

My sister had never cooked or done any housework, but she decided to take over those tasks. I think I told you about her decision to stay in the house and do the housework and the cooking. It was that or work in the fields. She hated the sun and would get heat strokes. She was gaining weight and didn't want to be around people looking at her. At my urging, my mother allowed her to stay home. She was about thirteen.

I stopped cooking for the same reason that I stopped obeying my mother: because it was a female role. As long as I liked to do it, it was fine. But I was really heavy into learning, into books and exploring, and the cooking and cleaning took time out from the books. There was another reason as well: once I become good at something, I give it up. It's real bizarre. I got good at working leather, and I gave it up. I got good at crocheting, knitting, sculpture, whatever. I've done it and want to do something else. There was a switch, I think, for me around the age of twelve, thirteen, fourteen—a switch from using my hands and doing fine embroidery to working with my mind. Part of it was rebellion against working in the fields like an animal, where the work was so brutalizing and made you into a numb animal where you only did mechanical things. You worked in the hot sun with the sweat, the dirt, and the thirst. It was sort of a rebellion against the body, which again was connected to the sexuality. Everything was connected.

CW: You mean not working in the fields was a rebellion?

GEA: Working in the fields meant time away from the books, which was the mind or the spirit. Working in the fields meant working with your body, with the animal body, and mine was always in pain. It was horrendous, because out of every twenty-four days—my period came every twenty-four days—ten of them were painful. I had fevers of 106, tonsillitis every time, throwing up. Horrendous pain all the time, all the time, all the time.

CW: Would you stay in bed during those ten days?

GEA: It didn't matter if I stayed in bed or if I was sitting or walking because the pain was always there. Often I missed school, but sometimes doing things—rather than staying in bed—would distract me.

CW: Did you work in the fields?

GEA: When my father was alive, I went to school and worked in the fields in the afternoon. After he died, we worked in the fields in the summertime, on Saturdays and Sundays, whenever we could. Sometimes my brothers would miss school to work because we needed the money.

CW: Who owned the fields you worked in?

GEA: Not my family. My family lost their land to whites because of taxes and dirty manipulation by these people, so my father was a tenant farmer, a sharecropper. He kept 60 percent, and 40 percent went to this corporation called Rio Farms, Inc. These white landowners had just incorporated and bought all the land from the mostly Mexican small farmers. My father would get in debt to them for the seed and the water. We were like slaves, Christine. When my father was alive we'd go out in the fields and cover watermelons with paper plates so they wouldn't freeze in the wintertime; we'd hoe and pick cotton. My father had braceros when they were still legal and later he had mojados— trabajadores sin papeles, workers without papers.

CW: What's that?

GEA: Braceros are people from across the border, from Mexico, who come and live here. We had some good relationships with some of those braceros, they were wonderful. When my father died we didn't have anything and had to work for other people. We worked for my Uncle David and for the farmers around the area, mostly whites. A Mexican, a Chicano, would come up and round us all up, put us in the back of a truck, and take us to the fields. Sometimes my mother was able to get a stretch of land only for us, so she'd load us up in the car and we'd go the fields and just work on our own, without a supervisor. The fields were not ours. Even when my father was farming, they weren't ours.

CW: When did your family lose the land?

GEA: Gradually. I had a very irresponsible grandfather, the one with all those women. He went through a lot of money and land through carelessness. Also, the whites knew how to take land away through trickery. My grandmothers, uncles, and aunts sold their mineral rights for a few dollars. This happened before I was born on both sides of my family. My grandmothers ended up with a little land which they then parceled out to their sons and grandsons. I ended up with around twelve acres which I deeded over to my mother. It's so senseless to chop up the land and give everyone a little piece.

But my other grandmother, Mamagrande Ramona, on my mother's side, her husband, her husband's father before her, and her husband's grandfather had amassed some land—land grants from the time when Texas was Mexico. It was shared collectively. At that time people weren't into private ownership. Private ownership didn't occur until the whites came. Because they settled there, it was their land. Their ownership was even acknowledged by the U.S. Land Grant but it was taken away through carelessness, through white people's greed, and my grandmother not knowing English.

CW: There must have been a lot of resentment involved with going to the fields, too?

GEA: Oh, yeah. To work in the fields is the lowest job, and to be a migrant worker is even lower. If you work in the fields but you stay home, you're pretty low down in the social scale, but if you work in the fields and move with the harvests—to West Texas, Arkansas, Indiana—you're even lower because you have to pull your kids out of school and you're at the mercy of other white growers who were considered worse than Texas growers. We migrated one year, during my second year of school. My father swore never to do it again because I missed two months of school. We went to the Texas panhandle, lived in three or four different houses and moved around. To me, it was a new experience, I have a lot of memories. After that year my father would go by himself. When my brother wanted to drop out of high school, he started migrating with his family. We were the kind of people who worked in the fields but didn't migrate. My father insisted we go to school. He wanted me to go to college. Nobody else did. They didn't even know what college was, but my father was different—probably because of this aristocracy (it's really weird, very poor aristocracy but aristocracy anyway) on my father's side and a sense of superiority, that the Anzaldúas were always different. We were the poorest of the poor and we were different, but not in a privileged way. We were different in being so odd. My mother's side was very india, working class, with maybe some black blood which is always looked down on in the valley where I come from. So here was this peasant-type with this aristocratic, Spanish-German, blond, blue-eyed, Jew, whatever on my father's side. (I told you he looks exactly like the man who runs the laundromat in Brooklyn, near my apartment—very Jewish features, curly hair, the nose.) Very proud, silent, doesn't want any charity, but I don't know where it's from because all I've ever known is poverty.

CW: What was the physical environment of your home like? You had a house, right?

GEA: We had several.

CW: Start with where you were born.

GEA: I was born and raised in Jesús María and in Los Vergeles, which means "the gardens." It was a little ranch settlement made up of several surrounding ranches. Our house was on my maternal grandmother's land. Her people had settled there when she was young. Schooling was in Spanish because Texas was Mexican territory then. Even when it became part of the U.S. the little ranches would gather money and hire a teacher. It wasn't like the government did anything. (My grandmother had been born further up into Texas, in Gonzales, and she'd traveled down and married my grandfather, who had brown eyes and was fair, a very handsome man. On my father's side, my grandmother was born in one of the first settlements in South Texas.) It was just a little ranch, no electricity, no running water. We got water from the windmills and the well. It was semidesert, lots of cactus until irrigation came ten years later and the whole valley was transformed.

It was very peaceful. I felt very much connected with the sky and the trees and the dirt; I have wonderful memories. Then my father started moving around, he became a tenant farmer, a sharecropper in different types of farms. Every two or three years we'd have a different house within a 30-mile radius. One was a dairy farm, one a chicken farm, they were all farms and ranches. When I was about to start school my father didn't want me to go on the bus, so he had this house built about two blocks from the school. Our house was really special because it had a toilet. We lived there one year, my first year of school, and I'd walk to school and come home for lunch. Then he got another tenant farm, so we all moved into the tenant farm and he rented out our house to white people who didn't take care of it: The screen started falling down; the toilet got this big hole in it; all the boards in the porch were broken; the grass and roses my mother had planted were ruined. They treated the house very badly. My mother was really upset. She's neat, she wouldn't treat furniture or doors like that. We rented the house out for about five or six years and returned to it when I was eleven or twelve.

CW: So you kept changing schools when you moved?

GEA: Oh, no. The same school but different buses would pick us up.

CW: How many people were in a class at that school?

GEA: About forty or forty-five. We were all Mexican. The whites wouldn't dare have their kids with us. All the whites were bussed to Edinburg which was the same school district but had better teachers and facilities. Once in awhile there'd be one white family, usually a family that had moved from another state and who weren't so prejudiced yet.

CW: Did you have Mexican teachers?

GEA: No. They were all white.

CW: What was their attitude? Were they prejudiced?

GEA: I had one teacher, Mrs. Garrison, who encouraged me. The rest thought Mexicans were dirty and dumb. I was very smart, so I was the exception. It wasn't that I was smart, it's just that I didn't believe in that stereotype. My aspirations were higher than those of the other kids and I knew I was smart. The other kids were smart too, but they believed they were dumb because that's what they were told.

CW: When did you have Mrs. Garrison?

GEA: I was seven years old when I entered school. My birthday falls

90

in September so I had to wait a whole year. I think I was in second or third grade. Mr. Leidner was another white teacher with whom I was real close. He taught me leathercraft, history, and I was sort of like his teacher's aide: he'd let me teach his class and make tests for him. When kids didn't know how to read or had problems with their arithmetic, I'd help them. If some kid was really dumb, I'd let him copy from me. I was such an outsider and felt so abnormal. I was super skinny and tall for my age because of the hormones. (I was born with a hormone imbalance, and it made me grow really fast.) I was a freak and had only two loves—books, literature, learning, and dogs. I also loved people, and I think I let them copy to get them to love me or accept my freakiness but also because I didn't want them to be dumb. The teaching career came very early in my growing up.

CW: Did the teacher ask you to help other students who were having trouble with reading, or did you do that on your own?

GEA: The students asked me.

CW: You helped them after school?

GEA: During class, during recess, after school, or in the morning before school began. Once the teachers realized that the kids were asking me, they let me help because I could explain things that they couldn't. During recess I'd rather do that than play. I was growing so fast that my movements were very awkward. I was always chosen last for ball games. The teachers liked me because I didn't give them any trouble, because I was smart, and because I helped them. The kids liked me because I was smart without being obnoxious about it. I didn't put them down for being dumb.

I was extremely sensitive, Christine. I was wide open to everything people were feeling, thinking, sensing. Everybody knew this, and they were extremely careful with me. Once in a while the kids would call me "the brain" or "teacher's pet" or "shorty." (This was later when they kept growing but I had stopped growing. When I was tall they called me "huesos" for bones.) Kids can be cruel, but they were very gentle with me. They weren't as gentle with my brother. They laughed at him because they thought he walked like a girl.

God, I must have been this walking sponge. It was amazing, Christine. I always felt so alien and so strange, because I was bleeding. I had these breasts I wasn't supposed to have, and I was smart. I think I survived by cutting my body off, by blocking certain feelings. I didn't know how bad it all was. And I always felt so alien and so strange because I bled. The kids didn't know I bled or had breasts.

Bodies and Health

CW: Did your brothers and sister know about the hormonal changes?

GEA: My sister suspected something was going on, but the only people who knew were me, my mother, and my father. It became such a good secret that we forgot. You know how that happens sometimes? You just put it out of your mind. I couldn't talk about it until '78, when I was operated on. I was in Yosemite and I went into this pain. I just fell on the floor and went into convulsions. My friends didn't know what was wrong with me. I'd have these very high temperatures and then I'd have these very cold flashes. It was the hormones. A year before my operation, '78–'79, I went to six gynecologists and they wanted to do a hysterectomy. They said my uterus was abnormal—lopsided or whatever; my cervix opening was abnormal, I had the opening of a woman who's had a child. The ovaries were enlarged, especially the left ovary. I had fibroids, scars in the uterus. I started reviewing my past and it just came back to me: "Oh, I had started bleeding at an early age."

CW: You mean you really had forgotten prior to that?

GEA: Off and on during my life. I remember thinking about it when I was a teenager and then forgetting it, but to really talk about it with my mother. . . I called her and told her what the gynecologists said, and she said, "Yes, you started bleeding when you were three months old. The doctor said it was because you were a throwback to the Eskimo." (I have a lot of that very old Indian blood in me.) She told me she had to make these little girdles so that the kids wouldn't see my breasts, and she had to make sure I had a piece of cloth in my panties in case I bled. Guess we couldn't afford Tampax or Kotex.

I remembered it all. I remembered washing the bloody cloths: I'd take them out into this shed, wash them out, and hang them really low on a cactus so nobody would see them. It was painful, Christine. I was a child with no way of protecting myself. Dealing with my sexuality was bad enough, without having to deal with the bleeding! It became a black monster and grew out of all proportion. And the pain was horrendous. Waves of pain would sweep through me. It felt like my insides were going to come out when I threw up. Then there'd be these jabs. When the waves receded I'd be really weak. In my auto-biography I describe it as a vulture picking my insides.

CW: When that was happening you couldn't really deny it because it was so painful?

GEA: No. But I got used to it and repressed it so that I had no way of gauging when I was hurting, when I was ill. In 1980 when Randy had hepatitis and everyone in our house got checked, I went to the doctor. He said, "You've had this virus for God knows how long. At least two months. Haven't you felt the pain?" I was in pain. I had an intestinal tract infection but I'd repressed the pain. Pain was a way of life, my normal way of life.

CW: Were you concerned about the blood showing, about people finding out?

GEA: My mother was, but I wasn't. She was scandalized because at a very early age, I was the only one in the extended family to wear shorts or a bathing suit and she'd say, "Oh, but your pubic hair is showing through the suit." No, I don't think I've ever been ashamed to show the body. The shame was something I internalized from my culture, from my mother and grandmothers. Women have internalized from men the belief that a woman smells and is dirty when she has her period. I had no defense against that belief; I was three months old. When I found myself, it was the beginning of my spirituality, because it was like getting in contact with who I really was, my true self. My body wasn't dirty.

CW: But you were a part of the big secret. You and your parents.

GEA: Yes I was, for the first thirty years of my life. That was the big secret, the big shame. During the operation—it came as an initiation—I discovered that I didn't feel that shame about my body but had internalized it. It wasn't innate. Even when I was little, I was very uninhibited about my body, and then I'd remember, "Oh, I'm supposed to close my legs." So for thirty years I repressed my body; I feared and hated my body. But it wasn't me; it was something I was taught. It's really weird, Christine.

CW: But children are usually at least part what they're taught. It sounds like you were always a rebel, even though you had the desire to be good, to be what you're supposed to be.

GEA: It was like there were two people in me—one part saying, "This is bad, this is dirty, you're evil. You're bleeding," and the other part saying, "No, that's their perception. I don't feel that way." The two didn't come together until '78, when I found out that I couldn't possibly have caused the bleeding because I was only three months old. Later I realized that yes, I had caused it: my soul, my greater total self, had chosen that I struggle with this imbalance. And that was fine. My greater self chose it. It wasn't me, the evil Gloria, who caused it; it was me, the total self. So then the guilt split and I didn't feel evil. Part of the reason I helped people by teaching was to compensate, because evil was always tied in with what my mother and sister called "selfishness." I realized that being selfish was being myself, and they called me selfish only because I didn't do what they wanted me to do. But it took me thirty years to realize this. During this time I had terrible guilt and I blamed the body. I thought I was bleeding because I'd done something bad, there was something in me that caused it.

CW: So you took on more your mother's view of it than your father's?

GEA: My mother as a personality, no. My mother representing the culture's laws, yes. She represents a whole culture: her mother, and my father's mother—all grandmothers, all women. I think it's because women are the law givers, the carriers of tradition. My mother is a pretty amazing woman. She gives lip service to the culture's laws, but it wasn't really her stuff, you know? When you're little, though, you don't distinguish. It's the mother. She's the one.

Religions

CW: What religion was your mother?

GEA: No religion. My family was not religious at all. We were all baptized as Catholics and made the first communion and confirmation. My grandmothers believed that if you hadn't had a first communion or baptism your soul might have to wait a while in Purgatory or somewhere, that the process would be slowed down, and that's the only reason they'd have us baptized. But my mother isn't the kind of woman who says, "If God wills it. If God wishes." Nothing like that. She believes there's a God, but we weren't religious. (I mean, I never heard about the Pope until I was eighteen.) My mother's upbringing was very Spanish and very Mexican and very Indian, which has always repressed women and sexuality. My grandmother was more pagan than Catholic. She had candles and la Virgen Guadalupe on a little altar, and sometimes she'd pray to or have medals from the different saints. My father never stepped into a church unless someone died and when his corpse was taken into a church.

Catholicism has survived because it's so loose and has incorporated indigenous religions. Everybody has their own brand of Catholicism. I always felt like the Crucifixion and all that has more to do with the religion of the planet at this time: whether you're Protestant, Catholic, Jewish, Buddhist. Cross-culturally, people have similar attitudes about sacrificing the body.

CW: How was God presented to you as a child?

GEA: The way it filtered down was that he was this very gentle spirit, that if you were true to him he'd stop your suffering, lighten your load in some way. The Mexican people always refer to God in very endearing terms, Diosito mio, very gentle, very feminine. It wasn't this God of the Old Testament—judgment, hellfire, brimstone, and punishment.

CW: You said that if you were true to God he would take away or lighten your load?

GEA: That's what the Mexicans believed.

CW: So what did you have to do in order to be true to him?

GEA: Believe in him, and this is the great ripoff: All religions impoverish life because they renounce it. They especially divorce the flesh from the spirit or the mind. To me, it always seemed like this division is where the oppression of myself as a woman, as a lesbian, as a brown woman, as a working-class woman comes in. To me religion has always upheld the status quo, it makes institutions rigid and dogmatic. Anything threatening—people like me (dykes, creative people, heretics of some sort)—must be eliminated. I saw established religions keeping the Mexican poor, keeping the Mexican satisfied with his life.

CW: So you didn't feel any conflict about not following church rules?

GEA: No, because I didn't have anything to do with the church. But I got very angry at the Catholic Church because of how they oppressed people who are different. I think religions are bad.

CW: Did you ever think that you should believe what the church taught you? Did you every try to integrate into that teaching?

GEA: No. It was just another system I could study, like mythology. When I was young, I went to several churches to see what they were doing. Baptists and Methodists had a lot of prejudice against Catholics, but the Catholics I knew didn't care too much about what the Baptists or Methodists were doing. I was outside looking at this rivalry between Protestantism and Catholicism. To me it was ludicrous, it was like looking at two sides of the same coin. They were similar except that the Catholic Church has kept a lot of the ceremonial stuff. Later I studied the life of Christ, the New Testament, and the Old Testament in college courses.

CW: Was there anything you took from those experiences with organized religions?

GEA: My religion was the stories my mother and father would tell, which had to do with spirits, with devils. I'd feel their presence. The folk myths like la Jila, la Llorona, the spirits riding in the wind. And those were more real to me. If you breathed them in, if mal aigres entered your body, you'd get sick. My religion was more like the earth religions of the Indians, which people now call witchcraft. I believed that certain people have powers, like the curanderas.

CW: What stories of spirits were important to you?

GEA: Stories where things aren't what they seem—supernatural powers, the ability to fly, changing form, transforming shape. (You know, my fiction shows this a lot.) These stories are indigenous, where a man becomes a cougar, a snake, or a bird. Very much like the don Juan books by Carlos Castañeda—stories of transformation, about powers and abilities existing and manifesting themselves in the wind, the ability to feel a presence in the room. A lot of my father's stories were about similar incidents where a black dog would race along the truck, and he would step on the gas. He'd be doing fifty, but the dog would still be right by the door. Then he'd be doing sixty, seventy, eighty and the dog would keep up. As a teenager I rejected these stories as superstitions, but I'd had similar experiences.

The religion of the Mexicans—Catholicism—is just a veneer. I don't know with white people, but with Mexicans it's a veneer for the old gods and goddesses. People only go to church, believe in Christ, and eat the host because that was happening in the Aztec religion: they ate the flesh of the sacrificial victim. If you eat part of a bear, you become fierce like a bear. That's what I meant about Catholicism being loose: it allows other religions to survive and it builds its churches in the sacred places of the older religions.

CW: Whereas Protestantism actually got rid of the gods and goddesses altogether?

GEA: Right. Protestantism exterminated the india. So did the Catholics but they incorporated them, intermarried, so that in Mexico, South America, and the Caribbean you have the mixture of white and black and Indian. But there's no difference in the oppression and genocide of the Indians. You know what I mean?

Religions always side with those in power. If you deviate, you're burned as a witch, as a faggot, as a lesbian. The great guilt forced on us is that they want us to merge with the normal, to cut off the unacceptable parts of ourselves—you know, our sexuality. We have to keep silent and can't say who we are. I really believe that religions have to be gotten rid of.

"Yoga of the Body"

CW: What's the earliest personal spiritual experience you remember?

GEA: Very early, Christine. I was maybe three: I was on the floor, reaching to get apples or oranges or something, and I was extending to get them; my body was extending. I had the feeling that I was two or three people. It's an image I use in the novel. It was like looking in a three-way mirror and seeing three parts of myself but all connected. But it wasn't me, it was almost like I could see sheaths. It was all the same body, but not in one place.

When I started hearing the stories I mentioned earlier, I became aware of presences and spirits, and very afraid of them because I thought they were evil. Only in the last few years have I recognized that what I sensed was actually the soul's presence, either that of my own soul or those of other people. I repressed all this stuff until I started taking drugs, which really opened up my memories of things. I had a childhood of spiritual happenings that I buried and forgot, and I'm still trying to dig them out. The drugs opened up a second phase of my life: I had out-of-body states and precognitive experiences, knowing that something was going to happen. My grandmother appeared to me the night she died, although I wasn't told that she died until two days later. I'd sense the presence of my dead father. I'd go into a trance and see things that have happened either in a past life to myself or to other people.

But the main spiritual experience has been a very strong sense of a particular presence. One of the reasons I don't get lonely is because I don't feel I'm alone. How can you be lonely when there's this thing with you? This awareness was the strength of my rebellion and my ability to cut away from my culture, from the dominant society. I had a very strong rhythm, a sense of who I was, and I could turn this presence into a way of shielding myself, a weapon. I didn't have the money, privilege, body, or knowledge to fight oppression, but I had this presence, this spirit, this soul. And that was the only way for me to fight—through ritual, meditation, affirmation, and strengthening myself. Spirituality is oppressed people's only weapon and means of protection. Changes in society only come after that. You know what I mean? If you don't have the spiritual, whatever changes you make go against you.

To me, being spiritual is awakening to the fact that you're a spirit, that you have this presence. Any spirituality that doesn't see that presence on a daily basis and work to awaken it, to give it more life and make it a part of your everyday life, is not spirituality. The spirit evolves out of the experiences of the body; it's not something finished and perfect. Spirituality has nothing to do with religion, which recognizes that soul, that spirit, and then puts a dogma around it, saying, "This is the way things have to be." Religion eliminates all kinds of growth, development, and change, and that's why I think any kind of formalized religion is really bad.

CW: Did you feel as though you had to break away from religion?

GEA: No, because I've never been in the clutches of religion. After my father died I waited four years for the promises of religion to kick in, but its rituals didn't bring him back. I thought it was beautiful to have faith, whatever you had faith in, but the words they gave to this faith were false. The kind of belief and faith they had went beyond any personal representation of God. It was like a real faith in the spirit, and they just gave it the wrong body, the wrong words, and the wrong forms. But I don't think of that kind of faith as religious; it's spiritual.

CW: What did you and your mother believe happened when your father died?

GEA: I think my mother believes he's in heaven, that he's part of this soul of God, this spiritual consciousness. I think he's returned to the creative life force. He didn't reincarnate for a long time because I felt his presence so strongly. When that happens, they haven't taken another form. I think my mother always felt that the masses to save my father's soul were more in celebration of his soul.

Very early I also believed that I could go through the wall. I'm writing a story about this woman who does walk through a wall. I've always believed we have the means to do so; it's a matter of believing. First of all, it's a yoga of the body. "Yoga" means union of body with mind and spirit. To do a yoga of the body and really walk through the wall, I would have to expand myself. Each cell is a miniature universe; the sun is like the nucleus, and the planets revolving are neutrons and electrons. Everything has this type of vast space within its cells. Everything in existence. So there's space. If you're looking at it from the perspective of a cell, there's millions of miles between the nucleus and the revolving electrons and protons. In water, there's more space; and in air, there's even more space. In iron, there's very little space. The denser something is, the more compact. So if I could expand, open up my cells and expand them, I'd go through this wall because there would be nothing. The molecules in my body would be flexible enough for me to go through the wall. It's like watching *Star Trek* when they energize; they decompose the molecules and recompose them in the place that they want to be. I think that process happens naturally when you sleep. You leave your body. You go out in the astral. The minute you think "L.A.," you're in L.A.; even though your body is over here, your consciousness is over there. I believe this can happen by doing yoga of the body, which means that instead of renouncing the body— wanting to leave the body and become spirit—you work the other way around, make the body divine, make every cell divine. And those kinds of ideas I was having at a very early age.

The idea central to my autobiography is the return of the spirit, the idea that God and the devil are the same person, that evil and good are the same. I've always believed that. Like the yin and the yang. If you go so far to evil, you get to good. They're one; we only separate them because of the duality, the way we work. I'd been having these ideas off and on, and I'd jot them down as poems or stories, or whatever. About a month ago I started reading *The Mother*. I told you about *The Mother's Agenda*.

CW: Who's that by?

GEA: Mirra Alfassa, a half-Turkish and half-Egyptian woman born in France. She died in 1973. She has these books called *The Mother's Agenda*. She was connected with Sri Aurobindo, an Indian sent to England when he was little. His father didn't want him to grow up with Buddhism's "superstition" and mysticism or with anything to do with India. So he was educated in England until he was twenty-one, and then he took up his language and his culture and all that. He was put in jail, where he had a conversion. He became a self-realized person by plugging into this oversoul or whatever. I don't know how to explain it. But he met the Mother around 1926. They became part of the same consciousness. Some people think he was the last avatar on earth. I started reading his stuff about two or three weeks ago. The ideas I already had were very similar to his, so I did a meditation. I said, "OK. Did I get these ideas from him?" I had never read or heard of this man. And this whole bunch of stuff came through, Christine. It's going to blow you away, because you're part of it. . . .

"Off the Rational Track"

GEA: I want to talk about the Bible verse, "In the Beginning was the Word and the Word was God." This statement, before it got corrupted by the church fathers, meant that in the beginning was the sound, the vibration—a rock, a plant, an animal, a human, a particular area. That vibration is like the song of its being, its heartbeat, its rhythm.

A lot of the ideas that have come up in the autobiography are spiritual ideas. Especially, the idea that everything is spiritual, that I'm a speck of this soul, this creative consciousness, this creative life force; and so is a dog, a rock, a bird, this bedspread, and this wall. In recognizing that soul—which is what Native Americans have always recognized, they've always respected the elements—nothing is alien, nothing is strange. Spirit exists in everything; therefore God, the divine, is in everything—in whites as well as blacks, rapists as well as victims; it's in the tree, the swamp, the sea. . . . Everything is my relative, I'm related to everything.

The church has taken the very essence of what spirit is and subverted it. The people who are "righteous"—the ones on the correct path, the lawmakers and lawgivers—those who profess to follow Christ aren't following Christ or Buddha, or whatever.

When I was reading this book by a man named Satprem I thought, "WOW! These are the things I'm trying to talk about." One belief is that your body, your mind, through dreams, through some sort of internal unconscious process, works things out. Sometimes even before they happen, you deal with problems. You make the inner changes first, and then you make the outer changes. I've always believed that. Sometimes you can do both at the same time: work to create outer change, through political movement, at the same time that you're trying to do meditation and developing yourself. And then I started meditating, and these are the things I came up with. Are you ready?

CW: Yes.

GEA: OK. There are about three thousand people being prepared in the astral realms—through dreams and even when you're awake but you're not paying attention to this other part of yourself. (Because the conscious mind is very small. There's this whole subconscious and unconscious that's really deep.) The preparation has to do with what I was talking about earlier—expanding the body. He called it "supermentalization." There's a little group of people, like fourteen people, that I'm supposed to be connected with. And out of those fourteen, seven were named, and you're one of them. There's a kind of preparation we have to go through. I don't know. It's really weird.

I started thinking, "When did all this stuff happen?" I already had these ideas, before I knew of this man's existence. How did I get his ideas? Maybe the ideas were everybody's. In the meditation it came through that I *had* gotten them from him, beginning in 1977, through the mental realm, through ideas and dreams I had when I was not really aware. So I was trying to figure out what happened in '77, but I can't remember. It was a time of great change in my life because I moved from Austin, tore up my Mastercharge and BankAmericard, and gave up the idea of becoming a university professor. I was teaching at the university, and I just threw everything out. I was going to be a writer full time, committed.

In the meditation I learned that this kind of preparation takes place on four levels: the spiritual, the mental, the vital (which is the emotional, like desires, cravings, hungers, likes, dislikes, fear, jealousy, envy, joy, happiness), and the physical. My preparation is on the vital. I was really blown away, because I thought I had to do the work on the physical. This preparation has to begin pretty soon. We have to become fully conscious, fully aware, and be fully ourselves. We've talked about this before. It's so hard to do. The first step is becoming aware that you're more than your thoughts and emotions. Superlaid on top is this thing that you sometimes get glimpses of, which I call "the presence." I used to think of this presence as the daemon, which is an old term that means the luminous spirit that dwells inside you. But then, probably during the time of the witchburnings, society made "daemon" synonymous with "demon," possession, like *The Exorcist* and other popularized, trivialized motion pictures.

I want to read to you something from my journal: "June 1: There's definitely someone in command of my life, and it's not the ego. The ego has abdicated, run for cover, is shrinking in the shadows and doesn't return except for clandestine skirmishes during the night." Of course, the returns are more often than that. "Something else pulsates in my body, a luminous thin thing that grows thicker every day, bigger. Its presence never leaves me. I am never alone. I cherish the time I am by myself, for then I can be with her, him, this secret lover, this in-dwelling spirit, the daemon, the divine presence within."

I had a type of conversion three years ago, during the operation and shortly thereafter. After the conversion, this thing that was hateful—that was ugly and put down and oppressed—was beautiful. The female body and serpents are two of the most feared things in the world, so I used the serpent to symbolize female sexuality, carnality, and the body. Snakes used to represent to me the body and everything that was loathsome, vile, rotting, decaying, getting hair, urinating, shitting, all the conditioning I've had—that all people have—about the body, especially the female body.

I made this little sketch: in the middle is the personality, which I called "Gaudi" because that's what I'm called at home all the time. Around the personality, which is like the nucleus (well, it's not really the nucleus, it's very small in the middle) is the body, the life or emotions, and then the mind. Each of those parts has a little ego. And then, around that, is the individual soul or the psychic being, the little speck or spark from the big flame which is life, which is consciousness. I'm this little flame which is part of a bigger flame, what the Buddhists call "the self." Some people call it the spirit. I call this part the "angelos" because my middle name is Evangelina.* Then there's the universal self—the spark—that's in me, in you, in the tree, in the rock. It's the same substance; it's universal. And then there's the thing that incorporates everything—the body, the personality, the little soul, the bigger soul, the self. Some people call it "God"; some call it the "creative force," whatever. It's in everything.

---

* From the Greek "eu" (well) and "angelos" (messenger). [GEA]

The people in training have to start realizing and acknowledging this soul, this presence. Instead of giving power to and identifying with one part of your being, the ego—the petty self, the emotions, the anger, whatever—people must start giving power to the total being. (Religion taught us to give power to the ego. It said, "There's parts of you that are not permissible and therefore they don't exist. You have to be like the rest of us.") We have to recognize the total self, rather than just one part and start to be true to that total self, that presence, that soul. And we have to work with the body. To not say "Oh, the body is dirty and vile and we should escape it because it's a prison. The flesh is a prison, and the spirit is all-important; we should discard the body and let it rot." No. It's the other way around. Matter is divine also. We have to start doing that on a daily basis.

Around '73 I spent a lot of time by myself in Indiana. I didn't have any friends. I had a job that required me to travel a lot so I was by myself in hotel rooms and motels, on the road. When you're by yourself things come up that you have to deal with. My way of escaping was to read romance books and novels. When it got too scary, I'd go into a book. I also did the opposite: I'd read scary stuff to confront these things. I used to love thriller movies and stuff that other people were scared to see. It was like I was attracted to this other world and what it had to offer, its visions and stuff, but I was afraid. So I'd take some little timid steps forward and then I'd run back and put my head in a book.

When I went to Austin I started having very intense psychic experiences. One occurred in December 1974. It was my first semester there, and I'd been mugged on November 7th. That mugging opened me up because it was a violation of my spirit, an invasion. I'd felt exposed; I realized that the cosmos was indifferent, that it's good and bad both, that it's just and unjust, that ultimately it probably balances out, but at any given point it could be one or the other. So, I was lying in bed, doing a brief meditation. (I don't remember what. It was some little thing.) Suddenly I found myself flat on the bed with my hands crossed over my chest. (I never sleep like that.) There was this weight on me, like a house that suddenly fell on top of me. I couldn't move; I couldn't even blink. I couldn't do anything. I was so glad that I'd left a night-light on in the bathroom because I wanted to see how much time had elapsed; it seemed like forever. It literally felt like I was in the bottom of the ocean, waiting. It had like a sound, a vibration. Do you know what the vibrations of fear or anger are like? Every emotion is like a vibration.

Well, this was a different vibration. It was very big—almost like you could crawl on it, it was so big. It was like oatmeal. I don't know what the correct metaphor for it is, but it was thick. I was sensing it, and it had an intelligence. Now here's the scary part: the whole time this amazing thing is going on, this thing is breathing—a rhythm like breathing but it was really a vibration. This presence, this very thick thing was testing me. I wasn't really scared of it; it didn't seem evil, but it seemed like it wanted to invade me. And I didn't want it to. It felt benign yet foreign. Somehow or other, I must have passed the test because then I was able to move my little finger and then—gradually, inch by inch—I was able to move my hand. And then with the right hand I started prying the fingers off my shoulder. And then gradually I unwound. It was so weird that I didn't even record it in my journal until a month had gone by.

These experiences, and others, showed me the existence of other worlds. If you focused a little bit differently, you'd be in them. I'd start trancing real easy. I just had to concentrate on something, like a little spot on the wall or a space a foot away from me. I'd just concentrate on the blank air, just one little point, and do my breathings. And then I'd be gone. I mean, I'd see other things. This started happening more and more frequently. Sometimes it would happen in public places. The whole thing just scared me, so I backed off. I thought it might be the onset of madness, insanity.

CW: What do you mean, it started happening in open places?

GEA: I'd be sitting in a restaurant or walking in the street and I'd look at someone; all of a sudden, I could see who they really were. Sometimes I'd see shadows or little layers around them, which I later learned was the aura. I could just see thickness around them. A lot of this was happening with Randy. We'd stop in the middle of the street and it would be like this world opening—like this abyss had opened up and the street was not the street anymore; the street signs were not the street signs. Everything had a different meaning, yet everything was the same. There are other worlds superimposed on this one, occupying the same space we occupy. Right here in this space there might be a city. We don't see it because its vibrations are much faster; they're much higher. It's sort of like looking at a hummingbird fly: its wings are flapping so fast that you don't see them. We're in these other worlds, but we don't see them. We're only aware of being in this world.

I was also experiencing strange intuitions. I'd think of someone and the phone would ring and it would be that person. Or I'd see a number in my head and five minutes later some friend had given me their new phone number and it was the same number. Also, there was this presence in my room. Sometimes it would say words in my head and I'd type them up. I thought it was the spirit of Cortázar, a writer I admire very much. This was just a vibration, a sensing, that would always be over my left shoulder. I clothed it in my imagination because it didn't have a form. I could have given it a female form, but at the time I probably wasn't a strong feminist yet, I still thought a lot in terms of male things. I didn't tell anyone about it. Sometimes I'd take walks, and it would walk two or three blocks, but it would always return to the room. It would never go as far as school with me. It was friendly.

CW: When was this?

GEA: It was 1974, '75. I lived in that apartment for a year and a half, and that presence stayed with me. I never told anyone, because they'd think I was crazy. One day Randy and I were walking to visit a friend down the street in another complex, and he said, "Oh, you know that presence? He's following us. Did you know that?" And I said, "What do you mean?" He said, "You know, that tall man." He described this presence exactly the way I had clothed it—tall and thin, almost cadaverous. And he said, "It's your father." But I said, "No, my father is stocky and he's not even 6 feet tall."

That blew my mind, that somebody else could see it. Randy had been seeing, feeling this thing all along, but he knew it wasn't harmful, that it was good. So he didn't want to say, because it might freak me out or something. Sometimes he walks into a house and he knows if it's haunted. Or you've seen the cat in this apartment? He'd see that. He'd see the whole history, all the people that had lived there. He reconstructed a house in San Francisco where I once lived. It used to be a mortuary. He described this whole scene of the ambulances bringing in the bodies which were then pulled up to the third floor with a rope on the outside of the house; they'd be brought in through these large windows. Nobody believed a word. It sounded really strange. But then they started checking on the people who had owned the house before. It used to be a mortuary, and they did use a pulley to bring the corpses up to the third floor and then in through the big windows.

I also experienced some negative presences—not presences, "apparitions" is a better word. The apartment complex where I lived at the time was sort of like a labyrinth, with columns, partial walls, and full walls. I'd be walking between these pillars and walls, and I'd turn to my left and see a man dressed in black pants and shirt walking. But then the wall would obscure him, and then he'd be opposite me walking in the other direction. Wherever I walked and looked, he'd be walking—sometimes to my right, sometimes behind me, in front of me, to the left. The man looked like a regular person. He had flesh and everything. I mean, I thought it was alive, a real person. It seemed really peculiar that this happened again and again. One day Randy was walking with me and he saw the very same thing. (Thus far nobody else had seen it.) We were both looking at the man, and I got this hint that it was Randy in the future, an evil Randy. Randy said no, it wasn't him. Julie came to visit in July, and—without me or Randy telling her— she saw the same man. She also thought it was a future or past Randy, and all the hairs in my body went !!!!!

It was evil. So Julie, Randy, and I did all kinds of cleansings, spells, and circles, and he disappeared. But this man didn't feel like the presence, like the apparition. This felt like a real man, flesh and blood. The other wasn't; it was just a feeling that I pictured as a tall, thin man. Later, as years went by, I started thinking of it as the muse, la musa, as a woman. I mean, it will always be whatever it was, but I can put different forms on it. And then I moved.

So that time in Austin was pretty weird. After the presences, I think I started doing mushrooms. Some of the things I'd felt were verified. When you're doing drugs, colors are different and things don't seem to be as solid. You make connections that you don't make when you're sober, so that you see behind the curtain. So I thought, "Well, I'm not crazy." The drugs put the ego—the customary glasses that you see the world through—down, and you see the world through eyes that aren't censored by the mind, by rationality. I wasn't afraid anymore of being crazy, because it just meant that I had opened certain doors.

CW: How did those things lead to your recent meditations?

GEA: I learned that what I was seeing was my soul. Because of the stories I was told as a child, I had clothed the soul as these evil apparitions. Not all evil. Some were good. I was also sensing the soul in other people. If you think you're evil, your soul is going to look real evil. If you think you're good, it's going to look good. So I think the soul is always neutral. I mean, it's got your best interests at heart. It's evolving and it wants you to grow, because it has to grow.

But however you see it, the mind is not in your head. The mind is the area around you, about 4 feet in diameter. When psychic people read you, they're not reading your mind, they're reading your thoughts—that area around you, in your aura—and then just translating them into words. So if you think you're bad and evil, that thought is around you, and people who read you, read it. Now, maybe somebody very enlightened would be able to go through the 4 feet surrounding you to get to the real soul, or whatever, and find that it's good, joyous, or whatever.

I was seeing these evil things because other people were; it was their fear. Not only did I have my own fears—and for me to see you, I have to look through my space, the 4 feet in front of me, so that everything I see is going to be colored by my perception—but I then have to filter through your perceptions. Also, I'd had all these horrendous experiences, like being mugged.

So of course I was seeing all this bad stuff. But somehow or other I got through. It's sort of like in swimming the breaststroke, where you extend your arms and make a little opening. It culminated March 20, 1980, when I had that operation. Right after the operation when I was healing I had a strong sense of this presence—my greater self or whatever you want to call it. Part of this feeling was the influence of having died for twenty minutes. It's like I was off the rational track and therefore could see more clearly. This feeling didn't last, but I started doing the psychic development class with Tamara Diagaleu, took some training in Tarot with Angie Arrien, worked with dreams. I was doing psychic readings. I set up an altar with candles. I consecrated the altar. I had my knife. You've seen my knife? It's shaped like a moon.

CW: Oh, yeah.

GEA: I went very seriously into finding out how to call forth this soul, this spirit, how to draw it out of me or into me, or whatever. And then I thought, "Well, the East Coast is not like the West Coast, and maybe my spirituality is going to suffer." But I think it's gotten stronger, because I've just developed it by myself. On the West Coast, if you want your palm read or your numerology done, it's real available, so you depend on external authority. And here, on the East Coast, there aren't courses I can go to. There's nothing readily visible; you have to hunt for it. Of course, there's a catalog that comes out with all the names of people doing things, and there's Santería. But they don't give information to just anyone who goes in and asks.

During the month of May—when I went into my sixth house where I was dealing with a lot of conscious growth of the self, really working at it—I had very strong meditations. And she appeared—this soul, whatever you want to call it. It's sort of like a light all around me, and I smile when she's there. Even if I'm depressed. If I was depressed ten seconds before, I just find myself smiling and feeling very peaceful. That whole month was beautiful, from May 5th to about the 29th.

CW: That was when you were doing all the spiritual work?

Meditations, Making Love to the Divine

GEA: Yes. And then I went into a depression. During this time in May I was doing a meditation which became a sexual fantasy. I was making love to the divine, to this soul. And she had a penis, Christine. She was a woman. She had breasts and everything was womanly. Even her penis was womanly. I thought it was so strange. It was like her little clit just grew. I thought, "Oh, what is this? I'm not supposed to be having these heterosexual fantasies. This is a regression. What is this Goddess? Why does she have a penis?" Then I figured out that she's probably neither male nor female. I don't know what the divine is, but I'm sure it's not a man. And if it's not a man, why should it be a woman? Maybe it's both. So that was really weird.

CW: And that was in a meditation?

GEA: I was sitting cross-legged on my little pillow there where I always meditate. It's a special, really thin pillow which I fold. I sit on it at the edge of the bed, and I cross my legs on the floor.

CW: What kind of meditation do you do?

GEA: To still my thoughts, I breathe very slowly into and out of my abdomen, relaxing and letting go of everything. Then, to be connected to the middle of the earth, I put a root down into the earth through my cunt. And then, to be connected with the heavens, I shoot another tentacle out of my head out into the sky. At this point, I just concentrate. It's sort of like locking in. You know how two magnets lock in?

CW: Yes.

GEA: But it's hard to lock in. I really have to search. It has to do with the focusing, and I have to cross my eyes. (I can't do it if my eyes aren't crossed, which is really strange.) Somewhere here, about a foot from my forehead, I'd lock in and just concentrate. (Sometimes I'd lose it and have to go back and do it again.) By then, the thoughts start, ideas for stories.

Either I'd do a visualization—like staring at a little spot, a little black spot or a white spot—or I see her shape. Sometimes I give her a form, like a woman, and she'll be this ghostlike figure that keeps moving. Or I use the words, the mantra, which I say to myself mentally. But sometimes I don't have to. I get to the point where I don't have to do that to keep the thoughts out. I'm just silent. And that's when it happens: it's this incredible connection. I think this is where the fantasy started, because the connection is so incredible that you feel like you're in sync: your heart is beating, you hear this heartbeat, and then your cunt is having an orgasm. The cosmos—the spirit, or whatever you call it—is like a fist, like a heart, and it's beating. In that beating of the cosmos my heart and my cunt are in unison, in one rhythm. It's so pleasurable that I don't want to leave. It's incredible. Sometimes I do have orgasms, but the rest of the time they're not physical orgasms. They start out in the mind and then after the meditation, I'm wet.

During that particular meditation, it was like I was fucking: the Goddess was fucking me and I was fucking the Goddess. She took me in her arms, and I was sucking her tits. It was as if I went through her body, like she was holding me in her arms, in her body, but I could also pass through her body and come out the other side, and move back and forth. There was no separation. Then she lay on top of me and we were rocking and rocking. Suddenly, I feel her little clit, which is like a little button, getting bigger. It's closer to a tit than to a penis. It looks like a long tit. I don't know if you know what I mean. Some women have really rounded breasts, but I see some women who have very skinny breasts that are like phalluses. They're very phallic, because they're elongated. (Maybe the phallus is really the breast. I don't know what the difference is between the penis and the breast, but they have the same kind of shape.) I'm clothed, but suddenly I feel this little thing entering me, and it's her. She enters through the vagina and the rest of her follows the little penis. It's like all of her came in through the vagina, and she's inside me. It was so intense that I just fell backwards on the bed and stretched out. I had this incredible physical orgasm. Forget the mind. It was physical.

I don't know. People would probably think I was—I don't know what they would think, to have an experience like this. But they must think it's pretty weird, because people think you need another person to be able to have this kind of experience. And maybe you do. But occasionally, I've found that you don't. Isn't that weird?

CW: Yes.

GEA: In the next few weeks when I had sexual fantasies, it had nothing to do with meditation, it had to do with masturbation. It was her again in different forms.

CW: Did she have a clear form?

GEA: Sort of like fog with a light shining on it. Sometimes her hair would be very long, and it would be part of her body, and other times it would be invisible hair. Sometimes she would be very small, like the size of a thimble or the size of a matchstick, but other times she would be as big as this room—and sometimes bigger.

CW: She kept changing size?

GEA: Not in the same meditation. In different meditations. Sometimes she's black and sometimes she's white. But in the meditation that went into the fantasy, she was like a flame. And a flame has some blue and some orange and some yellow and some white, depending on what it's burning and how you're looking at it. She was mostly like intense fire, almost whitish yellow at that time. But when I do other meditations, it's different. Lately, she hasn't had a form. It's just like a drumbeat or something. It's so hard to put into words. It's like a vibration. It's like the wind, listening to the wind, but it's a different rhythm. I put on my earplugs, and I still hear it. But if I put my earplugs on, I won't hear the subway rumble. It gets very intense, and I think, "Oh, it's going to wake up Gerry, two floors down."

CW: What does it sound like?

GEA: It sort of sounds like the ocean. All oceans have—I call it a breath because they come in and they go out. It's like a breath. Have you ever been in a forest, when the wind suddenly goes through it?

CW: Yes.

GEA: It's like that, but it's regular. It's like a machine, like a metronome. But with the feeling, like the chimes of the wind and the ocean and the trees. But it's steady, like a metronome or a pulse. It doesn't go real slow and then real fast. First you think it's a mechanical thing, like a motor. Then it becomes like a song, like music. That's why I think the stuff about the word is really about vibration. It's like a heartbeat and like your cuntbeat, but it's not. It sounds more like what the ocean would sound like if there were trees in the ocean and it was autumn and the wind was blowing. I don't know how to describe it.

CW: And that sound comes to you in the meditations?

GEA: If I work hard, yes. I have to work really hard, and you know how I am: I'm very lazy.

No matter how good the feeling is, the next day it's hard for me to meditate. It always is. Even if I say I'm just going to sit for half an hour. It's wonderful when I'm doing it. Now why do I have such a resistance? Do you have a resistance?

CW: Yes.

Spirituality and Power

GEA: The meditations where I hear the pulse are rare, but they've been happening more often lately. They haven't happened in about a week, because I've been a social butterfly. The meditations with the orgasm, of the heart and the cunt and the cosmic part, are much more rare. It's only happened twice in my life. Or maybe more. I think it started happening when I started studying under Tamara in San Francisco. I'd go home and do my meditations, and I'd have these incredible experiences. They're beautiful, you know? I mean, I can watch *Star Trek* or *Twilight Zone* for an hour, but I'd get more pleasure out of meditating for an hour. So why don't I do it? That's what I don't understand. It's the same with writing: I get so much pleasure from doing it, but it takes me a tremendous effort to get myself to sit at the typewriter and write. It's like something has made the creative act and the meditative act so out of our reach. I think it's this religion I've been talking about, that I'm so opposed to.

But I would have gone stark raving mad had I not had the spirituality. Because it helped me get over everything—being mugged and almost killed, being this very shy and timid little country girl. Before, I didn't want to speak. I'd hide when people came to visit. And now I put myself before classrooms and before hundreds of people.

CW: How did spirituality help you over that shyness?

GEA: It connected me to the strength—to the soul and the source of power—which I can channel into myself. Part of this power is myself. It's sort of like there's an ocean out there that you call consciousness, and I have a little part of that ocean within myself. I realized this when I was about ten years old, when I almost drown. I told you about that?

CW: Well, tell—

GEA: My father took the family to Padre Island. It was a Sunday, and we'd picnic there. We'd take the truck, and my father would put this big awning on it for shade. My mother would bring a little table and put out the food, and we'd have this freezer full of Coke and juice and stuff. We'd play on the beach. We were only allowed to go into the water up to our waists, because none of us could swim. But I'd always go in over my head. My mother had given up trying to stop me because I loved being in the water. I'd go to the lake by the house, and we'd go down to the Gulf of Mexico. All the time I was with water, water, water. People thought I was water crazy.

So that day, I was in the water and this big wave takes me a little bit out. I'm not worried because I can dog paddle back. But this undertow pulls me by my feet. To me, it felt like something had reached a hand and pulled me under the water. I got really scared. I'd been practicing holding my breath, but I could only hold it for three minutes. In my panic, I didn't even hold my breath that long. I lost the air and swallowed all this water. Then I was swallowing water through my nose. My body was not accepting the water; it wanted air. Just before I lost consciousness, I had the feeling that the ocean inside me had joined the ocean outside me. There was no boundary. There was no skin. Our two oceans were touching. My ocean and the physical ocean were touching. I felt very happy. It was very peaceful, and I loved just being there.

But then, my feet touched sand and I regained consciousness. I remember uncurling and my head coming out of the water. Thirty, forty, fifty yards from the ocean there's a sandbar, and that's what my feet had touched. I was able to stand up and, by standing on my toes, giving a little hop, and tilting my head, I could breathe. I don't think I was conscious, because I was so weak that I don't know how I could have done the little jumps. I was really out of it, Christine. I guess that was like the second death, the second time I died, and part of me realized that I couldn't die yet. I waited about three hours for the tide to go in.

The whole time I was doing these little jumps so my head would stay above the water and I could breathe. The sandbar was about three feet in width, so I'd put out my foot and try to stand on the ocean floor but I'd be under water. So then I'd jump back onto the little sandbar.

And at the end of three hours, I dived or pushed myself off the sand bar and paddled. When I came up, I was in shallow water and could stand. While I was on the sandbar, I looked for my mother in the red truck, but I couldn't see anyone. When I got to the beach, they were these little tiny specks far away. I started walking back. Before I got there, I had to figure out what I was going to do. I went into the sand dunes so that my clothes were caked with sand and then came out through the direction of the dunes. My mother wanted to know where I'd been all afternoon, and I said I'd been hunting for treasure. (The ships that used to go from Mexico to Spain would always stop off at Padre Island, and there were legends of buried treasure. Everybody was always digging.) She was very upset with me. I think she knew what had happened, but she didn't want to make a fuss. I mean, part of her knew. But if I had told them what happened, we would never come to Padre Island again. Ever since then, I've been afraid of the water.

In college my sophomore and junior years I took swimming classes. Every time I had to dive into the pool, I was terrified. It wasn't because that earlier experience in the ocean hadn't been pleasant. It had been very pleasant, except that the initial struggling was terrifying. But that horrible part stayed with me. I didn't remember the pleasant part until I started doing the autobiography. So to this day, I won't go into the ocean. I'll go into a pool, because the wave won't sweep me away. That's also the fear of sexuality, of losing your border, your border being swept away, engulfed. All of it ties together.

Becoming Lesbian?

CW: Tell me a little about your lesbianism, about being a lesbian.

GEA: I was a lesbian in my head, in ideas, before I was a physical lesbian with my body. It started a long time ago. There was a woman who lived in the lot behind our house. The townspeople would talk about her. They called her "una de las otras": for six months, she was a woman and had periods and for six months she was a man and had a penis. They were called "half and half." At the time I thought I was real smart and knew that wasn't true, but now I'm beginning to think it might be true. Psychologically, lesbians may be women with the potentiality to be whole, to be neither male nor female, to be both male and female, to be neuter, to be. . . . I don't know. But it's not the official way of being; it doesn't have the male-female polarity.

Two of my female cousins were having an affair. They only confided in me. People always confide in me.

CW: When your cousins confided in you, was that the first you had ever heard of women being lovers with one another?

GEA: No. I'd seen one of these trashy books that had the two lesbians on the cover, so when they talked about it, it seemed oh, yeah, it exists. But at first it was just an intellectual thing. That experience in Texas that I mentioned earlier—when I saw the two women fucking—made it more of a reality. It was the body. Before, all I'd heard was talk and words. Then when I was in school, I met this woman. I told you about my experience with her. We were really good friends and really close. I always felt this intensity, this energy, between us. This energy was similar to the energy I'd felt between me and my father, my brother, and sometimes between me and my mother. (I really repressed the stuff with my mother.) One day I asked this woman, "Why don't we talk about this feeling between us?" and she said, "What do you mean?" I said, "You know, the lesbian stuff. You know, the lesbian feelings." She just got up and walked out the door. The term was about twelve days away from the end of the semester, and the next day she had packed everything and left. I waited a little while and then wrote her a letter, but there was no answer. I waited a few more weeks, and then I called her home. Her sister answered and in the background I could hear the woman saying, "Tell her I'm not here." I waited half a year and then called again. Her mother answered and said, "She doesn't live here anymore."

Later, when I was teaching high school, there was a coterie of little baby dykes that formed around me—these little groupies, my first experience with groupies. They'd make jokes: One of them lived on a street called Gay Street, and they'd make jokes about Gay Street. They'd pass each other these notes which they wanted me to see. Teachers were supposed to intercept love letters, but I just let them get away with it. They'd show me their letters. They wrote to me for many years. They used to call me "Shorty." They were real confused kids. I mean, they thought what they were doing was bad because their religion said it was. They had no one in the whole school, but they knew I was OK, that I'd listen. So they'd come and tell me about their lover's quarrels. If they misbehaved, I wouldn't send them to the counselor. I'd talk to them, and it would turn out that the problem was sexual. They felt like creeps. There were also some faggots.

So then I went to Indiana and there was a woman who's a lesbian or a bisexual or something. She's not heterosexual. She and I get real close, and she starts talking about her attraction for women and all this and all that. Then I went to Austin and met Randy, who was this flaming faggot. He introduced me to a bisexual woman. He also introduced me to his roommate, Norma Funderberg. (She just recently wrote to me. I'm going to see her when I go to Austin.) And he took me to bookstores. He was always shoving me towards the feminist section, but I didn't want to be caught there. I was liberated, but I wasn't a women's libber, that kind of thing. There was a meeting at this place called the Y, which was where they had political meetings, organizations, and workshops. They put out this paper called *The Rag*, and the radical part of the city took place there. I said, "I don't want to go to the meeting—all those white women, all those lesbians." But I went. I was the only so-called straight woman. By then I had begun to wonder. I noticed that all my friends were faggots and dykes. I had one straight woman friend who had a crush on me. (I don't know how to explain it to you, Christine. This married woman had the hots for me.) Everybody else was queer. So in my head I started thinking that I must be one. To myself, I was one of them. I still didn't use the word "lesbian," but I felt like I was one of them.

CW: Why didn't you use the word "lesbian"?

GEA: Well, it wasn't part of my culture. We used the words "half and half." We used filthy words, like "culera," which means ass-licker. Even my cousin and those people didn't call themselves "lesbian." They didn't know what they were. "Lesbian" is a modern word, I think. I don't know what people call themselves, but others called them "queer." I wasn't sure what I was. All I knew is that I wasn't straight.

But also because I've always been attracted to men. Even now, I'm attracted to men. I'm attracted to children; I'm attracted to animals. When I was at McDowell's,* I made love to a tree. "Lesbian" is the nearest thing that identifies me, but I don't know what I am. "Lesbian" is not an adequate term. I know that I consciously chose women. During

---

* Artist colony in Peterborough, New Hampshire. [GEA]

that period of time, I consciously chose that I was going to love women. If I was attracted to other beings, I was going to consciously change that attraction by changing my fantasies. You can do that: You can change your sexual preference. It's real easy.

I made a conscious choice. But I think that my Self had taken me to this place where I had to make the choice. I know it was meant. My whole head got turned around. I started seeing things from the perspective of the feminine. All my life, all the readings I'd done in literature, religion, philosophy, psychology had always been male. So I did a complete turnaround and chose feminist literature as one of my areas. I mean, that's how complete the turn was, changing from this person who didn't like the words "feminist" or "women's libber." I didn't think I was oppressed as a woman. Randy and I had this huge argument: "You are so oppressed," he said. I said, "I am not oppressed. I can do whatever I want to do. I come from a very poor background, and I was able to get an education. If I want to walk through that wall, I can. I can do whatever I want." Which is true. A lot of people can't do it, because they haven't concentrated; they don't have the ambition. But I was wrong in believing I had never been oppressed. I'd been oppressed all my life. So oppressed. So that was the complete turn. And I started looking at women's bodies. I think I'd always looked at women's bodies, but now I was conscious of it.

So I became a lesbian in my head first, the ideology, the politics, the aesthetics. I started looking at history differently; I learned that Christianity is based on a female religion, the worship of the mother. Psychologically, spiritually, philosophically, and politically—it was all women. The touching, kissing, hugging, and all came later. First was in my head. But I had a pretty terrible time, because these women fall in love with me, Christine. I don't know. I can't explain it. I wasn't a name in the community, I was nothing—just this little Chicana.

One of the reasons I was turned off to the term "lesbian" was because I only saw these motorcycle dykes. They wore boots, jeans, and big T-shirts with their big breasts bulging under their shirts. Those were the only visible lesbians, these truck-driver, stocky, masculinized lesbians. In the early seventies, that was the stage of the movement. If you were a dyke, you wore these awful boots and these awful jeans and you never changed them; it was a uniform. At that time I was still shaving my legs. (I'd stopped shaving my underarms.) I thought it was disgusting, the hair on their legs. Now look at mine! I'd go home and my mother would give it to me: "Why don't you shave?"

When I was in Indiana working with the school districts I had to wear nice clothes. I used to set my hair and I wore makeup. But after Indiana I stopped shaving. I stopped the mascara and the rouge. I stopped curling my hair. I started wearing this uniform, this awful uniform—not quite, because you know how I like color, so I'd have my red shirts and my wines. Even in queer community, I was queer. I didn't know there were other spic dykes like me. Now, there are a lot of spic dykes dressing up—wearing makeup and heels. You should see Sonia and Mirtha when they dress up.

Then I went to California, where I had my first sexual experience with a woman. I also had a very serious relationship with a woman, that I told you about. Again, she fell in love with me but I didn't reciprocate. I very easily could have, but I have these high standards, fears, and a very very picky Venus in Virgo. But my first sexual experience was with a woman who had a husband, a male lover, and a female lover. Another woman who was bisexual would give me massages. So then I became a lesbian in the flesh, temporarily anyway.

CW: Temporarily?

GEA: Well, my celibate periods are so long. I don't know if I'm a lesbian when I'm celibate. Do you think I'm a lesbian when I'm celibate?

CW: Are you?

GEA: To myself I am. For a while, people were suspicious: Is she or isn't she? And the extent of my sexual relationships with women has been brief, very short term. I have yet to have a full sexual relationship, a live-in relationship with a woman. Even the relationships with men were like that.

The mainstream community has laws that you're supposed to live up to: you have to be silent and you have to merge with this greater herd, these cattle or sheep. But the small community—the lesbian, homosexual community (which is not as small as you think it is. If everybody would come out, it would be half the population, at least in this country; I don't know about other countries)—has rules. Even within this community, I don't fit because I don't have these relationships. I don't fuck. I don't go to the bars. I'm not coupled, and I'm not looking to be coupled. Or if I'm looking, it's not with that kind of desperateness. So there's always something wrong with me. Why don't I go to the bars? Why don't I pick up someone? Why don't I fuck more often? Why don't I have a lover? Am I afraid of sexuality? Am I afraid of relationships? And the answer is yes. But the answer is also no. It's like they're missing some of the picture.

Within that lesbian community is the smaller community—the third-world dykes and faggots. And then within that community is a smaller one—the spic dykes, the Spanish-speaking ones. Even in that community, it's like I'm not a Latina. I'm not from South America, Puerto Rico, or Mexico. I'm from the U.S. My Spanish is different. My customs are different. Everything is different. So if I'm with Juanita and Mirtha, I'm still different. But when I'm with Chicana dykes, there are some mutual territories that we experienced, that we had grown up in.

Ethnic Pride, Worldwide Oneness

GEA: But I'm sure that with the Chicana dykes I've met, I'm odd, an outcast. Because a lot of them are nationalists and I don't believe in nationalism; I'm a citizen of the universe. I think it's good to claim your ethnic identity and your racial identity. But it's also the source of all the wars and all the violence, all these borders and walls people erect. I'm tired of borders and I'm tired of walls. I don't believe in the nationalism. I don't believe that we're better than people in India or that we're different from people in Ethiopia. One billion people go to bed hungry every night. One billion, with a "b"! There are droughts in Ethiopia, Kenya, and Eastern Africa—a three-year drought, Christine! People are dying every day. And then people talk about being proud to be American, Mexican, or Indian. We have grown beyond that. We are specks from this cosmic ocean, the soul, or whatever. We're not better than people from Africa or people from Russia. If something happens to the people in India or Africa—and they're starving to death and dying—then that's happening to us, too. Because what I see in meditations is that if I can see this presence, which is my soul, and that the substance it's made of is in everything—in the trees, in black people, in yellow people, in red people, in white people—why should I be proud to be Chicana? Yes, I'm proud to be the different ethnicities that are in my blood. But I'm not going to kill for that. Do you know what I mean? It's like saying, "Oh, yeah, air exists, trees exist, roses exist, Chicanos exist, Basques exist, the people, the races that are in my blood exist." So there's a mystique.

If everybody was thinking like this, nobody would starve, because it would be like you were starving. You'd be this little baby in Ethiopia dying of hunger. So you'd make sure that baby didn't starve. If people thought this way—that the soldier dying in Israel or wherever was you—you'd make sure to stop that war. There'd be no more violence because it would be like taking a dagger and plunging it into your own heart. Because we're all from the same speck. We're just different specks from this big fire. You know what I mean? We just have different forms. Some of us are black, some of us are white, some are short, some are tall. Some of us are in vegetable flesh, some of us are in animal flesh. It's a matter of the vibration of consciousness: The vibration of the consciousness of that plant over there is different from that of a towel and different from that of a person.

So for me, to say "I'm a lesbian"—I say it because there's nothing else. But I'm also all these other things: I'm that plant, I'm that towel, I'm the little kid starving in Ethiopia. You know what I mean? But you use the word because you have to, because if you don't say what you are—if you don't say "Look, I'm me. I'm a lesbian"—then that part of you gets killed. If the world was different, we wouldn't have to say we're lesbians. We could just be whoever we are and fuck whomever we wanted to.

CW: And nobody would care.

GEA: Right. But we haven't gotten to that point yet. So when I go off into this future I have to be pulled back to reality because the borders exist, wars exist, starving people exist. Whenever I eat a salad, I remember the one billion people who go to bed hungry on this planet, and all the little children who are starving. I hate to go into restaurants because I see all these people throwing away food.

"The Gathering of the Tribe"

CW: What kind of spiritual work do you see yourself doing in this lifetime?

GEA: In the meditation it came through that in June of 1985 I have to call a meeting. I already knew I have to do this: years ago a psychic reader, a man named Eric, told me there'd be a gathering of the tribe. He didn't give me the date. In a recent meditation I received the names of seven people who are going to be under preparation; they're going to be training themselves, working out towards recognizing the spirit, awakening it, promoting it, and living it. They're going to be working on different levels. It's a meeting of kindred spirits. What's so funny is that I'd already written about this meeting in my autobiography; I called it "The Gathering of the Tribe." It's just really weird how the stuff comes out in the writing before it comes out in real life. The same thing happens in dreams: first, it happens in dreams and then, months or years later, it happens in real life.

So, the work I see myself doing is being a channel. I can either be a channel for the oral or the written word, probably through the writing. The kind of channel that I am is in these points of view I've just given you in this five-hour interview. Those are the kinds of things I need to communicate but not in the way I communicated the ideas to you. I'm writing a story about the idea that the soul is a luminous thing. The story is about a woman who fears the soul and thinks it's a demon. It's inside her and comes out; it's so repressed that it has to leave the body. Then she's nothing without it. I sort of fictionalize the idea that the luminous spirit dwells within. I communicate the ideas. They're not my ideas; I don't know where they came from. I *thought* they were mine, until I started reading Sri Aurobindo.

So my spiritual work is a path of self-discovery. If I discover it, I communicate it in the writings or in talking. It's being a teacher from a very early age; I always teach what I have to learn. Also at the same time that's happening, there's the Aries part of me (my moon is in Aries), the trailblazer that initiates new projects. So I look at a person, think of their potential, and say, "Oh, you should learn to do this. Why don't you try astrology, or why don't you do the I Ching, or why don't you read this book?" Or I'll say, "Oh, you should really contact this person, you don't know each other, but . . ." I'm a connector, I connect people to each other. I have to make sure that the ego doesn't take over because there's two people connecting it: me, the little petty ego that gets a good feeling from having put someone on the right path or said, "Look, have you thought about this?" and the higher self. It's like picking up the lamp and lighting the dark places.

I have to make sure it's real spontaneous, that it's from the higher self. It sees a person's spirit, soul, whatever, and automatically thinks, "Why don't they do such and such." Sometimes the mother archetype, the all-powerful mother, is in me, looking after people and taking care of them because it gives me control over them and because it makes me feel that I'm better than they are. But I'm no better. Mostly I love doing it, I love the people, it gives me great pleasure and it's part of who I am. There are always two motives. The one from the ego is the source of all my problems because I get on my high horse and I have to be knocked off of it. I think you can tell which me it is.

CW: Do you think most people can tell?

GEA: I know you can tell. The people I'm close to can tell. I don't know if strangers can tell. I usually can tell. If I'm riding in a subway and some man is speaking forth on something, I know if he's fake or not.

There's an ego of the mind, an ego of the emotions, and an ego of the body. If we shut those three egos up long enough, then you can hear the vibration of its presence, of its soul, this music that I was telling you about. Quieting the mind is fairly easy. Well, it's hard, but you can do it by concentrating on something, by having a mantra or something, where you shut it down. The breathing helps to shut it down. The emotions, however, are something else. For me, they're much harder because I get confused about whether it's a legitimate desire working for my good and my growth or whether it's a habit I've developed out of fear, greed, jealousy, or laziness.

And then the body is really hard to tackle. I think that aspect is going to take two thousand years. So when you've got the three egos quiet, then you can start the supermentalizing that Sri Aurobindo talks about: instead of operating from this mind, you operate from the supermind which is outside of the body and slightly above. Certain people have certain connections to it. There's the higher mind, which is slightly above your head. After that, there's the intuitive mind and then the illuminated mind. Then there's the overmind. (You sometimes plug into the combination of the intuitive mind and the illuminated mind in your writing, like that card that you wrote to Gerry and some of the things that you said about poetry. That's when you're connected.) I have to work my guts out for thirty hours and then I get this flash the last second: it's the perfect metaphor, image. I say the thing, and it's the right thing to say. But then it's gone and I'm back to using the rational mind and the right brain and the left brain.

When you came in, I was working on this one sentence, trying to take the emotion of fear in the story I'm writing about the soul, and to present it in a palpable, concrete way. You know what I'm talking about? So then I have to write—what is fear? It's a stench, a metallic taste in the mouth. It's like being wrapped up in tentacles of an octopus. I'm trying to put all of that in one sentence, so that people will read it and say, "Oh, yes, that's what fear is."

"La Facultad"

GEA: I think lesbians and faggots have access to this other world. In my autobiography I call it "la facultad." In Santería you call it "having the capacity, the faculty to." It's almost like cultivating an extra sense that straight people don't have, or that straight people who are insane or persecuted, or poor whites or creative people have. Most lesbians and faggots have it because it's a matter of survival. You're caught between two worlds. You're a half and half. You allow yourself to have the qualities relegated to the male—assertiveness, independence, going out into the world—you use those qualities, yet you're a woman. A faggot uses the emotional qualities of a woman—the feminine stuff. So we're like half and half. Because we're not supposed to be this assertive or this complete. It's not because we cultivated it; it's because the world forced it on us. And blacks, street people have it too. It's being connected to the other world, because we were pushed so far back, so far away that we had to confront what other people repress: their sexuality, their fear, their racism. We had to confront everything—all the stuff in them—that they projected onto us: that we're sick, we're vile, we're criminal, we're not good mothers. People like me get double and triple projections, because there's the Indian and the Mexican. Blacks get it even worse, because they're so black. I mean, the darker your skin color, the more projection because you're the opposite of white.

In my book, I call us "divine warriors" because we have to fight. But it's not a physical fighting. It's fighting with the spirit. To be healthy, you must awaken a sense of who you are and keep it strong and assert that you're OK, that you're not sick, that society—religion, political systems, morality, the movies, the media, the newspapers—that they're all wrong and that you're right. It takes tremendous energy, courage, and perseverance to keep that awareness awake. So you start tapping into your strength, your source of power. Some of us don't. Some of us go mad, get locked up, get knifed in the streets, kill ourselves, or pass for straight. To me, passing for straight is the same thing as a light-skinned black passing for white. If she said she was black her friends would reject her, she'd lose her job, her husband would leave her, she'd be an outcast among not only the white people but also among the black people. Some of us sell out; that is, we revert back to being straight.

I think there are some legitimate changes. Sexuality—sexual preference—you can change. But a lot of the changes, if they happen, happen out of the heavy oppression, not out of choice, not out of an equal free choice. You know what I mean?

I believe that lesbianism and homosexuality existed from the beginning. We've been strangled in Aztec villages. We've been burned alive in Incan villages. We've been hanged, put in gas chambers, concentration camps. We have always existed, but we've always been persecuted. And for some reason or other we have to exist, we have to survive. This is my idea, Christine, that there are certain things in the body, certain faculties that we haven't used yet. We use 10 percent of the brain. That's all we use. The other 90 percent—or even if it's 75 percent—we don't use. Its time of flowering has yet to come. It might be thousands of years but there will be a time where those capacities will be used, where the other 75 percent of the brain will be used, where we'll be able to fly. These capabilities are latent in us, in the human race. And I think that the ability to choose your sexual preference is also latent, but very few use it. Or maybe everybody does. I don't know.

I think gay people have a role. I have a double role: as a mestiza, a person of mixed blood, my role is to unite people—the blacks with the whites with the Indians. Not in any grandiose way but just in calling attention to the fact that we're all human, we all come from the same spark. And to show that humanity. Showing the white man something he doesn't know about the black or showing the black man something he doesn't know. Just through the writing. The me who's a mestiza, a person in the middle, between cultures and the me who's a lesbian, who's also straddling the culture of my people who are Chicanos, the me straddling the culture of my people who are queer people, and—in between those two extremes—I'm also all these other people. That is the spiritual to me. We are like crossroads, Christine. I think faggots and lesbians are crossroads, because we come from all colors, all cultures, all nations, all time periods. Every single people on the planet has queer people. So there's a way we can help ourselves and other people, and there's a way we can harm them. I think that's why there's a lot of pressure on us.

It's not an accident that creativity, music, art, acting, and stuff like that are activities for faggots. I think more of it is going to be attributed to lesbians. Lesbians haven't been as visible, because we're not as visible in the street as the flaming faggot. But I don't think it's an accident because when you're up against the wall—when you have all these oppressions coming at you—you develop this extra faculty. You know the next person who's going to slap you or lock you away. Then you make use of faculties that belong to the other realm so that you already know the rapist when he's five blocks down the street. We have this radar, and it's connected to the same thing, to the creative life force. It's creative. It's connected to creativity.

But there are straight people who have this creativity and are free from sexual bias. Many straight men are. I think all the great writers are. They're still indoctrinated by the culture, but when they write they give up being a man and become a woman too. Because they start using the left-handed side, the feminine side. To create you need both sides. People like Faulkner or even Henry Miller: at some point when they were creating their characters they had to give up being only a man; they became both, half and half. Without using the feminine, you can't be a creator. You cannot create works of art, music, painting, or films. Einstein, too. You don't have to be queer to have it. All I'm saying is that if you're queer you probably have it, unless you're in a real sheltered place.

It's not elitist. It's in everything. It's in everybody. But they start knocking it out of you when you enter school. If you talk to children, they have an incredible imagination. The smaller you are, the wilder your observations and images and the connections you make; everything is real. But the older you get, the more society knocks it out of you. So what I'm saying is that it was knocked out of us when we were six or seven. But some of us kept a little tiny part of that imaginative realm. Sometimes violence opens it up. Drugs can open it up, can give you access to this other realm.

CW: What is this training leading you towards?

GEA: Well, becoming myself. That's something I've just lately been observing. I've gone through stages where I was what people expected or wanted me to be. I had to leave my mother in Texas, go away to school when I was eighteen, to start being who I was. I had to leave. I couldn't be who I was at home because certain conceptions were placed on me—some true, some not true.

The development is leading me to greater awareness of who I am and therefore of what I came into this lifetime to do—my path, my function. It's leading me to pick up the pieces that were chopped off: reclaiming the body, sexuality, spirituality, anger. It's leading me towards wholeness. If you're whole, you're perfect. It might take us—this human species—another thousand years or more. We're at the beginning of moving beyond the mind, the vital, and the physical. We're also going to have the superconscience. Growing whole means becoming divine. If the divine is in everything, then we're also the divine. So, development is in recognizing that and working it out in the flesh. You can't go off into a disincarnate sphere and work it out. You have to work it out in a body. You have to work it out in life. If we were some other life form then maybe we could work it out in a spirit.

The development isn't about finding myself—because I've never been lost. It's about recognizing myself, taking the veil off. It's like building a bridge to the source—to the creative life force, the substance that's in everything, that has tremendous power, just like the nuclear bomb–and connecting to that strength.

CW: But you think in this process another spirit will enter you?

GEA: In the meditation it was called a "habitation." It wasn't like a spirit taking over. I talked to you a long time ago about avatars and the walk-in—disincarnate spirits that are enlightened, that have real life themselves. Like Sri Aurobindo dying. He's a spirit. He's a teacher. He can come and teach you through dreams or through meditation. Disincarnate spirits are enlightened souls, souls that have realized themselves, realized that they have a soul. A habitation is almost like putting on earphones and hearing instructions from a tape recorder. The instructions might come in other ways. Maybe through a coincidence: A book falls off a shelf and hits you on the head; you open it and read it. It might be overhearing a conversation. When the spirit inhabits you, then you get direct information. But it doesn't mean that your spirit leaves. It's like a teacher teaching you, except you're not in a classroom. You're not in a physical classroom. You're in a different kind of classroom, one you can reach when you're meditating or when you're quiet or when your conscious mind is asleep, like through dreams, if you can get a handle on your dreams and if you start working with them. So this spirit is probably going to be instructing three thousand people or more.

In the meditation it said, "Read *The Mother*." So I went and started reading it. The Mother, when she became a realized woman—it's like she had everything at her command. I mean, she knew what people were thinking. She knew what they needed. She knew that she was total consciousness. She was the earth. She was everything, this little skinny woman. She was the only one who could do the yoga of the body and work on the cellular level.

I had already started working with the cells when I broke my arm. (Sometimes the RNA sent the wrong messages to the DNA and there was all this foul-up, and that's why you need to take antioxidants—Vitamin C and Vitamin E, etc.) I was already working with this idea—ever since my operation—with the hormones and stuff. To read that was like—!!! And then to see all of my ideas in there. I thought, "Where did I get my ideas? This man copied from me." Then I realized that he had probably given them to me. So I meditated, and it said that in 1977 I had become acquainted with him and his work; in '83 I had become acquainted with him on the mental realm through dreams; and in '84 he was going to inhabit my body for short periods. And I got certain dates like that for people. He's just a teacher, except that he doesn't have a body. It's like me giving a creative writing workshop and people coming to it. He's doing this but in another realm. So it's not like the avatar. According to Buddhist traditional theology, the last avatar is called Kalki and, according to what some people think, it's divided into three: Sri Aurobindo, the Mother, and humanity—and it's going to take maybe two thousand years for humanity to achieve that. But in the meantime, there are these people who are getting this training, for whoever wants it or—I don't know. I don't know! I don't know! That's all I know. I was real suspicious of it because of the avatar and all that other stuff we'd gotten into before. I was real skeptical. But when I started reading, it was like—you know? All the stuff, it's all in the poems I've been writing for the last ten years. It's all in the stories. And this is one of the reasons spirituality is so important! It was so strange, and I thought, "What the hell is going on?" Was I right the other time when I said that the spirit had entered my body when I was three months old and then it got knocked out when I fell off the cliff? What was going on? I don't know. I only have my meditations to go by, the writings, the Tarot cards, the I Ching. I don't know. I could just be an egomaniac, thinking that the spirit is going to inhabit my body. But then I think maybe there's millions of those things happening because I really feel we're going to be saved. Maybe not the whole race. I don't think it's going to be an apocalypse or anything like that. Maybe that's what it's supposed to be. Maybe they've always been there. We just don't see them because we're so busy trying to stay alive. All these presences I've felt, all these apparitions and stuff—maybe they were this guy showing up for a few seconds. I have no idea. I could be totally off the wall. But then it said to tell people. And I've only told three people.

CW: Who have you told?

GEA: I've told Randy, Clover, and you. With Clover, I left it very, very superficial. I gave him the title of a book to read, and I said that he was going to be getting instructions, he was going to be preparing himself. This was about a month ago. The last time I talked to him, he still hadn't gotten the book. So he might never. Maybe he doesn't need the book. I wasn't going to tell you for a while, because of the stuff about the avatar. I wanted to wait and be sure before I opened my big trap. But then it came up. I really don't think you need to read any books. I just think you need to meditate more. Because your spirit is very evident. It's very much there. I see its presence. So I don't think you have to work on the mental. I wonder what you have to work on, whether it's the vital or the physical. I doubt it's the mental, because you're not the kind of person who gets stuff from books. I think you get stuff from life and from people and maybe secondarily through books. And Clover, I don't know. He's really messed up. He's really scared. Maybe this shock of being scared of AIDS and dying and stuff, maybe that will open him. Or maybe it will drive him away.

CW: Maybe he'll work on the physical.

GEA: He needs to work on the vital and stop smoking grass. So maybe my little job is just to communicate. God knows where these ideas come from. I know it's connecting the spiritual with the political and all those kinds of connections of what I told you, living in crossroads.

.

3

Lesbian Wit

Conversation with Jeffner Allen (late 1980s)

(1998 – 1999)

ALK: In this conversation with Jeffner Allen you suggest the possibility of creating some type of psychic, imaginal identity category that (in my opinion) crosses many of the more established identity borders. Could you say more about this type of identity category? For instance, how does it work in relation to other more commonly accepted categories based on class, color, gender, sexuality?

GEA: The problem is creating a new category with a new label other than one defined by gender, race, intellectual class, etc. There are aspects of personality that people aren't focusing on now, because they see only certain features and certain categories as having more importance. But what if race, gender, and intellectual characteristics didn't matter? What *would* matter? That you're a loving person and that there are many different kinds of loving? Often I'll be in a room filled with different ethnic groups and nationalities and I feel really connected to them, even if there are no other Chicanas or dykes in the room. In "To(o) Queer the Writer" I talk about my experience with a group of hippies in the Haight who in one way were *so* different from everything I had surrounded myself with, but in another way I could really connect with them. So, what was the commonality? What helped us get to the place where I could say, "This is the category and these people belong in it"? I know identity has to be rethought and reconfigured, but I don't have the answers.

129

"Lesbian Wit"
Conversation with Jeffner Allen (late 1980s)

Labels

GEA: "Lesbian writers writing about their own writing." [Laughter] Jeffner and I find the way the topic is worded in this call for papers problematic. In articulating some of the different areas, concerns, and themes, the underlying hidden text or the deep structure is almost as evident as the conscious structure.

JA: Yeah. If I think of myself as a lesbian writer, I can't find the lesbian part; I mean, where would I look to I find it? There's no place I can locate it.

GEA: You'd have to separate all the other aspects of yourself, distinguish them from one another, and therefore bracket them or make boundaries around them so that you could discover and articulate the lesbian.

JA: Like a carton of eggs, with each aspect discrete.

GEA: But the lesbian is part of the writer, part of class, gender, whatever identity you have of yourself and I have of myself. There's no way we can put ourselves through this sieve and say "Okay, we're only going to let the lesbian part out, and everything else will stay in the sieve." The sieve and all the different identities we're supposed to sift are part of the lesbian.

JA: The topic separates identities into wholes and parts and parts and wholes. Somehow the tissues where I feel a whole bunch at once don't come in there. Can you talk about how you feel about your writing and let's just see what comes up? Does that work better?

GEA: Yes. I have the same problems with the label "lesbian writer" that I have with the label "Chicana writer." I'm a Chicana, and therefore a Chicana writer. But when critics use that term they're looking not at the person but at the writing as though the writing, not the writer, is Chicana. They're marginalizing the writing as they marginalize the writer. But middle-class, white, heterosexual people go around saying, "I'm a writer." They don't consider me a writer. They consider me a *Chicana* writer. I'm exempt from the writer status; there's a little adjective placed in front of it. The same thing happens with the lesbian writer—not so much from white, middle-class, heterosexual groups saying, "You're a lesbian writer," but from the lesbian community itself, which wants to have pride in the fact that they have lesbian artists and writers and wants to publicize this fact. I see a lot of lesbians and gay men searching for queer movie stars and classical writers and ecstatically saying, "Well, you know, Proust or Whitman or Guattarí or Foucault were homosexuals." [Laughter] They put "lesbian" and "homosexual" in front of those writers because it legitimizes homosexuality. For a Chicano or Chicana it's done in an exclusionary way, but with the lesbian and gay communities it's a privileging and an inclusion.

JA: Both ways make hierarchy and function as judgments or evaluations that cramp what writing can be. I'm also thinking about a twist on this theme, which happens often among lesbians: "Well such-and-such is supposed to be lesbian writing and you're not doing it." Or, "Such-and-such are supposed to be lesbian concerns and you (whoever the 'you' is), you—a lesbian—aren't addressing them." As nifty as it sometimes can be to find a great lesbian writer, if there's this thing called "lesbian writing" or "lesbian issues," what if a lesbian doesn't do those? Is she not a lesbian anymore? This gets so hung up on definitions, judgments, hierarchies, and exclusions. But for me, the joy of the writing and looking to see what can be found out is in that there are so many different kinds of writing a single lesbian might do, or any person might do.

GEA: There are two instances of Chicanas critiquing my work. One woman looked at *Borderlands* and judged it critically as not lesbian, not dealing with lesbianism, not dealing with lesbian issues. Another woman, a straight Chicana, did a paper on *Borderlands* and kind of appropriated my writing, sucked the energy, its soul, out of it by comparing my experience with hers. She wasn't really looking at the differences of class and sexual preference. The first was a lesbian and the second a straight woman, but both in different ways dealt with only one aspect of the work to the exclusion of other aspects. They didn't see the whole and I think that's sad. It's a way of reducing the other person and her work, a sort of character assassination. Also it erases the boundary between writer/author and work, as though they equal each other. There's the assumption that the writing persona in the text is the same person as the author and that's not true. In some instances collapsing the boundaries between text, reader, and author is good, but not in these two cases which made *Borderlands* equal Gloria Anzaldúa. [Laughter] What do you think?

JA: Yeah, there's a question about reading too. If I'm reading somebody's stuff, how do I want to read it? Do I want to read a text by filtering it through a single identity point or do I look at it through multiple, shifting identities? If I read looking for a certain aspect or even looking for a handful of aspects, that's limiting. That kind of identity focus would miss the boat, at least on a lot of writing I enjoy. And if I read my own writing that way, I wouldn't know what it was about because it wouldn't be able to meet the test of having a specific identity. My writing couldn't meet the test—ever—and I wouldn't want it to.

Shapeshifting, Changing Identities

GEA: I've done a lot of thinking and some writing about shifting identities, changing identities. I call it "shapeshifting," as in nagualismo—a type of Mexican indigenous shamanism where a person becomes an animal, becomes a different person. For me there aren't little cubbyholes with all the different identities—intellectual, racial, sexual. It's more like a very fine membrane—sort of like a river, an identity is sort of like a river. It's one and it's flowing and it's a process. By giving different names to different parts of a single mountain range or different parts of a river, we're doing that entity a disservice. We're fragmenting it. I'm struggling with how to name without cutting it up.

JA: There could be a whole bunch of different names for the same thing, although often naming freezes. If I name something in ways that would freeze it, I'm naming the thing to conform to what I want it to be. Its other names—already existing or potential—will be lost. A lot of white feminist theory, especially in the '70s, talked about the power of naming, and it was important to name our experiences because naming somehow makes things real. I think naming can do that, but there's a question about the way that naming makes things real and the kinds of ways that I want to be naming.

GEA: And the kinds of things that the naming excludes or shuts off.

JA: That's right. So say that in the mountain range you have several different names, but what are the connections? How are dis/connections and connections happening all the time? Part of this piece I'm doing now is about what I'm calling "reverberations," sound or movement that continues and continues. It's not all one thing, but it's not necessarily six things that you could select out and identify. But it's not trying to aim at something like a melting pot or assimilation. This is hard to do because naming tends either to assimilate or to separate, segregate, marginalize, whatever.

GEA: I was trying to do that with the new mestiza. I was trying to get away from just thinking in terms of blood—you know, the mestiza as being of mixed blood. The new mestiza is a mixture of all these identities and has the ability, the flexibility, the malleability, the amorphous quality of being able to stretch, and go this way and that way, and add new labels or names which would mix with the others and they would be also malleable. But it's hard to articulate. I'm trying to find metaphors—like the mountain range, the river, the mestiza—but they're not quite what I want. Maybe in the process of writing it'll come to me: some new way of talking about these things without cementing them, without fixing them forever in my own writing. Metaphors that have exits and entrances, an open door so things can come in and go out, so that other people can enter and exit.

Bridges, Rainbows, Coalitions

JA: There's a notion I call "floating bridges," in this piece I'm doing now. [Laughter]

GEA: Is a floating bridge more like a ferry?

JA: It's a little nebulous, like a fairy, and somewhat magical.

GEA: Or like a rainbow, because a rainbow is a bridge . . .

JA: Yes. Like a rainbow, it's not completely clear where floating bridges are from or where they go. That doesn't mean it's completely unclear either, but it's not of the greatest concern.

GEA: Well the connotation/denotation of the word that's being used now politically by Native Americans is that a rainbow is a way many different kinds of people communicate with each other so that there's not a race separatism. It's Native Americans' vision of the red, white, black, and yellow communicating and making alliances. That's how they use the bridge. Jesse Jackson and company have also borrowed the Native Americans' metaphor of the rainbow bridge, but I don't know if groups in other countries have used that kind of concept. Native Americans claim they were the keepers of the Earth, the ones who would facilitate this rich multialliance, multibridging. That vision has taken quite a beating this past decade because of the reactionary times—the upsurge in racism and white supremacy with the Ku Klux Klan and the skinheads. But it might come up again in the '90s.

I also see lesbian and gay people as exemplars of the mestiza and mestizo, exemplars of the rainbow bridge, because we exist in all different cultures. Because we're persecuted we tend to look after each other so that you have more of an interracial mixture among gays than you do among the general population.

JA: Yeah.

GEA: But this interracial mixture is scary for certain people in the gay community; therefore some counteract that fear—that instability, that ambiguity—by making rigid boundaries around such concepts as "lesbian writer."

JA: Yeah. Like some parts would be the lesbian aspects and other parts would be the Chicano aspects or the black aspects or the Native American aspects.

GEA: Yes. Out of fear, they want to cement, anchor things down. And also because as lesbian or gay or whatever we live very unstable lives—emotionally and sometimes physically risky lives. I can understand that impulse to nail things down and measure up to a checklist of what it means to be lesbian, radical lesbian, or S/M lesbian. But when that criteria is forced on us, it feels totalitarian.

JA: It can kill off parts of the self.

GEA: Yeah. And different people—a straight person or a white lesbian or a lesbian of color—have different checklists and criteria. So you're dealing with two, three, or more different groups analyzing you for whether you're a legitimate this or a legitimate that. People used to look at class in that way; I don't know if they still do. You know—"Do you own a car or a house? Do you pay a maid to come and clean?" If you did these things you were frowned on by the community. But that kind of ideology was merely one of words and mind only, not something people would act upon. Politically it would be correct to be downwardly mobile and to have working-class modes or styles of living, yet that was not the reality. The reality was a double standard.

JA: Yes, I remember this too.

GEA: The same type of checklist applies to lesbians: Are you a lesbian who's in the closet? Are you a lesbian who's out? Are you a lesbian who's an activist? Are you a lesbian who's a writer? Are you out there being a model "good lesbian"? [Laughter] If you're not, if you happen to be a lesbian and you write a story in which the protagonist is male or a straight woman, you're criticized for supporting the patriarchy by writing traditionally, or writing about concerns not seen as lesbian concerns. They think traditional content or characters supports the patriarchy, but they fail to look at how the writing is done, at the form, at the style. Does it subvert the content?

Then there's another question: If you're a straight woman or man can you write a lesbian story? Are you a lesbian writer because you're a lesbian or are you a lesbian writer because you write about lesbian concerns? Is there such a thing as a lesbian language, lesbian style, lesbian terminology, lesbian aesthetics, or is it all up to the individual who's writing, whether she's a lesbian, a straight woman, or a man? Can a man write as a lesbian? [Laughter] This is the same question people have asked about whether a man can write or read as a woman. We all know that women read and write as men because that's how we were taught. We were trained to read as men. Little girls read the books boys read, but boys rarely read books with little girl heroines. We're taught to read westerns, spy novels, mysteries, and serious literature. We can also read women's literature and watch soap operas, but men aren't taught to read women. Can we apply this idea to the lesbian reader and the lesbian writer? What do you think?

JA: I'm not sure. If I'm reading something by an author I don't know, I usually have a feeling about whether the author is lesbian. Even with papers written by students I don't know, I have the feeling and usually the feeling is accurate.

GEA: Are you distinguishing between lesbian and feminist, or are you collapsing the two?

JA: Even collapsed, it's really weird, even collapsed—

GEA: Even collapsed, you can pick the lesbian writer?

JA: Well, I couldn't guarantee it every time, of course. But I have noticed this: Take a class with fifty or sixty students. I don't know them all and I go through reading their papers; when I give the papers back it usually turns out that the ones I thought were lesbian really are. But I couldn't tell you why or how I knew. The men and women separate much faster; if something's written by a man it usually separates out.

GEA: Recently I read dozens of anonymous manuscripts for a writing seminar I'm doing at The Loft in Minneapolis. I thought only two men applied because something—their writing or their little intro letter—gave them away. But when I picked writers, the program director said, "Oh this manuscript which you think is written by a black woman is really by a black man." There was another manuscript, one I didn't pick, that I thought was written by a woman, and it wasn't. I really was shocked. But I could spot the lesbians more easily by their writing samples and by what they said in their letter. I could distinguish that group much more than I could the feminist women and the men. Isn't that interesting?

JA: That's really interesting.

GEA: But this is just an isolated instance. I don't know if the same thing would be true if I was to do this experiment two or three times with different groups. I'm making this assumption based on one experience. With nonfiction I can usually distinguish the women from the men because generally women are more interested in the psychological components of their lives—the feelings, the inner life. Most men don't connect with their feelings or their inner self as much. But there are lots of exceptions. So then I wonder: In writings, in conversations, when lesbians talk to each other and when straight women talk to each other, are there certain things that each group brings out into the open? Are lesbians more apt to talk about their sexuality and that feeling component than straight women? Or are lesbians more apt to discuss relationship issues than straight women? Do lesbians always talk about issues like merging, separate spaces, and intimacy? Are there certain things common to lesbians that they talk about? Are there certain things common to straight women that they speak about? Do straight women always talk about children and husbands and job? Or am I making boundaries?

JA: Well, except for talking about husbands, which most lesbians would have a hard time doing, I'm not sure that it breaks down according to topic. I have these two straight women friends who I see a lot of. They have real conversations about sexuality, they discuss all the particulars. It's really kind of neat. But I don't know if that's typical. And I think, what do I do? I talk about so many different experiences. I don't know if there's one or two things I always talk about.

GEA: I think it depends who you're talking to—like you and I talk a lot about writing and a lot about race, class, and sexuality—

JA: —and the beach.

GEA: And the beach. And the future and current events and books, intellectual ideas. If you met with another friend, you'd probably talk about different things. Maybe not.

JA: I'm thinking of one friend, we talk a lot about intellectual ideas, but the talk is very different. There's a lot of playfulness when you and I talk, whereas with her, our way of talking is somehow less personable. She really gets into the particulars of layers and deconstruction. . . . She's real good at theory. She loves to talk about it.

GEA: More abstract?

JA: Yeah, more abstract. Whereas when you and I talk about ideas, I feel like I talk about theory because it's fun, because I want to see what you think about it, and also because it's making changes or differences, you know what I mean? That there's some kind of a movement going on.

Reading

GEA: So do you think that a lesbian reader reading your work—if I read your work—would that differ from a straight feminist reading it?

JA: For me it would differ because in a lot of ways you'd understand things about it or find things in it that a straight woman might not.

GEA: Such as what?

JA: Well, the particulars are so hard to come by.

GEA: What about the style? See, this is where it becomes hard, but would another mode of presentation be something that I'd be more in tune to? A straight woman might see it as a deviation from a traditional form, whereas I may see it as more of a lesbian mode.

JA: I think that could be part of it. And also sometimes—not always—straight women say that the things they read just seem unreal to them.

GEA: A straight woman reader would not catch a lot of the undercurrent that had to do maybe with sexuality and sexual experience.

JA: Yeah. I'm thinking of the last piece I did, which I read recently in a group with lesbians and straight women. There are things embedded in it—a few words here and there from late '70s lesbian songs and so on—to bring out the humor.

GEA: Because it's part of our culture we can fill in the gap and reconstruct it, but a straight woman might not.

JA: Yeah, these are cultural signs, in a way. Not signs of belonging, but they're signs that at least some lesbians will relate to. And then I tried to put some other signs that lesbians who weren't lesbians at that point would also find.

GEA: Identity formation is a component in reading, a component that a lot of people don't realize. When one reads something one is familiar with, one sort of attaches to that familiarity, and the rest of the text, or what's hidden, is not perceived. Difference also shores up identity.

JA: Sometimes a reader will fix upon one point and ignore all the rest—it might be a lesbian thing, or not. Usually it's something that really upsets a reader; the reader will fix upon that and the other dimensions get lost. Of course that's disappointing, because I try to write with several movements going on at once. If one moment gets lifted out, it's so disappointing.

GEA: Yeah. When my writing was first out in the world there was a danger that people with a negative concept and experience of spirituality might start reading me and then shut the book because of the spirituality. But there was also the impulse to say, "OK, I like Gloria's writing over here about class or race. Now she's talking about spirituality and I'm really turned off, but because I like this other stuff I'm going to keep on." So they access the spiritual and may find that it's not a turnoff for them. Then again, maybe there are some people who just can't read me because of the spiritual aspects and they'll shut the book. Or they may come across a sentence or passage that they think borders on essentialism or generalization or whatever. They look at that passage and are critical of it, it jumps to their attention. They keep reading but they're disturbed by it, and so it keeps them from perceiving the other stuff. That's one possibility. Another possibility is that they keep reading and find that I contradict the generalization or the essentialist comment. So then they look at my work as fiction. Anything is possible. The more entrances the piece has the better people can access it.

A lesbian will have more incentive to keep reading when she reaches one of these passages. There will be more doors and windows to enter the writing than for a nonlesbian reader. If it's a lesbian of color, there are even more entrances. Chicana lesbians have the greatest possibility of finding themselves represented in my writing. So there are different ways of hooking into and identifying with the writing. But sometimes academic women, outsiders—straight, white, whatever—can see through the writing and understand what I'm trying to say better than an insider. So for me it becomes a question of the individual reader, not so much whether she's white or straight or Chicana or a woman of color or a lesbian, but a mode of reading that can read between the lines and read the subtext. It's more a skill that a person has and not her ethnic, class, or sexual identity. She's trained to look at a piece of writing and read it in different ways. A Chicana lesbian working-class woman friend of mine who knows me and loves my writing may not have the skills or reading mode—methods of reading—may not see through or beyond whatever's offensive to her in any piece of writing. Maybe a middle-class white academic feminist can get it (if there's such a thing as "getting it"), or maybe not get it, but can be closer to my reading of my own work than this other Chicana.

I'm also a reader of my own work. As a reader do I have more in common with this Chicana lesbian working-class woman than I do with this white middle-class academic woman? Or can I have both? Can I have the working-class lesbian Chicana way of reading and the white middle-class way of reading? I probably have more training in reading as a white, middle-class academic than I do in reading as a Chicana. Just like we have more training in reading as men. So, what do you think of all this?

JA: Well, that's a lot to think about. When you were talking about the reader as critic who looks for certain points, I was reminded of my idea about reading in camouflage. The hunters where I live in the winter use camouflage. They're looking at something—like a wild goose or a deer that just ran by—and they don't see anything else because they're focusing only on the animal. And, the hunters say that because they wear camouflage they blend in and cannot be seen. A reader in camouflage would be a reader who didn't self-question where they're coming from, but just kept looking for one thing, trying to catch it, trying to bag it.

GEA: Like wearing blinders, it limits what you can see.

JA: Yeah, and so the reader claims to be invisible.

GEA: The camouflaged reader is only using certain faculties; she's blanking out the others because of the one goal to shoot bear. They're only looking for bear so if something else is hidden behind the bushes, all they'll see is the bear. I like that metaphor.

JA: I don't think the reading skills you mentioned would necessarily have to be linked with academia. It's sort of a feeling about connection—

GEA: It's probably acquired not through institutions but from a lot of different kinds of reading—

JA: —or maybe even friendships. Maybe reading skills can be acquired from ways of making friends or even ways of being by oneself or being with nature. There can be different sorts of overlap, like if I learn to hear something differently—say in music—somehow that will come into my reading too; I'll find some different shape of feelings or ideas on a page that I didn't find before.

GEA: Yes. Reading skills don't necessarily have to do with academic learning. If you're a street person, you go into an experience—say something taking place in a street: you're streetwise and can read the event in a way that a white academic feminist couldn't.

   If I'm writing about different ideas, those ideas are concretized. I don't come right out and say, "this is a theory," or "This is an idea." The working-class person, the Chicana dyke, will automatically identify with that experience and say, "Oh, yeah, I've lived it," or whatever. The white middle-class academic woman might see it in terms of where I position myself: Am I rereading certain patriarchal signs? Am I locating myself in a specific historical period? Am I being self-reflective about my writing? These are things she's learned as feminist critical approaches, things similar to the streetwise person reading the street. But the streetwise person is looking at an experience or event that's alive and moving, whereas the academic is looking at the flattened-out abstract theory on these pages that's not connected to the other. I consider myself standing in the borderlands of these two things; I can do both. I may be able to read the situation in the street from the point of view of a streetwise person, and I can look at these abstract theoretical writings and read them because of my schooling. Does that make sense?

JA: Yeah.

Compartmentalized Identities

GEA: But can I be both at the same time? Can I be both the academic intellectual person and also the streetwise person?

JA: They seem simultaneous. You didn't talk about learning one and giving up the other. For example, it isn't as if you have learned schoolbook study so you're giving up street observation, or as if you've found schoolbook study a 100 percent waste of time and gone back to street observation. Maybe this connects to something you were saying earlier about artificial downward mobility or pseudo–downward mobility, where someone claims to be giving up one thing in order to have something else.

GEA: Well, it's a bogus kind of move.

JA: Right, because both are there. It's like two hoops or frisbees that keep circling in different ways.

GEA: There's an awareness or compartmentalization that feminism is trying to get away from, but first it becomes an intellectual exercise. Later it becomes emotional, physical, and in all different aspects a more holistic exercise. But in the beginning there's a kind of a lip service paid to it. Now people are integrating that desire not to compartmentalize into their lives, into everyday activities. But compartmentalization has been a way of life for so long—to be different people and not even aware of it: life forcing us to be one person at the job, another at school, and yet another with our lesbian friends—that it feels really ambiguous to bring all those other identities with you and to activate them all.

Especially in school I notice that kind of separation between personal life and academic studies, even though the underlying foundation of women's studies is that the personal is political. But from what I've seen, it's been lip service except from lesbian women professors active in community things.

JA: Many of the women's studies programs I've worked with have spent most their gatherings talking in quite formal ways. In these meetings, I usually never say anything about my personal life. Nobody ever asks me, either. Nor do other women or even other lesbians—and there are other lesbians—share parts of their personal life. It would really be risky to do so. (How shall I put this? I've had so many horrible experiences.) In many ways it places me at risk if different aspects of my personal life get known, and I can't function very well in terms of the basic academic activities I need to do if there are all these ideas going on about who I am or who I'm supposed to be. It's much easier not to have to deal with all those ideas because they're usually not much about me anyway.

GEA: Especially when you're working on orals and dissertation committees.

JA: Yes. It's important to have good working connections, good professional connections, even if it's with other lesbians. This need outweighs what I really thought women's studies would be when it was just starting in the '70s. I was at University of Florida, and it seemed like women's studies was going to be this really wonderful place where women of real different classes, a lot of lesbians, and feminist straight women—most of the women were white, it was northern Florida—were going to get together, do things, and learn about each other's lives. But it didn't work. The women's studies program there had been going for about six months and at that point they refused to list a class I was teaching because it had lesbian content. Talk about coming to another topic! I was using this poetry book, *Beginning with O*, by Olga Broumas, and some regent saw my reading list, thought the book had to be "pornographic," and complained. I find it really a hassle to be an out lesbian in academia. Although I say I don't know what lesbian writing is, it is usually clear that my writing—whatever it is, except for the real academic stuff—is written by someone who's a lesbian. And it's a real hassle because there's all this static and prejudice—including, a lot of the time, by closet dykes.

GEA: At the Berkshire Conference we had a Daily Life of Lesbian Sexuality panel. They kept misplacing the sign and they put us in the wrong room. They did these things to occlude us, to obscure us. That happened to me again in the National Association of Chicano Studies Conference. But that's only one reality, locale, or space where that happens. In academia I find that my lesbianism gets hidden behind the overt race stuff. The race stuff is so dreadful, so horrible and painful, and I'm so busy dealing with it that it makes the lesbian stuff—especially in Santa Cruz—smaller by comparison. The Literature Board, women's studies, and His/Con people have an awareness of lesbianism and an awareness of not stepping on people's toes too much, but they have a blank spot about race and class. So the painful things I get hit with have more to do with ethnicity and class. If I went to South Texas, to Pan-American University, the lesbian stuff would really jar and stand out and be painful. So it depends on the location, the space I'm in.

JA: What do you do with the pains? Do you end up writing about them?

GEA: Yes. I'm writing an essay, "The Art of Bearing Witness: Literary and Artistic Productions and Class Identity," about the race and class experiences I've had here and in other universities as a graduate student and as a part-time lecturer or teacher. The crux of the article is that in these kinds of settings as a writer, a student, an intellectual, the personal—bearing witness to one's total history—gets pushed to the side. In asserting that part of myself into the Literature Board, into the university, I've run into a brick wall; into such blankness from these people who can't perceive anything but the institution and its hierarchies, its molds. It's like banging my head against this brick wall and I'm just hurting myself. I have to learn strategies and to some extent I've learned strategies that allow me not to beat my head against that wall yet somehow make chinks in the wall—not so much with my head, but with other things. It's just a real complex situation—being a lesbian, being working class, being Chicana, being a writer; different facets of that mixture come up depending on the space and the people I'm with.

Imaginal, Psychic Identities

JA: I also see stuff about dreams and images in your writing and these are also a kind of region of reality. In addition to the history, mythology, conversations, family experience, autobiography, there's also a lot of—

GEA: —fantasy and dreams and imaginings—

JA: —more nebulous realities. That is something that distinguishes your writing in many ways.

GEA: For a dreamer, the fantasy world can be a reality. In society the dreamer is not valued because according to the dominant mode of thinking if you're a dreamer you don't have your feet firmly on the ground in their "official" reality. They don't see the other reality of the dreamer. And I think that dimension is often in my stuff. People in society do categorize the realist, the dreamer, the idealist, the pessimist; so for a person who's into a kind of imaginal creative space—that can be an identity. It's just not an identity that people think of like a race or class or job or age.

JA: I think it's important to mention all those things; they're really key like race, class, age, and ethnicity. There are other areas too, although they may not have any name on them.

GEA: An inner reality, a psychic reality that a lot of us share could be an identity, a label, or whatever. But it's not something that's articulated, and therefore it's not a reality. And if it's not a reality, it's not an identity.

JA: Yeah.

GEA: Or they'll label it in a negative way: "mysticism," "New Age," "utopian." The person who uses her imagination—who images and visualizes and dreams—makes the connections between these different identities and realities. The dominant reality mode/academia wants to sever the dreamer's connections; it doesn't want to connect the personal and the academic, the spiritual and the intellectual, or the emotions and body. Maybe others find the kinds of connections we make in our writings hard to read and comprehend. I don't know.

JA: Sometimes our writings might be hard to read, but I wonder whether they're *really* so hard to read. In school, being taught to read in a certain way makes certain kinds of reading happen more readily. And, sometimes there may be blockades or walls. Or there may be expectations that a writing should be read in a certain way. Yet, say I'm talking with friends—we go on a walk or to dinner or something—the style of the conversation, no matter what it's about, usually isn't like reading a book, even though I may learn something in the conversation. In other words, my awareness may increase in that conversation, but the shape it takes formally isn't like the shape my consciousness may take when reading theory, or even some styles of writing. Sometimes styles of writing that rely more on image, on seeing a lot of images come out of each other, can be closer to patterns of informal conversation and further from patterns of formal writing. So why does imaginative writing look hard? Because imaginative writing may be closer to conversation—like if I'm just sitting with a friend and she says, "I just thought of something. It just passed through my mind," and then we go on to talk about something else, that quick changing of topic and sliding and gliding—

GEA: Well, I think it's because the reader hasn't learned to shift readily, the way that the mind works. If you're sitting there for five minutes, your mind goes through a variety of memories and ideas, improvises dialogues with people, restructures past events. Your mind is always shifting from one mode to the other. It's hard work when you're reading those shifts in a text. I've discovered that my literary assistants and friends who critique my writing want me to flesh out more of the gaps, show clear transitions so they don't have to do as much work. But for me, what's fun about reading is the gaps; I can bring my experience into the piece and use a concrete image to go off into my own experience, and that makes the writing richer because I can bring more into it. But we haven't been taught to do this. I can do it because I'm in my inner world—my psychic imaginary dreaming body—so much. I have a facility there because as a child I used that world to escape, to get away from stress, and also to nurture and comfort myself, for play and pleasure. So an image in a piece of writing can take possession of me and it becomes beautiful; it becomes meaningful.

I love to read writings with lots of images, writings that let me derive some meaning, connect the dots, figure out what's hidden in the foliage after I connect all the dots—writings with a certain sophistication, a playing with words, with little riddles. I get a lot out of that kind of reading. I also get a lot out of very simple straightforward narrative like oral histories. Reading and writing are enjoyable because I can make connections. When I write I know that certain people will make those connections with me and other people will think, "Well, this is messy. This is chaotic. I don't understand this." They don't want to work to make the connections.

[Pause to reconnoiter]

Lesbian Writings and Audiences

GEA: One of the things I find very boring about some lesbian writings, both fiction and nonfiction, is an almost formulaic impression or imposition about what lesbians *should* write and think about. A politically correct way of writing that feels sterile, flat. One of these impositions is the underlying belief—from both the straight and the gay world—that to be a lesbian writer you have to write about sexuality. There's the assumption that when you open up a book written by a lesbian a predominant concern is sexual relationships or sexuality. In one way lesbians have opened up the dialogue and an avenue for women to connect back to their bodies; lesbians really connected some of the political, theoretical, cultural, critical concepts with concrete experience. And that to me was really good—especially when I first started reading lesbian stuff and when I came out. But now it's become a unwritten law: To be a lesbian writer you've got to deal with sexual concerns. In the coming out story, certain themes are considered lesbian properties. Then there's the lesbian couple relationship, the breaking up—it becomes kind of formulaic and the formula is white and kind of middle class. A coming out story would be different if it was written from the perspective of some "other"—racial, cultural, ethnic, or whatever—in addition to lesbian otherness. A lot of ethnic-racial others take the white middle-class lesbian pattern—whether it's coming out or whatever; they take that pattern as a model. Instead of a fresh unique presentation of encountering oneself as a lesbian and confronting one's community as a lesbian, we copy this other model. It flattens our writing.

JA: One example of a writer who doesn't do that would be Chrystos in *Not Vanishing*. The poems and the writings are really beautiful; I'm not sure that they're saying something about coming out, I think there's a lot of—

GEA: There's a lot of honesty in her talk about relationships in her letters to me, where she's talking about her lovers or ex-lovers, her family, and the community. She calls it like it is and gets away from the utopian formula, the "It's great, we're all—

JA: —sisters together"?

GEA: Yeah. [Laughter]

JA: Which is part of her "not vanishing," maybe. She's not vanishing any part of her life; it's all there. Once I was reading my piece, "On the Seashore," to a group of mostly lesbians. On one page I say something about clitorises or clitori, several clitorises. (It's not done like that, but it's one of the images, it just flows through.) The passage is about two-thirds of the way through the piece, and all of a sudden there was a whoop and cheer from the listeners. Yet, I wasn't so happy—I guess I wanted the group to feel more than only that passage . . .

GEA: Well, when I go to lesbian concerts—Holly Near, etc.—and the whole auditorium is full of dykes, there's an assumption that this is our common culture, but here I am a Chicana and I don't identify with some of these classics, like the one about the gym teacher. All these women are cheering and getting up and screaming. It gives them this wonderful sense of identity and solidarity, but it leaves me out because first of all the songs are all in English, and there's nothing Spanish, nothing Mexican, and probably very few women of color in the audience. This happened when I was at the Michigan Women's Music Festival in 1981. There were some black bodies working or walking around, but for the most part all the performers—except for Sweet Honey in the Rock and a few black groups and maybe a Latina group— were white. So the kind of joy and spontaneity and plugging into one's identity that the majority of these women had—it made me feel left out, instead of making me feel good. I felt good for them, but their feeling good canceled my feeling good. Some of that also happens in the writing or at readings. I have a poem that I wrote about doing a reading at the Haight. I'd done a series of readings among the lesbian community and the Latino/Chicano Mission community. The Haight reading was full of white hippies and ordinary people and I felt so at home with them. I couldn't figure out why I felt so at home. Part of the reason was that they were very open to my work: If I was reading lesbian poems or stuff that was predominantly about being Chicana, they didn't have any preconceptions; they were just open. I felt accepted and valued in a total kind of way that I didn't feel in the lesbian or the Mission community.

JA: Because there were not presuppositions about how you should be?

GEA: Well, I'm not sure. See, the whole thing this poem is trying to figure out . . .

JA: Are you still working on the poem?

GEA: I just found it the other day while I was looking at the poems I have about reading—not just reading as the act of reading a page, but reading reality. This poem is about that. It's about me reading, but it's also about other people reading me and me reading them reading me. These people were straight and a lot of them were men, what you would consider chauvinist. Yet, they were there in a way that the other politically aware groups weren't. They were open and receptive, and they weren't reading me the usual way.

I don't follow the tradition of "the poet reads, the audience listens." So I don't do that. I dialogue. I read, they ask questions, they make comments, I read, I talk, they make comments. It's an exchange.

JA: Yeah.

GEA: They walk away with maybe less of me but more of themselves. That feels good. Sometimes I talk more and dialogue with them more than I read and people say, "Well, I wish you had read more." But it's never the other way around, where I read more and people dialogue less. Really it's become a balance. A very integral component to reading my work has to be the audience reading back, or the audience talking back. Otherwise I don't feel comfortable. And I think that goes along with what I said earlier: in the past, the reader was thought of as a very minor part of the exchange between author, text, and reader. The reader is now becoming *as*—if not *more*—important than the author. But I think the text is still primary.

JA: Yes.

GEA: So in reading like a lesbian, which includes listening like a lesbian, maybe one would distinguish a lesbian reader or a lesbian feminist reader or a feminist reader in the desire to interact, to add to the dialogue. That might be why we have such a low patience with texts and public events that don't allow us to do that. Many of the lesbian texts I feel bored with have this kind of sing-along quality where you're supposed to cheer, you're supposed to say "Wow!" and clap at certain points. Doing that invalidates other aspects of one's personhood.

JA: That cheering probably works for some people, but it doesn't work for me. I've never been part of a group that cheered like that. I've always sort of had friends, but a lot of times they don't even know each other.

They know of each other because I say things about one to the other. Maybe it's something about ways of making friendships that's just personal to me. But with friends here and friends there, maybe they read each other's writings or they certainly know that one and the other exists, but not even half of my friends are ever together in one place to be able to have a group cheer. Even if my friends all got together, it probably wouldn't be very interesting if it were to happen like that.

GEA: You know, I have these Libra parties, or birthday parties—

JA: Are you a Libra? I am too.

GEA: Last year I had two different parties. Because I have two friends who recently broke up, who couldn't be in the same room, I had to have two different events. Most people are amazed at how different my friends are from each other—in age, in class, in race, in a lot of different ways; they're amazed that I had so many different friends. It's possible for me to be sitting here talking with you and going for walks on the beach with you and have a perfectly good time, and then to do that with somebody who's a Chicana, and have those interactions be very different but also as fulfilling.
You're Libra? When is your birthday?

JA: The 11th of October.

GEA: Mine's the 26th of September. Last year I invited some other Libras and I think this time I'm going to ask not only Libra suns but Libra risings and Libra moons.

JA: What does that mean?

GEA: That instead of having a little party or a dinner for people whose sun sign is Libra, I'm going to ask people who are not Libra suns but might have a Libra moon or Libra rising—to see how that works.

JA: Oh, wow.

GEA: I'm going to be gone when my birthday comes along, but when I come back we're going to do that, and then I have a reading in the city [San Francisco], an inaugural celebration by Aunt Lute Books, and I'm going to have a birthday banquet afterwards, a Chinese birthday banquet. Have you ever been to a Chinese banquet?

JA: No. Have you done it before?

GEA: Yes. For a couple of birthdays.

JA: It's really neat, huh?

GEA: Yeah, my friend Kit Quan figures out how many people are going to be there, makes reservations, we go and then they bring out all these dishes! Lots of food. I loved it. How did we get into food?

JA: Making friends. All the friends in different places, and different friends; there's not a model friend, I guess. It's wild to end with a Chinese birthday banquet. It sort of takes things in a great direction.

4

Making Choices

Writing, Spirituality, Sexuality, and the Political

An Interview with AnaLouise Keating (1991)

(1998 – 1999)

ALK: In our 1991 interview you talk about "recogniz[ing] that our flesh is spiritualized." How does this idea of the flesh being spiritualized go with your health? For instance, diabetes has clearly had a huge impact on your life. And before the diabetes, you had many physical difficulties—the very early, extremely painful menstruation you discuss in the early interviews and the hysterectomy, especially. If the flesh is spiritualized, can you use spirituality to heal the flesh?

GEA: Yes, but you have to have tremendous discipline. Our mind, our flesh, our energy system are all connected. What people think affects the body, the body's physiology depends on how people think. If you have a belief system that modern medicine is the only answer to healing certain diseases, the diseased person is virtually helpless and dependent on the doctor who becomes an all-knowing God. The person can't participate in her own healing; it all has to be done with injections, drugs, and vitamin supplements. That belief system doesn't heal and has to change. You have to start believing, "I *can* effect healing in my body. I'm not going to give in to external authoritative figures." But it's very hard to change a person's belief system.

ALK: Because everything outside us is saying the opposite—that *doctors* heal us.

GEA: Yes. We have these belief systems because someone told us

151

repeatedly that we're bad and we begin to believe it. We can change these beliefs by telling ourselves the opposite: "You're a worthy human being. You're loving. You're worthwhile." You have to bypass the surface mind and maybe the middle-mind, go into the deeper-mind and reprogram it. You can do this using various techniques such as subliminal tapes. It takes a lot of energy and sometimes it takes trauma, like the trauma of a major illness such as diabetes. I have to open myself up to the belief that I *can* heal myself, that my body can heal itself with the help of the spirit. I don't know how long it's going to take. Maybe with some people it can take place instantaneously. With me, I spent the first year or so denying, resisting, the fact that I had a chronic disease that could kill me and then another year being angry: "Did I deserve this? Where did I fuck up?" I'm now at the point where I can detach myself and say, "Gloria has this drama, this chronic illness because she gets out of balance." I don't have that detachment yet, but I'm working on it and I'm waiting to see if there's a meaning to this disease, to this struggle: What is it teaching me? What am I learning? What's the pattern I'm repeating, the belief system I'm hooked into? I'm not at the point where I can detach completely and see myself struggling with this disease. If I activate the spirit, discipline the spirit and ask it to heal the body, I believe that it will heal the body. Some people heal themselves—people who have remission, who are supposed to die from leukemia. I think that self-knowledge and knowledge about the external world, both inner and outer, will give us the means to be able to heal our bodies.

"Making Choices: Writing, Spirituality, Sexuality, and the Political"
An Interview with AnaLouise Keating (1991)

This Bridge and *Haciendo Caras*

ALK: It's been over ten years since *This Bridge Called My Back* was first published. Has its impact on both feminist of color and white feminist thinking met your expectations? Exceeded them?

GEA: I think that it did meet my expectations. At that time I had just gone through a very major operation and before I started *This Bridge* I had gone through a very frustrating time with the middle-class white women who led the writing groups and organizations I was involved in—the Feminist Writers' Guild, the Women's Writers Union. In the '70s I went to consciousness raising meetings at the Y where I was the only Chicana. The frustration continued. When I was a grad student and nobody wanted to listen to what I had to say, I felt invisible. In 1978 when I was living in San Francisco, Merlin Stone did a workshop at a women's retreat called Willow. She offered two scholarships for working-class or women of color who couldn't afford this out-of-the-way nice, scenic middle-class inn.

I went to the workshop, but I started noticing that the people who ran the retreat were looking at me funny, and they moved me out of my single room and into a collective bunkbed-room, where I was the only occupant. Merlin and I figured that they had found out I was not a paying member like the other women—there were about twelve of us—and they started treating me differently. Like I didn't deserve a room to myself and I didn't deserve to eat what they ate. Their remarks were really racist and they weren't even aware of it. Merlin was bothered by the same thing, so we talked and it was at her encourage-ment that I started doing *This Bridge*. I put the soliciting letter together and I started telling people about it. Things were kind of slow so about six months after I started, I asked Cherríe to join me. We were still working on it in '80. We couldn't afford the costs that it takes when you're putting a book together—not only making copies but phone calls and postage and time, you know. . . . I got very very ill and almost died and at the end of March the doctor said, "Don't take on any heavy duties. Don't do any major projects." But that summer we had to put it together.

So those frustrations—similar frustrations like those I've just described—compelled me to do *Haciendo Caras* nine years later. I actually started *Haciendo Caras* in the fall of '88 when I began grad school for the second time. The frustrations this time around came out of my search for materials to teach a U.S. women of color class at UC Santa Cruz, and having to do this all over again—searching for an article here, an essay there, a story there, a poem here—and I thought "Ahh." I couldn't rely on teaching *This Bridge* again because people had been teaching it and people had been taking it in class. One person told me that she'd had it in four of her undergrad and grad courses. So I thought, "Well I have to do it." There wasn't anything out there other than single anthologies of particular cultures—Native American, etc., etc. So I started looking at magazines, quarterlies. I went to the library, looked at my bookshelves, asked other people, put together a reader for the class, and decided it was going to be a book for publication since I'd already done all the work. I'd been waiting for someone to do a similar kind of text but nobody had. I wanted it to be a textbook for women's studies classes or classes like the one you teach—but I wanted original things as well. Early in the fall of '88 I put together the reader and asked people to submit. I told Mariana Romo-Carmona to do something about being Latina and working in the U.S., living in the U.S., having had a child taken away from her because of her lesbianism, working with *Conditions*, putting together *Cuentos*, and all those intersections. She was working on an essay for *Haciendo Caras*. Barbara Ruth—who's half Jewish and half Native American and also disabled (environmental illnesses) and a dyke— she was going to write about that. I had all these wonderful essays planned and some people came through. Barbara Ruth didn't do her essay, so I chose a published poem, "The Eskimo." The book didn't have as many original pieces—poems, stories, and essays—as I had hoped. I thought it's not time for these women to publish, they can't take the risk or something else is holding them back. After nine years there *has* to have been some improvements, right? And the fact that *Bridge* had become a widely read book in the women's community said to me that people were listening to the voices of women of color— that white women were listening and that women of color were listening to each other. But it seemed to me that the stories, poems, and essays in *This Bridge* were being addressed to the white feminists. In *Haciendo Caras* I wanted us to be talking to each other more. And sometimes that's true and other times it's not.

ALK: You mean that sometimes it seems the writers are addressing themselves to white women?

GEA: Well some of it—like the Ann Mi Ok who wrote the poem to her birth mother. She's talking directly to her birth mother, but I think incidentally she was also talking to her white adopted mother as the other negative and I don't know how fair that was. Papusa in her letter—when she wrote me this letter because she couldn't write the essay I wanted her to write about her antiracism work in Iowa—I think she's talking to us and not just me. It's addressed to *us*.

ALK: "Us" being?

GEA: Us, the people in *Haciendo Caras*—the women-of-color contributors. Chela Sandoval's report on the NWSA conference against racism, I think it's speaking to white women and it's also speaking to us, so there's a change from *Bridge* in that there's more of the debate among women of color. You've read it. What do you think?

ALK: Yeah. I think sometimes the debate is more among women of color. Your essay "En rapport, In Opposition" very much is. Others seem to be self-expression, they're just going out and seem addressed to whomever reads them.

GEA: A more general audience? For me one of the differences is that in *Bridge* we were reacting against the white feminists' theories and words, it was more of a reactive kind of book. *Haciendo Caras* feels to me like—yes, that part is still there but now we've gone off on our own paths and we're utilizing that energy to work things out amongst ourselves. We're still bridging with white women, but a lot of the energy is just staying here.

ALK: Like you say in the introduction, you're building a culture.

GEA: Yes. But that's just my vision of the book. I may have read it in a way entirely different from you or from other people because my particular reading of it was that I had certain themes I wanted linked so that I could create a whole out of all these disparate voices and hundreds of concerns. That I could somehow focus, highlight certain areas so that then I could say "These are the concerns of the book, this is what these women are saying." As an editor, I tried to create an entity out of all these different arms and legs and eyes and ears. That's always hard because there's bound to be things you have to leave out in creating a picture of this total entity, so if it had been a different editor it would have been a different book. Even if it contained the same pieces but somebody else had edited and written the introduction it would have been a different book—you know what I mean? Because the title pulls it together, *Haciendo Caras*, making our own identities.

ALK: Yes. And the order you arranged the pieces in.

GEA: Right. I really didn't want to intercede or interpret too much so I didn't do a little intro for each section, like we did with *Bridge*. And I also didn't want to do a typical introduction where you say, "This author does thus and thus and thus, and the next author" . . . you know?

ALK: Those are so boring. . . . I'm going to read the stuff; I don't need to be told . . .

GEA: Out of all the things that were in the book and my own ideas, I wanted to create another little essay that was not a traditional introduction. A professor at University of California who saw a preliminary draft told me that I was centering myself too much in the essay, that I should take three-quarters of myself out of the intro. But I said, "When people ask me about the process of putting together *Bridge* these are the things people want to know: 'How did you do it?' 'What was your process?'" So I went ahead and did it my way.

ALK: I think your intro anchors the anthology, it tells your position. I thought the description about your students' reactions to the material was really useful. It also gives the reader some idea of what's coming up.

New Interconnections: Moving from Unity to Solidarity

ALK: In "En rapport, In Opposition" you say that you've "come to suspect that unity is another Anglo invention like their one sole god and the myth of the monopole." This essay was first published four years ago. Do you still feel this way?

GEA: Yes. I especially feel this way when I go to Hispanic Heritage Week events. Once a year in different universities they have Hispanic Heritage Week and their big thing, you know, is "Latinos unidos," "Jamás seran vencidos," and I think, "Why is there such an emphasis on unity? What about just plain being in solidarity with each other? What about just maintaining our own separate ethnic groups yet coming together and interacting?" You know—the Chileans, the Mexicanos, the Chicanos, the newly arrivals, the Puerto Ricans. Why does it have to be this Hispanic or this Latinos/Latinas umbrella? Why this thing about unity? After five hundred years we haven't achieved it. The reason we haven't achieved unity is because we're so different—geographically, culturally, and linguistically.

So then I thought if we don't achieve unity we're going to have such a sense of failure. Such a sense of "Oh we've been struggling for years and we can't unite, there must be something wrong with Chicanos who can't get it together to present a united front." If you take Chicanos there are differences between the ones in California, Arizona, New Mexico, Texas, the Midwest. Yes, we have a lot in common, but it's a big burden to put on an ethnic group that they should get their shit together and unite. White people aren't united. They may be united under capitalism or some other imposed system. What is it in our mentality—and I say "our" because I've been trained in the western way of thinking—that there has to be some kind of hierarchical order and at the very top there is the one: the one law, the one god, the one universe, the one language, the one absolute? That absolute may be "Do unto others as you would have them do unto you" or it could be what the physicists are now searching for, the one general law that everything happening in the universe—biologically, physically, and so on—will fall under this one law. And then I look at the U.S. American-ization of the total planet through the media of television and radio (mostly television). There's this whole gathering of peoples' minds on the planet. It's very attractive—anything American from Coca Cola to Levi's. In terms of a capitalist commodity market, a unity through clothes or possessing particular products could be possible, but I don't think it can happen politically, aesthetically, psychologically, or any of the other ways.

ALK: So you see unity as homogenizing or monolithic?

GEA: Yes. I see it as homogenizing because it's used as the big umbrella where everyone belongs and can take shelter. If you don't achieve it— if you can't get under that umbrella and achieve unity—that umbrella becomes a club used against you: "Why are you as a black or a Latina or an Indian so divisive that you can't achieve any kind of unity with your own people?"

ALK: So it just erases differences?

GEA: Sí. This idea implies that we can't live separately yet be connected. But we can! We can live separately, connect, and be together. But I'd rather call it "in solidarity," "in support of," "en conocimiento," rather than "united." Unity always privileges one voice, one group. En conocimiento . . . everybody has their own space and can say their own thing and recognize that here's another group that has their own thing and says their own thing, but there are connections, commonalities as well as differences. And the differences don't get erased and the commonalities don't become all-important; they don't become more important than the differences or vice versa.

ALK: And also when you say people can say things *to each other* in terms of each particular group as well as speaking to bigger groups?

GEA: Yes, yes. And then I think of the human personality. It's supposed to be one. You know, you're one entity—one person with one identity. But that's not so. There are many personalities and subpersonalities in *you* and your identity shifts every time you shift positions. The other thing—and I'm fictionalizing this in a story called "La entrada de ajenos a la casa/The Entry of the Alien into the House." It's about the body and all the organisms that live in the body: the E. coli bacteria in the stomach, the plaque in your teeth, the millions of organisms in the eyebrow area—the roots of the eyelashes have particular organisms different from the ones in the forehead. You are not just AnaLouise, you're all the different organisms and parasites that live on your body and also the ones that live in symbiotic relationship to you. The *mouth*!!! The mouth has tons of bacteria and foreign stuff. Animals live in symbiotic relationships—the cows with little birds picking the ticks off. So who are you? You're not a single entity. You're a multiple entity.

ALK: So you're really talking about an incredible interconnectedness?

GEA: Yes, not just on the biological level. Anyway, the story is about having a wart.

ALK: Gross.

GEA: It comes from a viral infection. There are people who have athlete's foot and a lot of women under stress or taking antibiotics end up with candida. It's about a woman who becomes aware that she's not a single entity.

ALK: Prieta?

GEA: Yes, one of the lesser finished stories which may not make it into the book. One's own *body* is not one entity. You can take this idea from microcosm to macrocosm, from the microorganism to the cosmos and its thousands of systems of planets.

Spirituality: "Roots," Masks, Essentialism

ALK: In the introduction to *Haciendo Caras* you discuss the importance of spirituality to women of color. How do you integrate spirituality with your political views?

GEA: I think that most of us, *all* of us men and women of all colors,

158

go around thinking that this is who and what we are and we only see maybe three-quarters or maybe not even three-quarters of ourselves. There's an unconscious component, a nonphysical spirit part. But we've been told it's not there so we don't perceive it. It's like a little child is taught what to see physically. If we were taught to see differently we would probably see people from other dimensions sitting in the armchair, you know—interlapping universes. But we're not taught to see that way. There are certain traditions like the shamanic tradition that teach you to experience the interpenetration of those other worlds. According to the Olmecs, the Toltecs, the Mayans, the Aztecs, and other indigenous cultures, physical reality is only one facet or one facade of the spirit world. It's a mask for the spirit world. You and I are masks for the spirit. If you can take the mask off or go behind the mask then you catch glimpses of this other reality of the spirit.

I think with me it always happens with trauma, with a traumatic shock of some kind that opens me so brutally—I'm just cracked open by the experience—that for awhile things come inside me, other realities, other worlds. Like when I was mugged I became aware of things that had to do with the landscape and the trees and this particular ravine where I was mugged. I could almost hear their vibrations because every living thing has vibrations. Somewhere really really really far back in our history people got scared of this connection with the spirit and the spiritual world and put down the wall, concentrated on using our hands rather than our imaginations to achieve certain things. In the poem "Interface" in *Borderlands* Leyla can achieve things with her imagination. She doesn't need to move dirt, she doesn't need one of those cranes. We went a technological route of using outer tools rather than a spiritual route of using thought and imagination. If you want to move from here to New York you get on a plane. But had we gone in the other direction all we'd have to do is think "I am now in New York between Third and whatever" and there we'd be. This is why shamanism is so intriguing to people and so intriguing to me, because you can move yourself through your imagination, through your soul. Your soul is actually there. When you dream about some place like Manhattan your soul goes there and then returns back to your body.

So here we go as feminists—wanting to be practical, wanting to make a difference, wanting to make some changes. We're looking at everything that gives us strength: having roots, having a historical past that we can connect with and say, "This is the route that my particular group has walked and I can see how what happened in the past has affected the present and therefore affected me and who I am and how I feel about myself." So we've dug into the past for a history and models and women and stories that can give us some sort of ground to walk on, some sort of foundation, some sort of place to take off from and also to find positive stuff there that will feed us, that will inspire us. When you start connecting with your past racial history and your own childhood personal history, you have all these ideas about feminism and the rights of women, the rights of all people, trying to make the world a little cleaner and a little safer and stop the destruction. You want it so badly that the desire opens you up to being exposed to things that will give you the strength to survive and accomplish this. In these pathway openings—in these channels, tunnels, cracks, whatever you want to call them—you come up against an awareness that the universe is alive. It pulsates, everything's alive: nature, trees, the sky, and the wind. Once you connect with that, you feel like you're part of interconnecting organisms—vegetable, animal, mineral—and everything has some kind of consciousness. If this pulsating rhythm, vibration, is some kind of awareness, of aliveness, then it's conscious. You start looking at rocks in a different way—at birds—and when they appear and when they don't appear and you let your imagination act as a center that connects and sorts through all the data and comes out with what you want. I think the imagination does that: it will look at the clouds and project certain images in the clouds so that you see certain patterns, and the clouds stop being some kind of weather phenomena and become part of this force that pulsates, that's everywhere. Sometimes you come to this spiritual knowing as a result of a shock. Sometimes a dream or something you read triggers it.

In California it's such a popular thing right now. People pretend they've experienced this, what I call a pseudospirituality or New Age awareness. Pseudowitches and shamans don the costumes, wave their wands, ingest different kinds of herbs, dance naked in the woods. It's all performance. But for some it's a legitimate first step toward really becoming witches or shamans. And then there are other people who don't need to do that, who in some way have seen the part of their personality that's been hidden from them—the spiritual part, the unconscious part. They don't need to go to through any of those fancy retreats or elaborate rituals or drumming or entering ecstatic states. They just all of the sudden see it. It's like turning around and looking at your shoulder and realizing that you'd only been seeing half an arm. Does that make sense to you?

ALK: Definitely.

GEA: But right now in the academy with high theorists it's very incorrect to talk about that part because they're afraid it's something innate and therefore they'll be labeled essentialists. Because the women who talk about spirituality a lot of times will talk about la diosa, the goddess, and how women are innately nurturing and how they're peaceful. But they're not. It's all learned. Right?

ALK: Right.

GEA: So they equate that kind of essentialism with spirituality but I don't. Maybe in the past there was that in my writing but now I see it differently.

ALK: Related to the question of essentialism is your use of the image of the masks. It's like our outside parts are these masks and there's this underneath-thing. Right?

GEA: Well, I think the different personas that we are—the you that's with me right now has one face, the you that's going to be with other people tomorrow will have a slightly different one, but basically there's the you.

ALK: One person with many different parts?

GEA: Yeah. But the masks are integral to you. The other concept—the concept the Olmecs, the Toltecs, and the Mayans have—is slightly different. The reason you see statues of a person inside a jaguar's head or emerging from the mouth of an eagle is their belief that behind the animal, there's always the human. But behind the human there's the animal. In explaining this concept of the mask with the human behind the animal is their philosophy of life, their belief that this is the adornment for the spirit; this is how the spirit dresses itself. Behind this mask—this outer reality, this house, my clothes, my face, me—is a spiritual entity. OK that was *their* explanation. To me, the masks are no longer necessary. We recognize that our flesh is spiritualized whereas the ancients believed there was a separation: "Here is the so-called real world and there's a wall, a partition, and then over there is the totally noncorporeal world of the spirit and the world of the ideals." In *La Prieta* I'm trying to do away with the separation and say it's here and now, and at the blink of an eye. I don't know if you ever read "El Paisano Is a Bird of Good Omen," where the roadrunner blinks and Andrea (who's now Prieta) blinks and suddenly is not sitting on the fencepost but is over there in the lagoon. She's watching those little kids playing with the lizard and the horned toad, and in the blink of the eye she *is* those lizards and that horned toad and those ants, and she's feeling the bites. I don't think we need that partition. Does that make sense to you?

ALK: Yeah. It's not that it's somewhere else, it's just that right now we don't see it because of the way we're looking.

GEA: Because of the way we have been taught what reality is and is not.

ALK: Right. Because what we've been *trained* to see influences what we believe and therefore how we act.

GEA: Yeah. Let's use the analogy of a whistle. Humans can't hear it but a dog can. Certain species will pick up a wide range of frequencies and others won't. And the body itself tunes in to some of these frequencies but the reception remains subliminal. If only we learned how to retrieve the messages.

ALK: But nobody's really cared or learned how, right?

GEA: Yeah, a large percent of our brain goes unused, a very large percentage of the reality that we could take in through the senses is not sensed because we've been trained to limit what we can see, hear, and understand. The people who can sense the invisible are either crazy or they're shamans or creative people.

ALK: That's similar to what I believe. . . . There's this tree I communicate with, but I resist it. I really resist it and what'll happen is that as I resist it when I'm working, my writing. . . . I can't write. Or things will start to go wrong around the house and I'll say, "OK," and I'll go outside and maybe have a little wine and I just sit there and say—

GEA: —"talk to me."

ALK: Yeah. The rational side can always say, "Oh this is just yourself talking to yourself." But the other part says, "Well yes it could be that, but it just seems like something more."

GEA: Yeah, your self extends to the tree. The self does not stop with just you, with your body. The self penetrates other things and they penetrate you. What you were saying earlier, that you can't prove it—

162

it's not rational, it's not scientific—goes back to the model of objectivity which has been one of the ruling models of our lives. For something to exist you have to be able to test it. It has to possess some kind of physical manifestation or else—

ALK: —it's not real.

GEA: And that theory of objectivity—which has been proven false over and over by its own scientists—makes us separate because it makes us the watcher. It privileges the eyes, the visual. It causes distance, causes separation. So the other part of yourself that's objective says, "Oh no. You can't be experiencing this. It's just you talking to another part of you. It's just your imagination taking off." And so here come other people who say what happens in your imagination is just as real (or equally illusory) as what happens when you walk down the street. What happens in a fantasy, *that* reality has as much validity as external reality. A work of fiction when you're working at creating a story, what happens to those people and the setting is just as *real* as what happens to your mother and your brother . . . you know?

ALK: Yes.

GEA: And that's one of the points I try to make in *La Prieta*, that there's not just *one* reality but many different realities. Why should one reality—external life—be privileged over the others? Some cultures really pay attention to their dreams and their rituals and the imaginative parts of their lives, which they consider other dimensions of reality. These people are being killed off—like the Aborigines in Australia who have their dreamtime. It's just us that privilege the mechanical, the objective, the industrial, the scientific.

Once at a conference I picked up a pamphlet, "Alternative Responses to the Columbus Sesquicentennial." It had a map of the U.S., Mexico, and South America. I began the keynote talk by turning it over and asking, "Who's to say that up is up and down is down? We're whirling on an axis but we're also going around the sun. So why should the U.S. and Canada be on top and South America, Africa, and Australia be on the bottom?" Why does the U.S.—one country—take it upon itself to call itself "America," the name of an entire continent? I feel the same way about waking life, about external reality which includes alternate states. You can be sitting there and go off into alternate states— fantasies, memories of yesterday, and things that have nothing to do with external reality. Another division is between dream life and waking life. We spend eight hours sleeping and dreaming and the rest of the time in waking reality and going off into alternate states. When you write you go off into alternate states all the time. What's to say that on the other side, the dream ego—the dream self—is not looking at external reality as the dream, and the dream as real? Because sometimes to me the dreams make more sense in the way they connect, associatively like a poem, than this outer reality. It's getting too wild, right?

ALK: Not at all. Well, I don't think so. Some people might, I guess. Some people would object that spirituality is often passive and escapist. If you're going to say there are all these other realities, you could take the step of saying, "So external reality doesn't matter, oppression doesn't matter because you have all these other worlds." But you don't do that. You manage to have both spiritual beliefs and a very strong political agenda, and I think that's very rare. How do you do this?

GEA: Because I look at us and we're flesh and blood. We're corporeal. We occupy weight and space, three-dimensionally. We're not some kind of disembodied thought energy. We're embodied in the flesh so there must be a purpose to this stage we're living in, to this corporeal body which we lose when we die and which we don't have before we're born. The things that we really struggle with and need to work out, we need to work out on the physical plane. We can't escape. Just because those other realities are there we can't just escape and say, "Oh this is just a play on some kind of stage and it doesn't really matter." It might be a play on the stage of life, but it's a matter of life and death. These things can only be worked out in physical reality.

ALK: Like in *This Bridge*, "theory in the flesh."

GEA: Yes.

ALK: Also, if there's this kind of cosmic interconnectedness that goes with the spiritual dimension then that's another way people who are so different in so many ways can connect, through this other level. Does that make sense? I think I picked that up from your writing.

GEA: Yes. What I call "almas afines," that we're kindred spirits, and this interconnectedness is an unvoiced category of identity, a common factor in all life forms.

Becoming Lesbian?

ALK: In *Borderlands* you claim that your lesbianism is chosen: "I made the choice to be queer." You say for some it is genetically inherent but for you it was a choice. Cherríe Moraga, in a review of your book, interprets this statement to refer to your political decision to *identify* yourself as a lesbian, and her view makes sense. But I hadn't interpreted it that way when I first read your essay. So what did you mean, what kind of choice were you referring to?

GEA: I was thinking of how much of the basic personality, the basic self, is there genetically, and how much of it has been imposed, especially about sexuality and femaleness and what race and class have to do with it. Since *Borderlands* I've been thinking that there has to be a middle way. You can't get polarized between "You are born into this world as a blank slate and everything that's written on your body—including your sexual preference—has been put there by society" and the other extreme—"You are born female and therefore you're nurturing and you're giving and you're peaceful: You don't kill, you don't violate." When I finished *Borderlands* this is what I thought had happened. Since then I've revised my thinking.

I looked at the model of the heterosexual couple. I knew who was getting the strokes and who was getting the slaps. I knew the boys were privileged. Heterosexuality was a patriarchal institution. Women would have to constantly struggle, even if they were coupled with progressive feminist-oriented males. Men were trained to be macho and however much they would fight it some of it would bleed through, just like women fight against passivity and self-sacrifice, characteristics we were told we possessed. I would never be able to put up with that kind of shit from a man. Or if I did put up with it I'd be ashamed of myself and feel bad about myself. So the only viable choice for me was lesbianism. As a lesbian I would have *some* power—if my lover happened to be white she would have some privilege, if I was older I'd have some power. I would have more of a chance to have a meaningful relationship with a woman. This is common sense. The heterosexual model is the ruling model in all the countries on the planet. In some countries men have four or five wives and the wife is powerless, unless she's upper class, and then she has to maneuver, manipulate, and conform to keep that power. In this country a woman CEO has to play the game in order to obtain that position. So the women who have become equal to men in terms of power, it's been at a great cost to them and they negate a lot of stuff, repress feelings, get ulcers . . . not that the men have it that easy. Across the planet heterosexuality benefits the male, so isn't it logical for you that you would want to have a different relationship?

ALK: Definitely.

GEA: And if desire is something that you learn like you learn heterosexuality, you're supposed to like this little boy if you're a little girl. Desire is one of the concerns in "She Ate Horses." If desire is not something that you're born with but rather something you acquire—where to direct that sexual hunger to connect, to touch, and to be touched—if that can be learned, it can also be unlearned and relearned. Some lesbians, political lesbians, came out in the '70s because that was a viable other choice. Lesbians who at an early age were attracted to and lusted after women acquired the desire in childhood or adolescence. Women who came out politically as lesbians resisted the teaching that women desire men. Political lesbians are lesbian in their heads first. Informed by theories about sexuality, political lesbians started looking at women differently. Through theory they started relating differently to their own bodies, to their emotions, and to the bodies, emotions of other women. With girls who got turned on by girls resistance took emotional manifestations early on.

Some of us do choose consciously: "I'm going to give up men, I'm going to go to women, I'm going to come out of the closet and declare my lesbianism." For some it's unconscious, they may not know they've made the choice until afterwards. Maybe they think it's natural to be a lesbian or that it's natural to be a heterosexual, but all along there have been processes and decisions they may not be aware of or remember. Right now, in 1991, I don't think every person is born queer. I think there may be some genetic propensity towards some things—having a good ear for music, for example. If there are queer genes they'll be discovered soon. Queerness may be genetic, queerness may be learned, queerness may be chosen. My thoughts on this will probably change in a year or two but that's where I'm at with it.

ALK: So it's more than a political decision to *identify* yourself as lesbian; you were deciding a lifestyle?

GEA: Yes. In retrospect I look back at when I was younger and I remember my cousin who was a butch—how close she would sit to me and how we had this special energy between us. It triggers earlier memories of similar kinds of closeness I've had with women despite the fact that I was taught that women were spiteful, competed against each other, and that it wasn't worth it to make friends with women, that only men could make worthy friends. Todo eso. It triggers another memory. When I was teaching high school all the Chicana jotitas and the marimachas would hang around *me*, and all the Chicano maricones would follow me around and show me the love letters their lovers had sent them. The same thing happened later. Most of my friends were gays and lesbians. When I'd go to the Y and do the consciousness-raising feminist stuff I thought I was the only straight woman and there were all these diesel dykes. One time I turned around and asked a friend, "If I become a dyke will I have to become fat and drive a motorcycle?" It's sexist for me to say that, but that was the thought I had. I reviewed my life from this perspective, this particular waystation I find myself on. Did I give you the analogy of using the train, the tracks, and the terrain of self in order to construct identity or to track the construction of identity?

ALK: No.

GEA: Along your life's journey are turning points, new directions that lead you to certain way stations. The train will stop at this way station and stay a few years and then get on the road again and stop at another way station. In one station you are heterosexual, in another you may be lesbian. From a particular way station you look back down the tracks and you look at your past and all the events in your life and your friends. You see through lesbian eyes and you reinterpret your past. When I became a lesbian I looked back at my life and realized there had been queers in it, my cousin, my tío, the high school Chicanitas and Chicanitos who'd follow me around. All along I'd had these signals that I was one of them too. So that when I got to be a political lesbian which I thought *I* had chosen—had I really chosen it or had I been one all along but repressed it?

ALK: And when you were writing in *Borderlands* you thought you had just chosen it but now you're looking back . . .

GEA: No, when I was writing *Borderlands* I had the lesbian perspective but my thinking had not evolved to the place where when you realize that you like women, that you want to have primary relationships with women, that you want to have carnal relationships with women, you can still make the choice to stay with men. Many of us have done that. You can become a lesbian and be a lesbian for twenty years and then decide that you want to be sexual with a man. I don't know if that changes your lesbian identity, but . . . You make a choice. If you know you're a lesbian and you're married and have kids you say, "OK, I'm going to be with my husband and I'll be a straight woman as much as I can and be with my kids." Or you can say, "I'm going to leave my husband, I'm going to come out as a lesbian and take this path"—depending on how much courage you have. But I think there's only certain places where you can make that choice and those are the places of ambiguity, of change, where you're in nepantla, in a liminal, in-between space—you can go either way. Once you're on this track you're pretty much a lesbian and you think like a lesbian and you live with lesbians and your community is lesbians and gays, and the heterosexual world is foreign and that's the path you and I—well I don't know about you—but that's the path I'm on.

ALK: Yeah.

GEA: But when I reach these nepantla places I can make choices. I can say "I'm not going to be politically active at this time, I'm just going to retreat into my writing." I don't think I'll ever be that way; I don't think I'll ever make that choice but other people have. So it's not that I'm invalidating what I said. I'm saying that was my thinking then when I was in that particular track and the train has kept going and I've stopped at other way stations. The way station where I last stopped had to do with a change in class, going away from a campesino working class into an intellectual, academic, artistic class. With the money and royalties and speaking engagements coming in I am now a step or two away from middle classness. Being in this particular nepantla state—Coatlicue is right in the middle of it—is so agonizing. And at the next way station I will look back at our conversation and at *Borderlands* and *La Prieta* and *Bridge* and *Haciendo Caras* and the children's books and whatever other books I write and I'll say, "This is how to configure my identity now." The old ways of identifying myself are still part of me: the straight woman, the white woman, the nonpolitical woman. But basically my personality has always been a resisting one, going against what's not fair. The way cultures treated girls is not fair. It's not fair the way the white culture treats ethnic groups. So there's this strong sense in me of "I'm going to fight against it because it's not fair."

Always on the Other Side /del otro lado: Differences, Lesberadas

ALK: In *Compañeras* you have a poem where you talk about "the other side of the other side"—always on the other side. And in *Borderlands* you also use that metaphor of being on the other side. What can you say about this other side? Well, obviously it's the other side of heterosexuality, but . . .

GEA: It's almost like the differences in me from other women started at a very early age. When I was three months old I started menstruating. The differences weren't just psychological but were also physical. As I grew older I had horrendous menstrual pains. I had breasts when I was six years old—these same breasts that I have now—which my mother would wrap up so the little kids wouldn't notice. She'd tie a little rag in my panties so that if I bled it wouldn't be all over the place. And I had to make excuses at P.E. that I couldn't bathe with the other kids because they would see that I had pubic hair. So I was marked early on. It was painful for me to be so different physically because I already felt different in other ways: I felt different because of my race, I felt different because of being a farmworker. In the valley if you worked the fields you belonged to a lower class of people than if you worked in a department store or in an office. I was marked as inferior for being female, yet I was different from other women, and as a Mexican I was different from white people. Those differences were painful. They really went all the way to the bone. And because I was wide open as a child everything came in. (I think you're a little bit like that: where people's words can just wound you and you'll just be bleeding all over the place.) People would say something in the wrong tone of voice and I would take it *so* personally that I would be devastated for the rest of the week. I had very thin skin, everything came in.

ALK: When I was little I was fat and unattractive and smart, with very kinky, kind of nappy hair, so in a *different* way I can understand what you're saying. How does your childhood go with being on the other side?

GEA: When I went to school I brought these marks and experiences of difference which I'd been taught were bad because my mother kept abnormality a secret and my father was worried about me, and my sister kind of figured out something was wrong with me and held it against me. In school I saw that I was different from the other kids—

169

en masse—and that I could pick up knowledge. They called me "the brain." I was a "dumb Mexican" who was smart. It was such a shock to the teachers because weren't all Mexicans supposed to be dumb? I always felt separate in school, which was 100 percent Chicano with only the teachers being white. I already felt on the other side of the other side, of the other side within the other side.

ALK: Separate, different? Not belonging.

GEA: Yes. Not belonging. Always on the other side. It was the same in high school. I was placed in accelerated classes and the other Chicanas weren't. The white kids never spoke to me and the teachers never paid any attention to me. I'd sit in one corner or in the middle or in the front or in the back, and it didn't matter.

ALK: You were always on the other side.

GEA: Always. In high school I couldn't really be friends with the kids who would have been there for me because I didn't spend the majority of my classes with them, and besides they were from different towns. I would just see them at P.E. and homeroom. I had a few peripheral friends.

In college I also felt different and separate from most of the other students. But I also became acutely aware that other girls experienced other kinds of difference. I went to college in an all girls' school—Texas Women's University—where I first witnessed two women making love to each other. I had my first experience with an epileptic, my roommate who one day as we were getting dressed just fell on the floor and was doing these strange things. But before she fell she started coming towards me with her hands shaking and this *really* funny energy coming from her and this look in her eyes, and I thought she wanted to strangle me. Nobody had explained it to me and I'd never seen a person have an epileptic fit.

I became more aware of other kinds of queerness. I started connecting with other differences then. I no longer felt like I was the only one on the other side. In some way I felt an affinity to queers and epileptics. I wasn't the baddest little girl in the world—I'd always thought that I was the worst, that something was really wrong with me and that I must be so sinful or deficient to have this happen to me, that I must have *deserved* this kind of pain and problem, that there was nobody else like me. I began to think that other people had other so-called sicknesses and we weren't as bad as others made out. I started feeling better about being on the other side because now there were a few others on the other side. No matter which class or race you came from, you could be sitting there looking perfectly healthy and normal and your differences would be invisible, like epilepsy or lesbianism unless you announced it some way through words, clothes, or lifestyle. But I always felt like all my difference was visible, that somehow people could see I was marked, they could see that I was abnormal, subhuman, or whatever. My self-consciousness was agonizing. If I'm speaking in an auditorium I still feel like I'm on the other side even though I try to get rid of the lectern and other barriers, and I try to be as open as I can. I'm more comfortable with my differences, but there's a little part of me that feels that I'm too different.

ALK: You do have a certain vulnerability when you speak.

GEA: Some people choose to cloak themselves in a kind of self-defensive way and act real cool, others are more open and say, "I'm vulnerable." We're all vulnerable up there on stage, it's just that some of us wear armor and some of us do not. Though I try to take off most of my armor, I know that I still keep some shields.

ALK: Paula Gunn Allen describes homosexuals as "perverse" and defines "perversity" as "transformationality . . . the process of changing from one condition to another—*lifelong* liminality." It seems that you see homosexuality in a similar fashion: as *difference*, and because it's different from the heterosexual norm it opens space for change.

GEA: Sí. It's like saying "OK if I am queer and I am different, then I'm going to make those strengths and not liabilities." It's going to be a pleasure, not a chore.

ALK: And because "I'm 'outside' certain cultural inscriptions change becomes more possible"?

GEA: Yes. It's almost like "I'm going to be hung anyway and if I'm going to be hung I might as well be hung for multiple deeds." It's almost like once you've transgressed—once you've crossed the line, once you've broken the law—the punishment is the same whether you do it for a few things or for many. Probably it's not, but that's my rationalization. If I've already broken one inscription, gone against one law and regulation, then I just have to gather up my courage and go against another and another and another.

ALK: Then that goes with the "lesberada." You use the term in a speech you gave at the 1988 NWSA Lesbian Plenary session. I wonder if you could elaborate on how the term applies to your view of lesbians.

GEA: I see us as outlaws but not in the way that the S/M people see themselves as outlaws. The lesberada/lesberado—the outsider, the outlaw—may have been declared a stigma by society. Let's take that stigma, turn it around, and say, "As a lesberada, as a lesberado, I am proud of who I am." A kind of camping up of that identity. Of really doing it in—yahooing and throwing the lasso. Like the cowboy. If I'm going down, I'm going to go down not with a whimper but with a bang. That kind of attitude describes la lesberada. I guess it goes back to the western movies I would watch and the westerns I'd read. That's why I'm partial to popular genres—horror, mystery, spy, detective, romance, westerns, science fiction. Los desperados were always these few marginalized cowboys, the "bad guys." So if we're going to be the bad guy let's do it in style. Let's reverse the meaning and make it a positive sign for younger lesbians to emulate.

ALK: Allen also claims that dykes have both masculine and feminine energy. You say a similar thing in *Borderlands* when you talk about homosexuals as being "hieros gamos," both male and female.

GEA: The term "hieros gamos" comes from alchemy, for the "inner marriage" of the masculine force and the feminine force. Now, I'm not sure if there's such a thing as masculine and feminine energy. And I'm not so sure that's an essential thing we're born with. I think we're socialized into having male energy and female energy. We're socialized into assertive "male" ways—a male way of walking, a male way of *thrusting* into space—and receptive "female" ways—a female way of receiving, nurturing, giving, and providing the space. For queer, traditional femininity and masculinity didn't take completely. It also didn't take with some strong women, with some feminists.

ALK: That cultural training didn't take hold?

GEA: Yeah. Some of us also learned the "male" mode. Maybe not in the style, but the attitude of "We're just as proud; we're just as strong; we can thrust through space and assert ourselves." In the valley we're called *mita y mita*. That's what I talk about in *Borderlands*: Half a month we're male and have a penis and half a month we're female

172

and have periods. But instead of it being split like that, I think of it as something that's integral.

ALK: That works together?

GEA: It works together. Sometimes if the situation warrants for you to thrust out—forcing your words out because you're being excluded or oppressed—then you have the energy to do it. And in other situations you will have the energy to be a receptacle, to just take things in. Right now women privilege the feminine and say the aggressive masculine is all wrong, all bad. The men say femininity is inferior and *they're* superior. I think they're both wrong. It takes the two.

ALK: You're rejecting that either/or thinking.

GEA: Yeah. It's both/and, not either/or. It's like my theory of identity: all these personalities that make up the self, all the personalities are on the stage of life, but they take turns taking center stage. It's the same with female/male energy. In certain situations you need a particular kind of energy. But if you're short and of color you'll sometimes get ignored by the white person behind the counter. You had to learn to say, "EXCUSE ME. I WAS HERE FIRST." In my culture it's bad for a woman to assert herself. If my sister gets shortchanged she may not demand her money back. I've learned to demand.

ALK: I don't always go and ask. I'm learning but it's hard.

GEA: Well, we've been socialized not to.

Representation: Individual and Collective "We"

ALK: In one of the workshops this week you distinguished between an "individual we" and a "collective we." What did you mean?

GEA: Because individuals from ethnic groups are seen by the dominant culture as generic people, as belonging to generic tribes, we've begun to see ourselves that way too—as a representative of a group rather than as individuals. When you're seen as a member of a group rather than as an individual, when you speak—at least when I speak—I find myself going from the personal "I" to the collective "we." I know it's politically incorrect to be representing other people but in "The Poet as Critic, The Poet as Theorist" (one of the chapters of my book *Rewriting Reality*), I talk in more detail about why this is true. One of the things is that there are so many people—women especially—who identify with the ethnic writer because that ethnic experience is not represented in the dominant literature.

Women of color never see ourselves in these books, we don't see ourselves represented. So along comes a Chicana writer, and the Chicanas say, "Oh that's *me* you're writing about!" or "That happened to my mother." Chicanas really identify with some of my experiences. What happens is that these women—and this is all women of color and maybe even some white women—start getting a sense of who we are and a sense of our mission and a sense of the political work we have to do by reading Audre Lorde and other women-of-color writers. We no longer look towards the so-called politicos—the leftist movement guys who, in the past, told us "This is what's wrong with the family," "This is what's wrong with capitalism," "This is what's wrong with the economic system in this country," "This is what's wrong with the U.S. relationship with Mexico and Central America." We're not listening to those guys. The women are looking at women of color—Lorde, Leslie Silko, Paula Gunn Allen, the Asian-American writers. If we've had experiences in common, if we've had similar experiences we *identify*, so part of the reading process is formulating an identity for the reader. If we don't happen to agree—if we don't happen to identify with certain passages of a book or with certain people or with certain books—we *dis*-identify. As readers, dis-identifying is also a way of formulating an identity . . . by saying "That's not me." I'm a reader as a well as a writer. This process happens to me, it happens to all readers. When I say "we" sometimes it's a singular "we" I use in order to make a connection with the readers. But sometimes it's a plural "we."

ALK: Meaning speaking for?

GEA: For *them*. Speaking to them and for them and with them. It's much more speaking *with* them than *for* them. I see it as a dialogue between author, text, and reader. If the reader happens to write about the reading it's a dialogue between author, text, reader, and reader-as-writer.

ALK: And do you learn as you're writing?

GEA: Yes. When I write I get insights. Sometimes I get them when I'm speaking but mostly when I'm writing. I discover what I'm trying to say as the writing progresses. This is more true with fiction and poetry because I allow more freedom for those words to come whereas in a creative essay—yes, it's creative and I have some freedom—but theorizing has more restrictions.

ALK: When you write a creative essay do you know where you're going to end up?

GEA: No. Which is the problem with the graduate classes. They want an abstract, an idea, or an outline. I don't work that way. For example in writing my dissertation they expected me to finish one chapter. And I said, "This is my process: I write all the chapters at the same time and bring them up through the second draft, the third draft all together. I don't have just one finished thing because I don't know where things are going to go." They don't understand that process because they plan a book: they perfect the introduction, they perfect the first chapter, the second chapter; they publish those. I don't work that way. All the pieces have to be on the table and I'm adding and subtracting pieces and I'm shifting them around. So there tends to be a lot of repetition in my work, I put the same thing in two or three chapters because ultimately I don't know where it's going to end up. That frustrates them. So I wrote about my process in one of the chapters and I reflect on the "repetition compulsion."

ALK: Would you say that it's repetition with variation by the time you get to the final draft?

GEA: Yes. It's sort of like . . . it's like the earrings you gave me. I start at the center and spiral around. When I come back to that point where that particular idea is mentioned I touch on it but I extend it to another level, I apply it to another field or process, I might put it in Spanish, or whatever—so that it gets more and more complex. But sometimes I may have the exact same passage in another chapter—with a computer it's very easy to copy and duplicate. Later I'll rework it to fit that chapter.

ALK: I do that too.

GEA: You do that too? And I thought I was one of the few who had that process because I do the same thing with the novel. It was hard for my publisher to understand. She understands that now, that I can't really finish "She Ate Horses" until I finish the other stories.

ALK: Because you're learning yourself, you have to figure out where it's going to go. It wouldn't work if you just tried to finish one thing. I think you get a better whole by doing it your way.

GEA: I think it becomes more integral, more of a single entity rather than disparate parts. The parts are still there, but they're—

ALK: —different?

GEA: Yeah. And I have to have a central metaphor like la Llorana or la Prieta. Within that central metaphor are these concepts, like working with the interface between the different realities—nepantla space. Nepantla is kind of an elaboration of Borderlands. I use nepantla to talk about the creative act, I use it to talk about the construction of identity, I use it to describe a function of the mind. Borderlands with a small b is the actual southwest borderlands or any borderlands between two cultures, but when I use the capital B it's a metaphor for processes of many things: psychological, physical, mental.

ALK: A metaphor that doesn't apply specifically to *one* thing but that can apply to many things?

GEA: Sí. But I find people using metaphors such as "Borderlands" in a more limited sense than I had meant it, so to expand on the psychic and emotional borderlands I'm now using "nepantla." With nepantla the connection to the spirit world is more pronounced as is the connection to the world after death, to psychic spaces. It has a more spiritual, psychic, supernatural, and indigenous resonance.

5

Quincentennial

From Victimhood to Active Resistance

Inés Hernández-Ávila y Gloria E. Anzaldúa (1991)

(1998–1999)

ALK: In this interview and in several others you discuss your theory of conocimiento. Could you say a little more about it?

GEA: Conocimiento is my term for an overarching theory of consciousness, of how the mind works. It's an epistemology that tries to encompass all the dimensions of life, both inner—mental, emotional, instinctive, imaginal, spiritual, bodily realms—and outer—social, political, lived experiences. I guess it's a pretty ambitious project—and me not even a trained philosopher! I've been working on this idea for years. It's hard to explain it in a few words because it has so many layers and encompasses many fields and territories.

In part, conocimiento is a theory of composition, of how a work of art gets composed, of how a field (like anthropology or literature or physics) is put together and maintained, of how reality itself is constructed, and of how identity is constructed. When you watch yourself and observe your mind at work you find that behind your acts and your temporary senses of self (identities) is a state of awareness that, if you allow it, keeps you from getting completely caught up in that particular identity or emotional state. This awareness sees through it. (To not see is to be in a state of desconocimiento, of not knowing, either by willful intention, by setting out to remain ignorant, or desconocimiento by default, by expediency.) I use the concept of nepantla to describe the state or stage between the identity that's in place and the identity in

177

progress but not yet formed. Nos/otras and the New Tribalism describe the formation of personal and collective identity.

ALK: What are some issues of conocimiento?

GEA: How do we know? How do we perceive? How do we make meaning? Who produces knowledge and who is kept from producing it? Who distributes and passes it on? Who has access to it and who doesn't? Is there such a thing as counterknowledge, and if so who constructs it and how? My symbol is a serpent in the Garden of Eden or Tamansuchan, the one with an orange or apple in her mouth. This image represents the unaccepted, illegitimate knowledges and ways of knowing used by those outside the inner circle of dominant ways. I use the idea of outlawed knowledge to encourage Chicanas and other women and people of color to produce our own forms, to originate our own theories for how the world works. I think those who produce new conocimientos have to shift the frame of reference, reframe the issue or situation being looked at, connect the disparate parts of information in new ways or from a perspective that's new.

You could say that conocimiento is basically an awareness, the awareness of facultad that sees through all human acts whether of the individual mind and spirit or of the collective, social body. The work of conocimiento—consciousness work—connects the inner life of the mind and spirit to the outer worlds of action. In the struggle for social change I call this particular aspect of conocimiento spiritual activism.

I see conocimiento as a consciousness-raising tool, one that promotes self-awareness and self-reflectivity. It encourages folks to empathize and sympathize with others, to walk in the other's shoes, whether the other is a member of the same group or belongs to a different culture. It means to place oneself in a state of resonance with the other's feelings and situations, and to give the other an opportunity to express their needs and points of view. To relate to others by recognizing commonalities. Con conocimiento—speaking, listening. Receptivity is the stance here, not the adversarial mode, not the armed camp. Giving feedback, taking frequent reality checks, and clarify meaning.

ALK: Could you say a bit more about desconocimientos?

GEA: Desconocimientos are the opposite of conocimientos. A not-knowing, a refusal to know, an ignorance that damages, miscommunications with irreversible harmful effects, that betray trust, that destroy. Desconocimientos are the evils of modern life.

"Quincentennial: From Victimhood to Active Resistance":
Inés Hernández-Ávila y Gloria E. Anzaldúa (1991)

Claiming Agency

IHA: I guess we should just share with each other what we'd like to accomplish in this interview. I told you last night that I wanted to look at the question of originality, especially as it relates to the quincentennial and to ourselves as indigenous people. On behalf of women who happen to be Chicanas, mexicanas, mestizas: What can we say to those who need to hear some messages to pull them along? I don't mean that we're ahead, but perhaps there are some things we could say that would be empowering and healing. In the end, of course, that would happen not only for the women but also for our pueblo and for humanity. I'm thinking of the women because they're the key.

Maybe we could tie the question of origins in with what was said about this last eclipse in Mexico—that it marked the beginning of the sexto sol. We're not completely out of the quinto, but overlapping into the sexto. I was told by people within the dance tradition that during the eclipse the moon—como maestra—nos enseñó una lección. She was demonstrating what can happen when the egos of human beings become so powerful they become obstacles to transformation and change. When she blocked that light she was showing us what happens: There's darkness but the sun ultimately came through, and in the words of the people of the dance tradition down south the sun impregnated the Earth. The Earth is pregnant now. The last part of the message was "¿Quién sabe si el parto sea con dolór?" And that's part of what we'd heard for awhile: Change can come about violently or harmoniously, and we have a say in how transformation occurs. Just like we have a say as human beings in how we learn. Often I've learned a puros golpes, when maybe I didn't have to learn that way but because of the choices I made that's how I learned, by blows. I guess that's tied in with the first part of what I said, what I keep repeating to all my young nieces, to help them from our perspective so that they won't learn through so many blows. They're going to go through some, of course; I don't know that it's possible for them not to, but they don't have to be the same blows. Why wish that on anyone, if there's anything we can do to prevent it?

GEA: We've come to a time when we can no longer play the victim role, la mujer sufrida. Now we need to look at the legacy of colonialism

179

and Columbus not so much in negative terms even though yes—we have suffered for five hundred years. I've recuperated la Llorona to trace how we go from victimhood to active resistance, from the wailing of suffering and grief to the grito of resistance, and on to the grito of celebration and joy. My origins as a writer go back to hearing stories about her.

Cuentos de la Llorona were the first stories I heard. La Llorona is my muse, my dark angel. As a cultural figure she encourages me to take personal and collective setbacks, obstacles, and oppressions which the dominant culture puts on mestizas/Chicanas and turn them around into facultades, into positive aspects, into skills, into learning how to cope with stress and oppression.

IHA: I didn't really grow up with stories of la Llorona; I guess my relationship was with Guadalupe. I don't know if it's because I'm from another part of Texas, although probably lots of people in Galveston grew up with la Llorona. I didn't and yet I grew up in the middle of the Chicano community. But I also grew up with a Mexican grandmother who was a very strict Roman Catholic in the sense that she didn't have a home altar or velas; she saw all of that as superstition, probably too indio, you know. Her husband, my grandfather, was the indio, as she would always say. My relationship was with Guadalupe. I was raised Catholic by my dad, not by my mother; my mother left the church after she married my father. She became Catholic only to marry him and then she left the church after I made my first communion. But I never had a relationship with Cristo.

GEA: I didn't either.

IHA: He just wasn't there. There was an emptiness. But I would pray to Dios; I could deal with the idea of a god and Guadalupe. And so Guadalupe was always the one for me. She's been consistent in giving me that strength to go on.

GEA: My grandmother Mamagrande Ramona had a little altar of Guadalupe on the ropero in her dining room. For the last three and a half years I've been working on a book whose central figure is la Llorona, a figure which holds all the stuff about writing, identity, and ethnicity together. I've been collecting Llorona stories. Everywhere I go, I ask people if they know any Llorona stories. I've also been doing archival research and one of the first stories I found connects Llorona with the Conquest. Ten or twelve years before Cortés came and

destroyed Mexico there was a woman heard wailing in the streets—
"¡Ay, mis hijos, [sé que, sé que?]!"—predicting that tragedy would
befall the Aztec people. So then Cortés came and did his dirty deed.
Another story I found in my research takes place a few years later: it's
about a woman who gets raped by one of these Spaniards and goes to
a lagoon, a lake, a body of water to douche herself. While she's doing
that an axolotl, which is the larva stage of the Mexican salamander,
enters her body and she gets pregnant with little salamanders. For
women the conquest has always been about what happens to their
children and about what happens to their bodies because the first thing
the conquistadores did was rape the Indian women and create the
mestizo race.

IHA: Right.

Resistance

GEA: It was a conquest through penetration. Even now when men talk
about how they're going to get this woman, como van a chingarla, it's
about conquest. So for me the negative legacy from the last five hundred
years of living under colonial conditions is about women, about the
exploitation of women's bodies and what comes out of women's bodies.

Theories about the "discovery" abound, about who came here first.
We know the Africans and Egyptians probably got here before
Columbus. Anthropologists posit that it could have been the Japanese
or the Chinese. And then there was Lief Erickson. Everybody's busy
either defending Columbus, the whites because Columbus was a white
man from Spain, or—Chicanos and Natives—bashing on Columbus.
It's actually the white Anglo dominant culture that privileges the white
in us, that tries to erase, to hide the fact that we have African blood,
the fact that we have Indian blood and only a very small percentage
of Spanish blood. While everybody is busy speculating about who
discovered America, let's concentrate on asking, "Why is Columbus
privileged by the dominant culture? Where are the voices of the Native
Americans and Chicanos? Where are the voices of blacks?" Columbus
started the slave trade. Why aren't we putting more energy into that?
Why aren't we discussing the effect all of this has had on women for
the last five hundred years?

IHA: And why has the Chicano community, in particular, been so
silent? For the most part they've been quite silent at the level of the
National Association of Chicano Studies. I realize why: The whole

Hispanic movement was started or rejuvenated in the late '70s and promoted by Coors and the Coors Foundation as well as the federal government. If you want funding, if you want anything in this society, you have to play by the terms they set and not by anything that will remind you of who you really are. It's amazing to me that they've been so indifferent.

The other thing we need to mention is that the Conquest is tied, as you said, to women's bodies. There's a relationship with that whole issue of right of conquest and the fact that people don't challenge it. If someone has overwhelming power—military or physical force—does that give them the right to violate, invade, penetrate, terrorize, and overtake someone else—whether it's an individual, a people, a land, or the Earth—just because you have the material, economic, technological power to do it? If you have the force, does that give you the right? Does it give you the right to say also that the victim really wanted it?

GEA: Big business, the corporations, and the U.S. government want to make money out of promoting these commemorations, fairs, and festivities such as Mexican Independence Day and Cinco de mayo. Common Chicano folk are ignorant of their history because it, and we, have been kept out of the history books.

IHA: Right.

GEA: On the news the other day, right after Mexican Independence Day, this newscaster went around asking people what they were there for. And only one man, one Chicano, could talk about what Independence Day was. The others were just saying, "Well we heard there was a parade and I know it has to do with Mexico." Many educated folk who have gone through the system from kindergarten through post-docs have been brainwashed and conditioned to accept what the dominant culture wants us to believe, which is that we are "Hispanic," the Spanish. Whites don't want any reminders of lo indio in Chicanos or Latinos, don't want to be reminded that they almost exterminated the Indians and are still doing it. Quite a few whites— progressive whites, proponents of multiculturalism—are doing stuff on imperialism.

IHA: And the Native American community is doing lots, hemispherically.

GEA: In one chapter of my book I reflect on the five hundred years of resistance, of reclaiming America, intellectuals, artistas, escritoras cultivating a certain kind of awareness—esa facultad of looking and seeing through all the lies, the veils, and the hidden stuff. The tongue has always been the symbol of speech, the symbol of communication, and I use it in my theory of conocimiento: using the eyes for seeing and the tongue for communicating, writing, and speaking of what is seen. La mano, the hand, is the active member of the body, the part of the body that does things. Con los ojos y la lengua en la mano: you tie in the sensitive, conscious political awareness with the act of writing and activism. La mano surda, the left hand, is the symbol of activism accompanied by a deep awareness. Margo Glantz, a Mexican Jewish literary critic, wrote a book on la lengua en la mano but I added los ojos and I added her symbol to my concept of El Mundo Zurdo and the deep awareness of seeing. Later I added the ears to symbolize the attentive listening to oneself and to others that is necessary to this kind of conocimientos. I'd like us to be more attentive to women's resistance. Rather than saying, "Oh poor me, I've been oppressed for five hundred years," we should get the anger out, lay the facts where they fall but also say "We are active agents. We never were passive." We've always been resisters.

IHA: Right. We resist by looking at what's called cultura—or Mexican culture in particular, Chicano culture and tradition—seeing and undoing that, unbinding that, ripping it apart at the seams, taking it all out and saying "Okay, let's really look at this and see." Both white intellectuals and some Chicano and Chicana intellectuals have held la cultura accountable for the position of women, for the image of women, or for the way women are treated in our community. The finger is pointed at the cultura, and yet that same cultura has given those women the strength and courage to resist; it may not be just from the cultura but it's not completely independent of it either. As you said in *Borderlands*, let's look at what we have to throw away and then ask "¿Qué es lo que nos pertenece? What is valuable for us to keep that would give us strength and ways not only to resist but to triumph?" Because I agree with you that we have to go beyond victimization.

Originality

GEA: Is this where your idea of originality comes in? What *is* your idea of originality?

IHA: Again, this reminds me of something you said in *Borderlands*: to look deeply, profoundly into your sources—and that's not to say that our makeup is predetermined or that we have no say about who we are because of where we came from—but to really look at and investigate our origins. I see the term "Chicanos" itself as almost synonymous with Pan-Indian or intertribal, because we're not all Aztec. Certainly many of us are. You, for one example, because you really have gotten into this; you're saying, "This is mine," and exploring it. That's what I respect about you: You really have looked into it; you haven't just taken the easy way and used surface allusions to Aztec philosophy, thought, and culture—which is what too many people have done. And that's why they're dismissed, because they've only just touched the surface; they put forward the image everyone is familiar with.

We need to go beyond surface allusions because it's not about romanticizing an Indian past, either. It's about really coming into touch with what that Indian past means and what it means to have raíces in this continent, in this hemisphere. Because we were interrupted in our relationship with the land, there are many people who don't know what it feels like to be connected to a land base. But look at all the Native people who've been relocated and urbanized, and some wiped off the face of the Earth, and yet they still have that connection to the land, to this hemisphere. They're very clear that's the one thing they have: "I am from this land. I am original to this land." What is it that happened with Chicanos? Obviously I know, I can say some words to explain colonialism and invasion and so forth, but what is it that happened to make them forget that land base? And to not be able to remember themselves as Native peoples? Yes, it's internalized racism. That's one of the things I'm exploring—that sense of place as land base. And I think tejanos—of course I'm biased—but I think tejanos have that sense.

GEA: I think you're right. La gente de Tejás, rural, agricultural people, have kept that link with the land, with a particular place, more so than urban people. Part of it is due to internal colonialism or neocolonialism, a psychological type of being taken over. Beginning in the sixteenth century, colonialism was material, it appropriated bodies, land, resources, religion.... Everything was taken over. Psychologically, that kind of colonization is still going on. If you live in the inner cities your children haven't had the physical concrete experience of touching the Earth, but they may feel connected, for example, to East L.A.

The New Tribalism

GEA: Another thing I want to touch on and see what you think is what happens when our sense of tribe and identity changes, when it expands to include a new kind of tribalism. Chicano history has gone through different stages which sometimes overlap. Periods of being forced to assimilate, encouraged to forget all about the indigenous roots, alternate with periods of resistance—especially during the Chicano movimiento, a nationalistic movement of claiming Chicanohood as central to our lives. It was followed by the movement dying down and un movimiento macha surging up. Chicana feminists, artists, activistas, and intellectuals, many of us dykes. We looked for something beyond just nationalism while continuing to connect to our roots. If we don't find the roots we need we invent them, which is fine because culture is invented anyway. We have returned to the tribe, but our nationalism is one with a twist. It's no longer the old kind of "I'm separated from this other group because I'm a Chicana so I therefore don't have anything to do with blacks or with Asians or whatever." It's saying, "Yes I belong. I come from this particular tribe, but I'm open to interacting with these other people." I call this the New Tribalism. It's a kind of mestizaje that allows for connecting with other ethnic groups and interacting with other cultures and ideas.

IHA: Which is the way it happened to begin with, right? Which is not what anthropologists would like us to think because they believe that each of the pueblos was in some sort of vacuum. That's why they look at Native Americans today, for example, who've gone through some cultural, social transformation and say, "Oh, you're not real Indians because the real Indians are only up in the mesas, in the kivas." And you go, "Wait a minute. Who are you to tell me that I'm not real?"

GEA: Sí.

IHA: It comes back to the whole idea of tradition. Tradition is not static, it's dynamic and it's always been dynamic. Otherwise it would have died. There has to be adaptation, interchange, contact, sharing with neighbors and newcomers. You find out what they're about and they find out what you're about. You borrow from each other and you give to each other. It's inconceivable that it would have been otherwise in the past.

GEA: People were isolated and separated mainly because it took a long time to travel from one tribe to another.

IHA: Right.

GEA: Now we live in a global village; we live in each other's pockets and not in isolated ethnic plots. We depend on exchange of goods, ideas, and information. Modern life goes on and we can never go back, we can never completely isolate each group from other groups.

IHA: The only thing I wanted to add is an extension to what you're saying in your idea of the New Tribalism. If I'm understanding correctly, it allows people to be comfortable, really trusting themselves, validating their choices and saying, "It's okay because I'm in this global community and I come from this tribe, but I'm having this meeting and I'm sharing with these other peoples." The other part of that is that if Chicanos really looked into their ancestral heritage—I'm talking about a revindication of each person's lineage . . .

GEA: Yes, of the differences not being erased.

Mestizas as Bridges

IHA: Yeah, and of knowing them. It doesn't mean you have to go back and live in the past, it means a validation of each individual's lineage. It means finding out where you came from. For example if you find out that you're Yaqui or Tarahumara or whichever tribe, you become aware that members of that community are still struggling in this world today. It doesn't mean that you have to go and live with them or become their supreme advocate or anything. But if not Chicanos, who? That's what was always said about us, right? That we were the bridge. And we *are* the bridge, you know? Not just us, but any Native person, mestiza or any mixed blood who has had to negotiate within and between the various communities, ¿verdad?

GEA: Sí, any mixed blood but especially people like yourself, people half Asian and half Italian or half Native and half black. The experiences of biracial and multiracial people are very important and we need to hear about them. For a lot of these people it's like juggling all these cultures and none of the cultures want them. They're asked to emphasize the Filipino part of themselves rather than the black part. People who have a little bit of the different tribes in themselves have something valuable to tell us. As a Chicana my tribes are more internal and integrated from centuries of mixing, but those whose mixing is more recent—half Chicana and half white, for example—have unique experiences and I'd like to hear more about and from them. In fact an Asian-American woman who was my intern, Jamie Lee Evans, is doing a book on these half-and-halfs, particularly if they have a white parent and an ethnic-other parent. What happens to the dynamic between the parents and the child?

IHA: Because of my Nez Perce heritage, I'm insisting on this particular point. I don't know what it would be if I were "only Chicana."

GEA: We have to listen to the Native people, we have to listen to the Indian and the Chicana, to people like yourself whose mother is Native and father is Chicano. We have to listen to the indigenous part of ourselves.

IHA: Everywhere in the world today multinational corporations and the military industrial complex want to erase indigenous peoples off the face of the Earth. Why is it so necessary to wipe them out? Why are they so expendable? One: Because they're not in any position to resist the superpowers' military, technological strength. But two: It's also because of their philosophies. I don't want to romanticize; I'm not saying that they're perfect, that there's nothing wrong with their worldviews. There might very well be. But in terms of—say, the idea of human beings as caretakers of the land—that's a useful precept for humanity, one indigenous peoples have in common: to live in harmony with life, to recognize all that lives around you as life, to not see human beings as superior to all other forms of life, to not see all other forms of life as expendable, to know pain when an oil spill destroys all the habitat and the life around it. There are some things intimately related with the worldview of indigenous peoples that are very threatening both to the world the way it is right now and to the powers that be.

For Chicanos and Chicanas it's getting back to the point of originality. How do we come in touch with that? Many Chicanos aren't even particularly environmentally conscious. It's sort of strange: Here are Chicanos letting 1992 come and go, letting environmental concerns come and go. These are things that you think we'd be pushing to the forefront, and yet it's passing us by. And I say "us" because I count myself in that community. I know it's not all of us because I know you and others are doing things.

GEA: One of the things that I—along with a lot of other people in many different groups in this countermovement—would like to see is the $87 million the U.S. government gave to the committee in charge of the quincentennial given to Native peoples. Give the land back to the Native people. The quincentennial committees had replicas of the *Niña*, the *Pinta*, and the *Santa Maria* built. The plan is to have them do a transatlantic voyage. Why not sell those ships and give the money to the Indians, give all the money they're going to spend on commemorative festivities and parades and—

IHA: —mementos.

GEA: Museums and art galleries who are hyping up stuff about the discovery and the voyages should put the emphasis on the other, the Indian, the groups oppressed by colonialism. I just got a postcard of an Aztec two-headed serpent from a friend of mine traveling in London. I want to see all these museums in Europe give all the treasures they stole back to the Native Americans.

IHA: Well yeah, a lot of people have been wanting to see that and they've been working on it. Down in Mexico in the late '70s they were saying that that would be one of the signs of change. When things started coming back to who they belong to.

GEA: We cannot undo the encounter, the contact, because you and I would disappear as mestizas.

IHA: But we would still be here as Native women.

GEA: When the *Pinta*, the *Niña*, and the *Santa Maria* want to dock in San Francisco, I wouldn't let them land. I would not let them land. Maybe I'd like somebody to sink the ships. I just can't believe they're spending all this money on this stupid—!!! The government and the dominant culture are doing this because it gives them a sense of control; they can control us, they can control the other peoples of color. It makes white Americans feel good to have a history that's five hundred years old, they can say, "We're not such a young nation anymore. We're coming on and this is our legacy." So they're emphasizing the legacy of whites, they're emphasizing the myth of the conqueror, the pioneer, the trailblazer—

IHA: —the new man.

GEA: There's this heroic fallacy that it's OK to penetrate a country—

rape it, conquer it, take it over—and not only to do that but to tell the inhabitants that they aren't who they are. This to me was the greatest injury: to take the identity away from these indigenous people, to put a foreign identity on them, then make them believe that *that's* who they were.

IHA: Take their names away.

GEA: Not only did they name them falsely—because "Indians" weren't from India—but in imposing this identity they also almost completely took away that integrity and sense of knowing who one is. And again this was done through writing, through the letters that Colón wrote to Isabella, through the chronicles kept by the friars and others. It was through writing that this Conquest was enacted. These documents were sent back to Europe saying, "The natives are thus and thus, the terrain is thus and thus, the riches are ours for the taking."

IHA: "The wealth is thus and thus."

GEA: Not only did they completely reconstruct people's identities but they also falsely constructed the whole of America. So now here we are, mestizas and Native women who use the pen—or should I say the keyboard?—as a weapon and means of transformation. We're reclaiming the agency of reinscribing, taking off their inscriptions and reinscribing ourselves, our own identities, our own cultures. The very weapon that conquered indigenous America, we're using it against them.

IHA: Which they never thought would happen.

GEA: No. Because you and I were never supposed to write.

IHA: We were never meant to!

GEA: We were never supposed to write counter to their ideologies!

IHA: I tell my students it's like those pictures of Native people that people buy to put on their walls: it never occurred to anybody that we'd come off the walls—literally come out of the walls, walk out of the pictures and start talking. Many feel very threatened—white intellectuals in the field of Native American literature (the field is controlled right now mostly by white male critics, some white female critics)—because now there are more Native American critics and writers protesting, saying, "No you can't do that. We're going to say what's what with our literature." So they do everything they can, once again, to keep us in our place. When you go to the MLA, if you go to one of the sessions on Chicano/Chicana literature or business meetings with people working in Chicano and Chicana literature, the room will be full of Chicanas and Chicanos. But in the Native American sessions, the room is mostly white. Some people are sort of startled when a dark face shows up, as if to say, "What are you doing here?" They determine if they're going to accept you or not, still.

GEA: When I was writing my children's book I read a lot of children's literature. I looked for Native American, Chicano, African American, and Asian American. More than any ethnic group most of the Native American books were written by white people. Some were beautiful and some were racist and misrepresented Native Americans. The same with Chicano children's lit. Here were these white people writing about Chicano themes, using stereotypical scenarios. That really upsets me. From the first year in school, these children get indoctrinated, get used to seeing themselves through the eyes of the dominant culture. It was just so blatant.

IHA: Yeah, it is blatant.

GEA: Those young minds are absorbing everything, just like we did.

"Las Tres Madres"

IHA: Just for the record today I want, at least briefly, to get at how we relate the Conquest to the individual woman, to the individual Chicana of whatever age. Because we've been talking about invasions and she's the key. And the invaders knew that, right? The mentados conquistadores knew that and that's why they put the women in boarding schools, indoctrinated them, made them forget about the diosa and about the fact that life is dual, it's a duality. They wrenched that knowledge from them, violently. What do we say to the individual mujer?

GEA: Yeah. That's a whole book, Inés. What's happened to her and how it's affected her psychologically, economically, intellectually. It's really hard to say it in a few sentences. But I think that a lot of the Anglo and Spanish conquest was the fact that the natives were femininized, made and treated like women.

190

IHA: Because many Native peoples understood and respected the female principle—they were in touch with it, the men as well as the women—and the invaders saw that as a weakness, a reason for scorn.

GEA: Underneath that was that fear of women's strength. Even now the ethnic groups of color, the people of color—whether male or female—are still feminized, kept in their place, domesticated, tamed, controlled. Or tried to.

IHA: To be told what to do.

GEA: Because we're unruly, supposed to be wild, uncontrollable, too spontaneous—

IHA: —too emotional—

GEA: —all the things dangerous to them, characteristics they associate with females. So it's been the woman—to me she's the epitome of resistance. We all have various ways of resisting. Often women who feel powerless have to resort to manipulation, women who feel stronger come right out and fight straightforwardly. Everybody has different tactics.

IHA: Yeah. As I said earlier, I didn't grow up with la Llorona, but in my adult life I understand her power as I begin to look into her and realize who and what she was. But I need to acknowledge that this was learned. I couldn't just say—like a lot of Mexicanas and Chicanas do—"Oh, yes, I grew up listening to those stories." Well, I didn't. But once I knew of them I realized what she was.

GEA: Yeah. We've always been on the negative side of the binary. Mexicanas and Chicanas got hit with the patriarchal interpretation of la Llorona—that she was a bad mother. OK, right away that belief is suspect because who are the bad? The bad are us. Then there's the interpretation of—say, the common Chicana, the average woman forced to buy into the patriarchal story: to her the Llorona is a warning to be a good mother, not to fool around because she doesn't want to be that stereotype. (Not unlike women who don't want to have anything to do with prostitutes because they think they're so different.) Then there's a feminist interpretation saying, "This woman was a danger to the patriarchy." La Llorona goes counter to the patriarchy, which says the nuclear heterosexual family is the most important thing, wife and children under the control of the patriarch, the man. I read her differently, I read as a lesbian. In some stories she punishes men who beat their wives. She appears to drunkards in the middle of the night and scares them to death. She lures some of them. They follow her at night and think she's their beloved. When they get close to her, she turns around and has a horse's head with long pointy teeth. They die of heart failure, whatever. There's a revenge element against the male in the same stories.

Potentially as a symbol, metaphor, and cultural figure la Llorona can be very empowering to the Chicana and the Indian because she was not only found in the Mexican tradition, but also in the Mayan and other cultures such as the Nigerian. There's a Native American figure dressed in white who cries and wails. She's transcultural. Hers is an empowering image when we reinterpret her story on all these levels and use it to mark five hundred years of colonization. At one point in history la Malinche and la Llorona become the same person. And (as I said in *Borderlands*), their ancestor was Snake Woman.

IHA: Who is also Guadalupe.

GEA: Who is also Guadalupe. So there's a connection between all these, las tres madres.

IHA: I'm so used to bringing up la Malinche that I just didn't bring it up and you didn't either.

GEA: Again, because they make her the bad person, the person who betrayed her people, the person who sold out.

IHA: Right, and en la danza, todavía yo soy una malinche, en la danza. So I understand her from this whole other perspective. Well, la Virgen de Guadalupe, la Malinche, la Llorona, Coatlicue, all—

GEA: Tonántzin.

IHA: Tonántzin—all manifestations really of the mother Earth. The original mother. Originality, that's the connection, it helps us to remember our mother. Chicanas are really in control even more so than they often realize despite the lie in the culture that favors the man, that says what the man says is central. Well maybe, but who really carries on everything, and who can change the men if not the women? It's up to the women to say no to their sons. "No, you don't do that and no, I will not favor you over your sister. And no, you cannot have this privilege just because you're a boy, because your sister is doing this work and then she's going to get to do this" and so on. It's the woman who is the key because the husbands are sons of women.

GEA: But we also need to take some of that responsibility placed on women and place it on the culture and on males. They also have to do the childrearing, they also can become new mestizos . . .

IHA: Exactly. Some of the older men think it's hopeless, but anyway—

GEA: Back to what you said in the beginning, about the sun impregnating the Earth. To me that's like the male impregnating the woman and one of the things I've seen—especially in the eco-feminist movement—has been women healing the Earth. So I'd like to see, with this sixth world sun, a new woman-to-woman impregnation, rather than male to female, because we, the women, have been taking care of the Earth.

IHA: I never see the sun as completely male. I never see anything as completely male or female because they're both. So when I think of the sun I think of the duality and then the Earth as the duality also. It's the double duality I mentioned earlier. That's how I think if it. Otherwise it would be very hard for me to accept it. Whether I accept it or not is sort of irrelevant; that's the way the message came through. It came to me like that, so there's not much I can do about that. But the other part of that message is that the eclipse affected the women. It affected everyone, but it's had an interesting effect on women in Mexico because quite literally women are organizing more. I don't know if it's more or if people are just noticing it more. To me they've been organizing, but they may be talking about new groups of women, which would be really good.

GEA: The sources I read say that the fifth world will end and the sixth begins on December 24, 2011, according to the Mayan and the Aztec calendars. But you're saying there's a little bit of an overlap—

IHA: This is like the beginning of the beginning and we're still in the ending of the fifth.

GEA: I think it's up to people like you and me, and other writers and artists and thinkers and everybody to create the new stories so that we can get away from the symbology and the metaphor of male and female, with the male being stronger and more active and the female being the receiver and passive. This privileging of the male has been passed down to us from both the indigenous cultures—or some of the indigenous cultures—and Western civilization.

IHA: Well, even if the predominantly male sun is dual, it's the perception of society that he's privileged and superior because he impregnates, when really it's a deflection of our attention because that's all he does. She—this incredibly active creative force—is somehow then dismissed.

GEA: You and I can give it that kind of reading, but people like my mother, my sister, my aunts still read it the patriarchal way. We have to make up new myths and new stories, we have to create more of a balance. Another theme you suggested we could touch on but haven't said anything about is the creative and the critical process.

IHA: I don't know how to hook this into '92 except possibly with what I said earlier about questioning the right of conquest at any level, whether it's individual or global. For me—and I think for you and for most of the writers I respect—the creative process is critical and the critical process is creative. You couldn't really have one without the other.

GEA: Except that the university tries to separate them.

IHA: The university and the critics try to separate, and that frustrates me sometimes. It would be nice if more critics would try to write creatively—because some of them never do, I guess, ever.

GEA: Or they're closet poets.

IHA: And then they take it upon themselves to pull everything apart and look at it. But I guess somehow, if we look at the creative process as a critical process of self-realization, a taking of conci . . . toma de conciencia—then we come to the same kinds of understandings you were talking about just now, about what we have to do. We can begin to see ourselves not only as the subjects but as the creators. The connection to that source, that origin—which does go back to that Mother—can work itself out in us, through us, in a life-giving, healing, empowering way: that's what women haven't had, what Chicanas haven't had. That's what's been kept—

GEA: —kept us down.

6

···

Making Alliances, Queerness, and Bridging Conocimientos
An Interview with Jamie Lee Evans (1993)

···

(1998–1999)

ALK: In this interview you state that you're "very hopeful" about the possibilities of alliance making, and you associate that hope with your belief that "to be human is to be in relationship; to be human is to be related to other people, to be interdependent with other people." You made this statement almost six years ago. Do you still feel hopeful? Has your hope grown? Diminished?

GEA: I've expanded that hope as well as the theory of alliance making I discussed in this interview. I now believe alliances entail interdependent relationships with the whole environment—with the plants, the earth, and the air as well with people. We relate by going inward and relating to the different parts of ourselves. If I can relate to the negative, depressive Gloria, the greedy, stingy, starving-for-affection Gloria—if I have a good relationship with my different parts, my different selves, I can carry this inner relationship outward and have good relationships with others—with you, my sister, my mother, my lover, and the community. But one doesn't come before the other; they're all simultaneous. I can have a relationship with a fence or with the plants and the cats.

ALK: So you still think that the alliance making is possible?

GEA: Yes. When I had the drawbridge or island model, I was thinking in terms of groups of people—the marginalized, disenfranchised groups hooking together and building a network, El Mundo Zurdo, where we could help each other. I've now taken into account the inner hand, the spiritual hand, the inner voice. So you're listening to your leaders, to the committees or the groups you're organizing with and you're also "tuning in" inwardly, to their subjectivity and to your own. You're examining what's not expressed outwardly, what's not voiced—which is what I mean by the inner hand.

ALK: Are you saying that you think alliance making would be more effective if people would pay attention to both of those things?

GEA: Yes! Alliance making is already more than just a rational, physical action. It's already an emotional, psychological action, and now I'm seeing how the imaginal, the creative facet of mind or consciousness, is interacting with the older alliance making energies.

"Making Alliances, Queerness, and Bridging Conocimientos"
An Interview with Jamie Lee Evans (1993)

JLE: Why don't you begin by saying how old you are and the kind of work you do with others.

Making Alliances

GEA: I was born and raised in Texas but consider myself a Californian as well. I just had my fifty-first birthday a couple of months ago. The kind of work I've been doing with women and men is participating in diverse kinds of conferences, visiting and talking in college communities and local communities of women working in violence against women organizations, coalitions, and rape crisis centers. I've worked with women activists who organize conferences on gay, lesbian, and bisexual studies and also Chicana/Latina Chicano/Latino communities—especially campus communities—in all different parts of the U.S. The third major group of people I've been working with—and sometimes these groups overlap—are writers. Women writers. I travel around the country addressing issues of alliance, power, and how we can work together to get our work out and create a stronger force so that the community or the academy or the world can hear our words, our histories, our needs.

What's really interesting to me is a kind of a paradox: there are groups of people who really want to work with other people and then there are other groups who want to separate and isolate out. One reason I'm doing this kind of work is that I've always been a mediator, I've always been a bridge. I think that ignorance is one of the enemies we have to combat—ignorance of power, ignorance about each other's histories, ignorance about other ways of living and other perspectives. Ignorance is a form of desconocimientos, an intentional kind of ignorance.

As a bridge and a messenger I open myself up, listen to hear what these people are experiencing and what they're saying. I have messages I want to impart to other people. Some of these messages are about how we can work together, how we can strategize to accomplish certain goals.

I guess my chief motivation right now is to get women-of-color voices to be heard in writing, in talks, in action, in terms of organizing and coordinating with other organizations so that certain goals can be accomplished. In my talks and in my writing I lay down a foundation and a context for these discussions. Sometimes it's giving a historical overview of certain history, certain struggles, and of adding my own theories and ideas on the topic, and then creating a dialogue between my listeners or readers and each other and myself.

JLE: What about writers and writing?

GEA: Since you've been working as my writing assistant, we've discussed a lot of issues. But we always come back to the writing. Writing is my way of making alliances. I say, "Here is this piece of work, it has these images and ideas. It has these beliefs, it has this perspective. What is your perspective? What is your history?" I get the dialogue going—either get them to talk, right then and there, or give them ideas so that when they have coalition meetings they can use these questions or focus on these issues and start the ball rolling. Or I say, "Write about this. Reflect, react to what I'm saying"—so that what I'm saying can just be a little kernel of corn they take and make into whole stalks and ears of corn. I'll offer the idea that we're all mestizos because we are of mixed blood, so that means we have certain commonalities, but it also means we have a lot of differences. In this society differences are collapsed. They take that idea and expand on it, giving their own history and perspective on it. All of a sudden there are fifty ideas about mestizaje, rather than just mine. In working with these groups—either having them speak or having them write—the aim is for them to communicate, for them to share their histories and to see that there's a political agenda we all have in common and to start thinking of ways that we can strategize to fill our common needs—health care, a roof over our heads, the ability to defend ourselves against the muggers and the rapists and the molesters, having a voice in the workplace. The needs are political as well as personal.

I work with a lot of marginal groups—Latinos, Chicanos, blacks, queers, Jews. Often they're up against the mainland, the masses of dominant culture. A few of these people in the mainland want to reach over and bridge with the marginal group. One of the first things we do from the margins is question their motivations. To distinguish the false allies from potentially good allies, we ask them why they're interested in bridging with us. But even then we mess up. They may snow us with a good con act, or they themselves may be unconscious that their motivations are not altruistic. Here are groups of marginalized people up against this huge mass of whiteness. Often, it's people from this huge mass of whiteness who ask me to come and speak because they want to draw people of color into their organization or into their conference or into their classrooms or into their colleges. So they asked me to be a visible third-world person, a token. I look at their motivations. Do they really want a multicultural university or do they just want to fulfill their requirements in order to get to funds, in order to hire teachers, in order to earn a salary? Often those who invite me to be a bridge are bridges themselves—like progressive whites, working-class whites, who've been working with civil rights movements and are part of the multicultural movement. Very rarely do I get asked by a conservative white male heterosexual. It's always people who have read me and respect my work or who would like to meet me. So the weeding-out process in terms of who to work with kind of takes care of itself on the phone when I talk with people. OK. I'm going to Minnesota to talk about the antiassault movement. My sponsors are dedicated feminists who are very much aware of the increase in violence against women. They tell me about their struggles and experiences.

JLE: When working with others, what kinds of things do you consider?

GEA: People who do the kinds of work I do need to figure out what these people want. Issues to consider are: If I go in with these people will I lose part of my identity? Will I be overwhelmed by their political views? Am I going to be brainwashed and taken over, or am I going to be left in relative freedom to express myself and to say where I'm coming from and what I want? It's a power struggle: Am I going to influence you or are you going to influence me? I don't usually run into that problem. I have a credible reputation as a writer, so they're respectful. I'm an elder to them. They listen to me. But does the school listen to its undergraduates, to its community people who don't have a standing in their community? No, it tries to win them over, seduce them into mainstream ways of thinking.

Part of my message to the young people struggling and making alliances is both the necessity of holding onto their beliefs and the necessity of changing their beliefs. I present them with my hit on things. But they have to choose which way they're going: Will they change in ways that the group in power wants them to, or will they seek out their new identity and follow their own direction? It's complex. It involves the emotions. When a person is slighted that person knows it. Something in their gut, in their heart—hurts. It's like someone pricking you with an ice pick. The assumption is that you have to remain calm, cool, and rational and not let your feelings overwhelm you, not let anger take over. I tell them, "You have to look at those feelings. There's a politics of the emotions behind each feeling. Behind guilt, behind anger, behind shame—those feelings are tied to specific experiences you've had. There's always a political context to those personal experiences." What I tell them goes against the grain, which is that you're supposed to be cool, calm, and put on a face when you're doing coalition work. You're supposed to play a role.

Alliance making is therapeutic. You're trying to heal a community or a culture while healing yourself. That's all alliance work is: you're trying to heal the wounds. You're trying to bring in justice, human rights, to people who have been wounded and disadvantaged in their lives—whether it's monetary, health, disease, mental illness, whether it's lack of knowledge, education, or training for higher-paying jobs. These are wounds—emotional and psychological as well as political wounds. Becoming allies with people is really about helping each other heal. Basically. And that is the vocabulary. I don't use the vocabulary other people working with alliances use. Because it's hard for people to expose themselves and their wounds to a stranger who's potentially an ally but could be an enemy. Jamie, if we were good allies to each other I would have to expose my wounds to you and you would have to expose your wounds to me. We would have to start from a place of openness. Anywhere along the working out of the alliance there's always the closing of doors, and then you have to open them up again.

We close doors when we hurt each other out of desconocimientos, such as ignorance. Or the hurt may be intentional, a way of taking back control. People want to keep their personal feelings out of it. But you can't. You work out personal problems while working out the problems of a particular group, community, or culture. You work on two fronts: inner and outer.

Shifting Power

JLE: Can you say more about interconnections between the personal and the political?

GEA: I use images to help people connect with different experiences. One of the images I use for this idea of who has power and who doesn't is the image of the shadow and who's stepping on the shadow. So I'll have something like this. [While drawing.] This is the body of the person and when somebody is stepping on your shadow—in Spanish it's called "pisan la sombra"—they're stepping on your face but they're doing it in a covert way. They're putting you down and walking on you without acknowledging that they're doing it, and you sometimes are buying into it. Women of color especially because we've been taught to be in this kind of oppressed/oppressor role—slave and slave owner. So when somebody who has control over us is in dialogue with us, we unknowingly fall into assuming a subordinate role. And the other automatically assumes the role of control, the role of the oppressor. You see this dynamic between students and teachers, between whites and colored, between middle class and working class. Always people fall into the roles they've been indoctrinated into. Decolonizing oneself from this kind of oppressor/oppressed role is both personal and political, inner and outer. As a bridge I'll say, "This is a scenario that happens often." Or "This is an assumption we all buy into." Or "These are some dangers when you're doing alliance work."

My role is that of teacher, healer, translator, mediator. That's my job as a writer. People look to me for images, for ideas. They take these ideas, think about and expand on them. They think of me as a model. It's alright for them to think of me as a model. But there's a danger, the danger of the pedestal. They give me their power and in return I'm supposed to tell them what to do. So when I'm communicating my ideas I try to turn it back: "What would you do if you were in this situation? Think about it or talk about it or write about it." "What does it mean for me to be on this pedestal up on stage, looking down at you? And what does that mean that you're down there looking up at me?" Be aware of the roles you assume for others and for yourself. My goal is to encourage them to challenge every assumption, to question everything, and to always, always look at their positions—where they're speaking from.

I have another image: una boca (a mouth) with feet. Perspective is where you stand. When you speak, you speak from a particular world. In a classroom you're speaking from the world of the academy, from an intellectual identity. In your workplace, at your job, you're speaking as employee, menial, management, or top of the heap. What comes out of your mouth changes every time the place you're speaking from changes. So when you're doing alliance work it's very important to say, "This is who I am: I am a Chicana, mexicana, dyke—whatever. I come from a campesina background, but I now have one foot inching into middle-classness. I'm part of the intelligentsia and the artistic class, and I'm speaking today to you as all these people but primarily as a Chicana or as a dyke or whatever." You position yourself and say what your stance is on particular things so that the other people you're working with know exactly where you are coming from. They can then say, "You say that you're talking from a working-class perspective but look at you: you have a house, you have a car, you have privileges, you're a professor, you're a publisher, you're a known writer." They challenge some of these positions. It's the first step in finding out whether a person who wants to be your ally is for real. Is she speaking from where she's standing? Is she putting her feet in her mouth or vice versa? You get a sense of whether or not you can trust a person. You go with your gut feeling. Sometimes they'll say all the right stuff, but you know they're trying to put one over on you or on themselves.

I think that in the last ten years, ever since *This Bridge*, white women take their courage in their hands and say it: "I am a white woman, I am middle class." It used to be so hard for them ten, fifteen years ago, but now they're able to say it. The question to ask yourself is are they saying this because they know we want to hear them say it? Or are they really examining their positions and privileges?

Anthologizing Alliances

JLE: Who would you say you're in alliance with?

GEA: With women of color, lesbians of color, queers of all colors, lesbian and straight white women, white men and men of color. I've

edited or coedited three books: *This Bridge, Haciendo Caras*, and *Signs'
Theorizing Lesbians' Experience*. With the first two I saw anthologizing
as my way of making alliances with women of color. My experience
working on the *Signs* issue was of white women wanting to make
alliances with lesbians of color and lesbians of color not trusting *Signs*
and therefore not submitting material. Many dykes of color I had
encouraged to submit did not. They knew *Signs* as elitist, abstract, and
racist. My work is anthologized in a lot of books. Some editors, women
and men, genuinely want to diversify the community and include diverse
voices, especially those that have been excluded. Other anthologizers
call on me so people like you, Jamie, won't challenge them with, "Look:
you have one contributor of color and ninety white contributors." Some
attempt to tokenize me and try to pull a fast one on their readers. White
culture is an amoeba that swallows its radicals, sort of tries to
domesticate us. I think that some of my work is hard to assimilate. The
language, the code-switching, and the way I write are not readily
assimilable. I write about particular, specific cultural things. Some are
hard for them to swallow. Though they ignore some of the issues, my
work makes them confront other issues. I don't write like a white
person. I don't write like an academic. I break all the rules.

If they can't assimilate the writing, they try to assimilate me by
tokenizing me. They'll try bringing me into their book, their conference,
or their alliance but acknowledge the easy stuff and ignore the more
controversial. When this happens I respond either by phone or letter
and ask them some questions. A new quarterly, *New Chicano Writing*,
started by Charles Tatem, asked me to participate. I called him and
said, "You wanted me to be on your editorial board, but these are the
things that I object to: You have 'Chicano' but not 'Chicana' in the title
yet the groundbreaking writing in the Chicano/Chicana community is
by women. Another is that you will only accept work written in
English." He gets back to me later. He's changed the name of the
magazine to *New Chicana/Chicano Writing* and accepts submissions
in English, Spanish, bilingual, Tex-Mex, whatever. I agreed to be on
his editorial board.

JLE: Somebody who makes the right decision, the right compro-
mises . . .

GEA: Yes, if the magazine's guidelines are opposed to my ideas about
writing and politics, I refuse to be on its editorial board. I'm on the
board of San Diego State University Press. It publishes books on border

issues. This kind of alliance is working with a university press or magazine or journal rather than with local communities or organizations.

JLE: You're not assuming familiarity with these people?

GEA: No. Usually, I don't work with them on a daily basis nor in the flesh. Some of these people are straight Chicanos and Chicanas. Our differences have to do with the way they identify themselves, academically and professionally. Even when my allies are Chicana dykes we may be worlds apart: regional differences, generational differences, and language differences.

Identity: The Power of Self-Invention

JLE: Can you talk a little bit about lesbian alliances? What are some major issues that come up for you, not just within the Latina/Chicana community but mainly with other communities?

GEA: Identity is one of the major issues. What you call yourself or what other people call you, makes you; it's an aspect of identity formation, a process that constructs or invents you. You can take your identity into your hands recognizing that you don't need a white person or a Chicana middle-class person to tell you who you are. You have some say in it. Constructing identity is a collaborative effort. What you name yourself comes up—you know, do you call yourself "dyke," "lesbian," "marimacha," "jota"? You can decide what to label yourself. What does it mean when a Chicana calls herself "lesbian"?

When discussing identity you get into the controversy of the social constructionist verses the essentialist. What do you think—was I born a queer or was I made a queer? Is there something in my genetic makeup, a queer gene? Why are some people in the family queer and others not? There may be a third or a fourth way of conceptualizing identity. What is the history behind your identity?

I explored what queerness was in Native cultures, how they treated same-sex orientation or whatever you want to call it. (The vocabulary changes every day.) The Nahuatl word for a dyke is "patlache." Queer sexuality was prevalent in some Indian societies, taboo and punished by strangulation or stoning in others. I could connect my queerness to my Mexicanness. So now I have the white traditions but I also have my own. When I think of myself as a queer woman, my queerness is not just white, but Indian, Mexican, Chicano, a regional queerness, a working-class queerness of my growing up in South Texas. Kids of color growing up now don't have a sense of roots. Their identities are secondhand—derivative from the white—so they're floundering. They know they're not white, and the issues of language keep coming up.

Agreeing on what to call ourselves as queer women is one of the hardest things to do. The word "lesbian" has different meanings to different people. Adrienne Rich defines it in one way, Pat Califa defines it another. So what is a lesbian? Is a lesbian identified by sexual activity or by cultural orientation or by political view? Take the word "queer"— What is queer? The word "queer" has been taken over by the academy, queer theorists have borrowed this working-class word.

JLE: Have they borrowed it?

GEA: Taken it over. Stolen it. For you "queer" means something, for Lisa it means something else, for me it means growing up in South Texas where the word was used for somebody who was different sexually. It was a working-class word, a word I feel more comfortable with than with "lesbian" or "gay" or "homosexual" or "invert." So language becomes an issue that accompanies identity. As does one's economic station. Money and sex are the two main issues in alliance work. Who has control over what, who has the resources? Who has the power, who has the big club? And how is that club being used— to shuttle resources to people who have need of it? Or to hit people over the head to keep them in their place? Issues of class ultimately have to do with money. Money is energy and people with money have the means, energy, and resources to get other people to do things their way. People who don't have money are expected to give their energies, resources, to the power holders who siphon them of their life's blood. The three major issues are: who I am, what language I speak, and how much money I have. Money, sex, and identity.

JLE: So when you say "sex" you mean female or male? You don't mean how much sex you have—say, four times a week?

GEA: No. And heterosexual sex is always a power thing, who is bottom and who is top. I shouldn't use those terms.

JLE: No, that's fine. I think that there could be a lot of disagreement.

GEA: In sexual relationships there's always a stronger person, the one with more power. The person who's more needy will make concessions to the person she loves because of that need, which gives the other person more power. It may not matter who's on top and who's on bottom. The bottom can be in control.

JLE: You've been reading too much psychology!

GEA: Whether in a homosexual, a lesbian, or a bisexual relationship, the power issue is still there. Somebody needs or loves the other person more. It's never equal. I think it comes closest with lesbians because they kind of take turns. But in your average relationship there's always a stronger party. The controller. Isn't it awful?

JLE: Of course my lover is sitting here. I have no comment. I'll call you later.

GEA: If the relationship breaks up it's because of the sex, which is actually about power, and that power can be about money or it can be about class which adds up to identity.

JLE: So you're saying that sex is all about power and money and class?

GEA: No. I'm saying that when a sexual relationship doesn't work, when it falls apart, the straw that broke its back is money, power, class issues of identity. If something goes wrong in your relationship, you can look back and it will be one of these: sex, money issues, or class which is language. Maybe I'm totally off the wall.

JLE: We could have a long conversation on this; it's very interesting, I don't know that I would agree. Do you consider the basic relations of love—two lovers—as being in alliance?

GEA: Yes. That's why the issues I'm talking about in speaking to Latino Heritage Week about identity are the same kinds of issues I'd be talking about to two dykes who were breaking up or trying to work the relationship. You just take the microcosm and expand it to the macrocosm, and you're doing the same thing. What I see happening between two lovers is what's happening between two or three different groups of people, nations, continents. It's no longer a house of two people but all the different communities trying to work together, the United States, the planet. But I may be generalizing.

JLE: You said a lot.

GEA: What I'm saying is that when you're doing process work on yourself or facilitating somebody else's healing, it's the same mechanisms that would be at issue and talked about in couples' counseling, and the same kinds of things I'd be talking about to these groups of people in alliances. I say "I" because other people would not be addressing this issue. That's my hit on it. Like I said before—activists want to divorce their personal feelings from their organization. They want to work in a reasonable, cool, collected manner. But I say that all of those problems and issues—the origin goes back to particular feelings and experiences that these activists have had when they've been one-on-one with their parents, with their boyfriends, with their friends, with their classmates. So the two of you are, in miniature, this country.

JLE: And all of the oppressions and power struggles.

Conocimientos

GEA: But the two of you can work together and be allies. People bond because they want to work together. I'm hopeful because to be human is to be in relationship; to be human is to be related to other people, to be interdependent with other people. So that's what we have to work at. Sometimes in order to be human and to relate to other people we have to cut ourselves a little slack—separate out, regroup, and recharge our batteries so that we can continue the work. That's where my model of the bridge, drawbridge, sandbar, or island comes in. My model is conocimientos. My pictogram for it is la lengua, los ojos, y las orejas en la mano surda. At the end of the tongue is a pen. "Conocimiento" is the Spanish word for knowledge and skill. It has to do with getting to know each other by really listening with the outer ear and the inner ear. Really looking at each other and seeing with our eyes and communicating orally or with the written word. It means always putting ourselves out on the line by raising our hands. The hand is the symbol for activist work, for doing. You raise your voice, you raise your hand. Because it's not enough to see and to understand. You have to go out there and take action. Whether it's to write a book, make an anthology, attend meetings once a week, mail flyers, or picket—it has to be done. Con la mano. With the hand. Activism. Writing is a form of activism, one of making bridges.

JLE: So when you talk about being a bridge . . .

GEA: One of the drawbacks to being a bridge is being walked on, but one of the pluses is that it's two-way—oncoming and outgoing traffic. It's being in different worlds and getting the best from those worlds—white and colored, gay and straight—and benefiting from those connections. But you also get damaged in some ways. This work bends a person, wastes a person; the wear and tear is stressful. Stress makes your body ill. I got diabetes. I have to watch that I don't get stressed out and overwhelmed. With the job of being a bridge comes another perk—of getting my name out, of people buying my books and believing in my work. I don't know if there's a balance.

JLE: You've made a career out of being a bridge?

GEA: Yeah, of extending my identity. It's not enough for me to be just a chicanita farm worker from South Texas. I have to see other worlds, experience other things. It's not enough for me to be a Chicana dyke. I am also a writer, an intellectual, an artist; I am also middle class, or will be.

JLE: Can you talk about the risks involved in being an ally?

GEA: The biggest risk is betrayal. When a person is betrayed she feels shitty, feels stupid: "Why did I trust this person and allow her to stab me in the back? It's all my fault." You know—the victim syndrome. I beat myself up over the fact that this person betrayed me. With Chicanas, betrayal is a big thing. We were betrayed as women, as Indians, and as a colonized group in this country. Along with the betrayal, you feel less of a person, you feel shame. Feelings of betrayal make you a smaller person, reduce your self-esteem. Betrayal is politically deadening. It's dangerous. It's disempowering. When you lose that self-esteem you no longer trust yourself to make value judgments about other people. "If I instinctively trusted this woman for over a year and she stabbed me in the back, what's to say I'm going to be right about this other person? What if I'm wrong? What if my gut feeling is wrong again?" So I lose confidence in myself and my values. The whole person is slowly destroyed, and this is what women of color are suffering from: their personhood is chopped off at the knees by these wounds.

JLE: What about betrayal in the lesbian community or with lesbians of color? Is it a problem there also?

GEA: Well, it depends on what stage of coming out you're in or how long you've been out, how much experience you've had in the greater lesbian world or whatever. At first I felt really good belonging to the lesbian community, even though it was mostly white. Before I'd had no home; I now had this new home. But after a few years I started looking at the power dynamic, at who had power, and who was trying to define for me what I was as a Chicana lesbian. I saw that my voice was silenced and my history ignored. Those issues drove me into looking at my queer roots. I had to get a positive sense of being queer from my culture, not just from the white culture. Now I can look at both the white lesbian community and my own culture beginning to have groups of lesbians organizing. Chicana dyke organizations are beginning to form, are beginning to come into their power. So now I'm trying to position myself, looking not just at my culture and the white culture, but at the whole planet. I'm looking at other nationalities and how they deal with their queer people. I'm trying to get a global perspective on being queer. Sometimes I feel very comfortable with a bunch of white dykes and other times I feel totally invisible, ignored. I feel that they only see the queer part of me and ignore the Chicana and working-class parts. As long as I leave my class and my culture outside the door when I walk into the room I'm OK. But if I bring in my race or my class, then education starts.

JLE: You're not as welcome.

GEA: I think that the white dykes really want a community that's diversified. Sometimes they want it so badly that they want to put everybody under this queer umbrella: "We're all in this together and we're all equal." But we are not equal. In their thirst and their hunger for this diversity, the issues of class and race are issues that they don't even want to examine because they feel those issues can be divisive. So they're hungry for being politically correct and having women of color in their organization and women of color lovers and women of color in their syllabi and women of color performers, singers, writers, or whatever. The greater our numbers the more power we have as queers. Bringing us under this queer umbrella is a kind of survival tactic. But often in order to bring us under the queer umbrella they ignore differences, collapse the differences, not really deal with the issue. Just sort of pay word of mouth attention to the issue and when it comes down to the numbers of who has power and how many women of color are in this anthology—in terms of the real work, they fall short. The vision is good—the greater numbers, the greater strength kind of thing—but they want us to leave our rage and our class in the checkroom when we walk in. I wrote an essay called "To(o) Queer the Writer" that deals with these concerns.

JLE: Do you think they really want a multicultural world or do they just want to stop being called racists?

GEA: They really want a multicultural diverse world. As a group, dykes are more progressively political than any other group. Because they've been oppressed as dykes and because of feminism they're more apt to see the oppression of women of color. There are always the false ones, of course. Dykes' politics are more progressive than most other groups, but they have a lot of work to do because of that very assumption: that they're enlightened and politically progressive. This assumption blanks out the trouble spots. Some don't want to really look at race or class issues. But I see some honest motivation about wanting to be allies. Sometimes they don't contend with their *unconscious* motivation, that they're doing it out of guilt or whatever. As a group, white dykes do a lot of therapy and therefore are always questioning their motivations; I think they really do want a multicultural diverse group and world. I am very hopeful. I think I'm one of the few people who are hopeful. Most people my age or younger have burned out and become disillusioned. It's the pits right now. Many young people of color have no hope, do not see alliances working, do not see white people reaching out, and do not see the possibility of white people changing perspectives or allowing change to come into their lives, but I do.

7

Doing Gigs

Speaking, Writing, and Change

An Interview with Debbie Blake and Carmen Abrego (1994)

(1998 – 1999)

ALK: You describe speaking at conferences as a type of oral writing in which you "expose" yourself. Do you feel this way about interviews also—like you're exposing yourself? Do interviews require you to expose yourself even more extensively than do speaking engagements or writing?

GEA: Yes, I discover what I'm trying to say while I'm being interviewed just like I discover what I'm trying to say when I write. I don't sit down and say, "I'm going to write a certain thing." Instead I say, "I'm going to explore this idea and see where it takes me." Often when I prepare for my talks they go less well than when I don't prepare and just open myself up. At such times I find myself saying things that surprise me. So I do both kinds of things: sometimes writing an idea beforehand makes it easier to communicate in an interview or a keynoter. But other times I get the insight right in the middle of the speech or interview and later explore it in the writing. Most of the time the writing comes first because I feel less distracted and can go inward into the thought.

"Doing Gigs: Speaking, Writing, and Change"
An Interview with Debbie Blake and Carmen Abrego (1994)

¿Queer Conference?

DB: In your keynote speech at the Sixth North American Lesbian, Gay and Bisexual Studies Conference you addressed the dangers of "performing the neocolonial" in writing to, for, or about the other, which you describe as a subtle form of racism that reinforces Euro-American privilege and cultural imperialism. At the conference you gave some specific suggestions about how academics can be more aware of what they're doing.

GEA: I urged academics to look at their own white race privilege and deconstruct it, to examine it, and in examining it, to become more aware of how they present the other culture. The ideology they were raised with privileges whites, credits whites with superiority, intelligence, and civilization. I called for a conocimientos, a type of looking at the ways they construct reality, the ways they construct knowledge, and in particular how those ways of constructing knowledge and reality violate other people's knowledges and sense of reality. I had a number of specific things they could do when reading and writing the other: deconstructing whiteness, deconstructing class privilege, economic and intellectual privilege, and being aware of how they'd be neocolonizing the other. By neocolonizing I mean taking over the other's intellectual ideas, artistic symbols, experiences, religious rituals, spirituality—how whites would consume and commodify these things by marketing them under their name as their knowledges, their ideas, their theories, their work.

Basically that's what I was trying to address. As I told you over the phone the other day I don't think I did a good job. People go to these conferences and expect a lot. They expect to be shaken, they expect to be stimulated, they expect to be wowed. A lot of times I can come through but at that conference I felt some kind of un-at-easeness. I couldn't seem to get it together. I think people felt the talk was OK, but I know when I mess up.

DB: Can you explain that feeling of being ill at ease? Did it have something to do with the conference participants or issues and the way they were or weren't brought up or dealt with? Or did it have to do with the particular audience at that speech?

GEA: I'm comfortable with a lot of audiences. I'm comfortable with males, with bisexuals and transsexuals, with white people, but I also experience some discomfort with all groups. When I'm in South Texas with my familia I feel an at-homeness with them, but I also feel like I'm so different from them now. And I always felt very different from them. So I'm very familiar with occupying this kind of borderland space. My life is usually in those kinds of in-between places. And I also feel very much at ease with high theory.

I started writing my reactions to this conference as part of an essay I'm working on called "Doing Gigs." I don't know what was missing. An aspect missing for me was a connection with the spiritual and the psychological, the emotional and the body. The dialogue and presentations were mostly in the sky, in the head. I also missed a community of women, even though the Latinas (Carmen—you and Rusty and the Latinas from your organization at the center) were very receptive and warm to me. I'm used to having more of an emotional connection with people.

This conference was a good conference and it succeeded in doing what it set out to do: To showcase the cutting edge of theory. A lot of the presentations were really exciting, the events worth going to. I was happy to be part of it. But something was missing. Or maybe it was just me. Have the two of you have talked about the conference? Does what I'm saying resonate?

CA: I talked to a friend of mine in Chicago and asked her how she liked it, and she said what was missing were class issues. The conference was too intellectualized for her. She wanted more on class issues and what the community was doing—the community of women, the community of lesbians in Iowa City, things like that. More of the grassroots efforts.

GEA: Papusa Molina's presence there was very important to me and so was Jacquie Alexander's and the Latinas' presence, but as soon as I'd get out of those little groups and go into the greater conference I'd feel this disconnection. I don't understand it because I generally feel comfortable with theoretical conferences, but this one was different. But you're right; I noticed the class issue wasn't addressed.

CA: And the issue of AIDS was put aside. It's not a priority anymore. The priority now is the transgender issue. Many years ago it was the bisexual issue, and so on. After talking to my friend I thought about it and wondered, "Yeah, where were the women from the community, the working class lesbians?" Also she said she felt a sense of who could be more outrageous in the way they dressed.

GEA: There was a lot of competition.

CA: Yeah, the competitiveness of who could be more gay, more queer. It was like a show. I had no problems being with men or anything but I felt that it was a performance. This conference was about who could outdo the other queer and vice versa.

GEA: Yes, that competitive edge in the papers, presentations, videos, and art. They want to make a name for themselves as cultural producers or be known as important presences in queer studies.

Does that answer your question about my uneasiness, Debbie?

DB: Yes. I think that's a great discussion of the conference.

The New Tribalism

DB: I'm also interested in something else you said in your speech that I'd like you to expand on. It's the anecdote about the "New Tribalism." How did you come to use this term to describe your work?

GEA: It goes back to the start of my participation in the anticolonial movement when I was young and a farmworker. As an undergrad, in the late '60s, I joined the farmworkers, participated in their demonstrations and marches, La Raza Unida Party conventions, and in MECHA. Before that I was with the Catholic Youth Organization and attended CYO meetings held at the Catholic Churches. I got my B.A. in '69 while still working in las labores. Right around that period I felt there was something missing in el movimiento Chicano, which was basically an important nationalistic movement for Chicanos, our civil rights movement. But it didn't address the oppression of women. Our struggle focused on securing the culture, securing the race, but to me it felt like the movement was trying to secure the *male* part of the culture, the male ideology. I was critical of this nationalistic movement but I didn't quite know why. As I came into feminism and began reading—when I became a lesbian, when I had a little more time to grow—I realized it wasn't enough to fight, to struggle for one's nationality; one also had to struggle for one's gender, for one's sexual preference, for one's class and for those of all people. These issues weren't addressed in any of the nationalist movements because they

214

struggled for ethnic survival and, because the male leaders felt threatened by these challenges women presented, they ignored them.

I began to think "Yes, I'm a Chicana but that's not all I am. Yes, I'm a woman but that's not all I am. Yes, I'm a dyke but that doesn't define all of me. Yes, I come from working class origins, but I'm no longer working class. Yes, I come from a mestizaje, but which parts of that mestizaje get privileged? Only the Spanish, not the Indian or black." I started to think in terms of mestiza consciousness. What happens to people like me who are in between all of these different categories? What does that do to one's concept of nationalism, of race, ethnicity, and even gender? I was trying to articulate and create a theory of a Borderlands existence.

I read an article by a white guy hostile to my writing and *Borderlands* in particular who wrote that I was romanticizing and idealizing the pre-Hispanic cultures. He called this the "New Tribalism." He may have been the first person to coin the phrase. My tribe has always been the Chicano Nation, but for me, unlike the majority of Mexican Americans, the indigenous lineage is a major part of being Chicana. Nationalism was a good thing to seek in the '60s, but in the '70s it was problematic and in the '80s and '90s it doesn't work. I had to, for myself, figure out some other term that would describe a more porous nationalism, opened up to other categories of identity.

Want to hear my rationale for my use of "New Tribalism"? I use the word nos/otras to illustrate how we're in each other's worlds, how we're each affected by the other, and how we're all dependent on the other. Existing language is based on the old concepts; we need a language to speak about the new situations, the new realities. There's no such thing as pure categories anymore. My concepts of nos/otras and the New Tribalism are about disrupting categories. Categories contain, imprison, limit, and keep us from growing. We have to disrupt those categories and invent new ones. The new ones will only be good for a few years and then somebody else will come along and say, "These categories don't work, you didn't take into account this other part of reality." Someone will come up with their own concepts. To me these categories are very much in transition. They're impermanent, fluid, not fixed. That's how I look at identity and race and gender and sexual orientation. It's not something that's forever and ever true.

Look at what "Mexican-American" means, what "Chicano," "mestizo," and "mestizaje" mean. The definitions change from decade to decade, from generation to generation. We constantly have to redefine and say, "This is what I mean when I say 'Afro-American.'

This is what I mean when I say 'Aztlán.'" The identities and histories people have are not the same as those of our mothers or grandmothers. We're exposed to more in the world now. We're living in overlapping intercultural, multicultural societies. So how my mother sees reality and how I see reality are different because the age I'm living in is the age of the Internet and of instant live video replay of news events, information deemed worthy by corporations like CNN, NBC, and CBS. These corporations affect me, by providing certain knowledges and information and withholding others. The status quo determines who has access to information and who does not. The electronic age is a greater part of my reality that it is of my mom's. See what I'm talking about?

Knowledge, Conocimientos, and Power

GEA: Another thrust of my writing is to look at who constructs knowledges, realities, and information and how they control people's identities through that construction. What's the relationship between knowledge and power, between conocimientos and power? How do they create subjectivities? Not only in people like us but in institutions like universities, public schools, the media. I'm constantly worried about how these knowledges get deployed and impact on people's everyday reality, on people's bodies in a way that other generations didn't have to be concerned about. What was of concern to them was the patrón— was he going to fire them or not pay them? My patrones now are the cyberspace corporations that are like the new elite, the new power mongers. It's no longer specific people. Am I making any sense?

CA: Yeah you are.

DB: Yeah, I think there might be a connection between past generations and the current generation as far as technology if we think of farmworkers being sprayed by pesticides. It seems to me that a similar kind of violence occurs. Then it was more physical and now it's maybe more psychic and emotional.

GEA: Right. It's a new colonization of people's psyches, minds, and emotions rather than a takeover of their homes or their lands like in colonialism.

216

Fighting/Theorizing Racism

CA: I've been thinking about the issue of racism lately. I've been working on a piece of poetry where I state that white women theorize about racism while women of color fight against it. I wonder if you have the same feelings sometimes?

GEA: Yeah, but I think that in theorizing about racism white women are johnny-come-latelies because in order to survive we had to deconstruct their racism. We started writing about our reactions and our experiences and we told the white people: "This is your problem, you need to take it up. You need to become antiracist. You need to do this work." So now they're theorizing but in general they haven't gotten to the level of hands-on dismantling it. They're just thinking and writing about it. There are some actively involved progressive whites doing coalition and alliance work. But I think you're right. We live it and they think and write about it.

One of the books I recommend is Ruth Frankenberg's *The Social Construction of Whiteness: White Women, Race Matters.* Other people are also doing this kind of work. But I think that's where we need to go. It's been my belief in the last fifteen years, or right after *Bridge* came out in '81, that we need to work on the internalized domination, racism, and prejudice we have among ourselves. There are internal affairs that we need to be dealing with: issues like facility with the language, crossing class lines, color—who's darker, who's lighter—the internal symptoms between straight women of color and queer women of color. I wrote about that a long time ago, around '87. I reprinted the essay, "En rapport, In Opposition: Cobrando cuentas a las nuestras," in *Haciendo Caras.* Instead of putting a lot of energy into second-guessing white people, we should put our energy into making alliances and coalitions with our own people and then with white people. Take care of some of the internal business first.

With *This Bridge* we were in direct dialogue with white women and I didn't see much change for many years. All that energy was going out, out, out. The dominant culture—Euro-American women—were sucking all that we had to say, all our experiences, all our writings, symbols, rituals, and we were being drained. I wanted to see an exchange between me and you, and me and Debbie, and the people working together in our community so that energy wouldn't be given to the oppressor.

Yes I have to understand racism because I have to survive it. But I also have to look at my own psychology as an oppressed woman, take that psychology of oppression and add the liberation and the empowerment to it. So that it's not just dwelling on how we're fucked by the dominant culture. It's about how we can turn these things around in a way that will make us feel stronger, more self-confident, and give us more self-esteem. This is why I keep going back to the cultural terms such as conocimiento and the goddesses like Coyolxauhqui, the moon goddess, Coatlicue, and others. That gives me a sense of being a person who's not just oppressed, not just a victim, but a person with pride in my culture—not in all of my culture but in some of it. I can take these symbols and myths that have been defined by the patriarchy and Mexican culture, see where these figures have been misinterpreted, and connect what's going on in my day-to-day life with what went on during the time periods when those figures were worshiped. There's a correlation between how women were oppressed back then and how they're oppressed now.

Coalition Work: Bridge, Drawbridge, Sandbar, Island

DB: You've touched on a number of things that I'd like you to expand on. You've just listed some of the risks and problems of coalition work. At the conference during your workshop on alliance building you mentioned a model you've developed for coalition work that addresses the issues of protecting yourself as well as going out on the limb. Can you explain the bridge, drawbridge, sandbar, and island model?

GEA: For some people, crossing from one world to another—from one culture to another, from one physical location to another—is very natural. They're very mobile in terms of feeling agile, able to migrate. Sometimes it takes work to make this crossing comfortable. You have to get used to moving around, get used to switching from one world to another. Very few people I know are predominantly bridge people or activists. It's a hard place to be, a hard identity to take up because there are very few boundaries, very few borders, and you're inundated all the time with the white culture or with other cultures. Being a bridge was a role that chose me or that I chose. If you're a teacher, an activist, or an artist, the bridge is a natural.

But there are people who prefer to do that bridge work only temporarily and I call those the "drawbridges." Then there are people who don't want to work with people different from themselves and those are the "islands." The "sandbar" comes in as a different kind of bridge, a more selective bridge. For me the bridge metaphor translated into Chicanos who live in the borderlands between different cultures—especially between the Spanish and the English, the Mexican and the American. With the Chicana, this is the kind of space we occupy just because we're in between the Mexicans in Mexico and the norteamericanos in the U.S. We're a kind of bridge people.

CA: The person you described as living on the islands: Isn't that perhaps the person who has been the drawbridge and retreats to being the island because of the frustration and the hurt of not getting positive feedback?

GEA: Exactly. For drawbridge people the intervals between being in retreat or with one's own group and then making the connections with the other group are shorter intervals, whereas the island people will go and live like this for twenty years. It's a matter of degree. I guess the drawbridge is like half of the bridge and half of the island. I wrote that essay quite a while ago, in '88 I think; I started a sequel that will be one of the chapters in this book I'm working on.

Revisionist Mythmaking

DB: I've noticed that many Chicana writers use Amerindian goddess images and symbols in their works. In *Borderlands* you used Coatlicue to a large extent. Can you talk about the significance of the goddesses in Chicana literature and specifically about the significance of Coatlicue in your Borderlands conception?

GEA: Myths and fictions create reality, and these myths and fictions are used against women and against certain races to control, regulate, and manipulate us. I'm rewriting the myths, using the myths back against the oppressors. An example of how a myth has created reality is the stereotype that Mexicans are dumb. For decades people have said that Mexicans are dumb and after a while it becomes part of the cultural perspective itself. There was the myth and the fiction that blacks were less intelligent than whites and therefore should not be given education, not be sent to school.

There are certain myths—the stories of Coatlicue, la Llorona, la Chingada, la Virgen de Guadalupe, and Coyolxauhqui, the moon goddess—that I associate with women. I want to take these figures and rewrite their stories. The figures we're given have been written from the male patriarchal perspective. Right away these figures are divided.

For example the Virgin of Guadalupe's body and sexuality were taken away from her. In the case of la Llorona the culture projects all its negative fears about women onto her, making la Llorona the bad mother who kills her children. Coyolxauhqui, the daughter of Coatlicue, who had four hundred brothers, was such a threat to Huitzilopochtli, one of the brothers, that he decapitated her, cut her up in pieces, and buried the pieces of her body in different places. To me that's a symbol not only of violence and hatred against women but also of how we're split body and mind, spirit and soul. We're separated.

I think the reason this image is so important to me is that when you take a person and divide her up, you disempower her. She's no longer a threat. My whole struggle in writing, in this anticolonial struggle, has been to put us back together again. To connect up the body with the soul and the mind with the spirit. That's why for me there's such a link between the text and the body, between textuality and sexuality, between the body and the spirit.

The dominant patriarchal culture betrayed these female figures. This is what I meant in *Borderlands* when I wrote, "not me sold out my people, but they me." First of all the indigenous males sold out their goddesses by driving them underground, by making them bad, by making them insignificant. The contemporary Chicano and Mexican culture has done the same thing by making one woman, la Chingada, responsible for the loss of the indigenous tribes to the Spanish conquerors.

Another level for me is that Mexico was forced to sell half its territory to the U.S. My people just happened to be on this side of the border and so Mexico was forced to sell me out. But now a lot of Mexicans look at Chicanas as agringadas, that we're not really Mexicans because we've gone over to the gringos. And the U.S. has sold us out because instead of honoring its treaty for us to keep our land, our language, they stole our lands and they stole our language by prohibiting Spanish. So there are all these layers of being sold out.

In general, men have sold women out by undermining them, by not being loyal to them, by battering and raping them, by presenting the belief that women are inferior. In the Chicano culture we grow up feeling it's a given that guys have all the power and privileges, that guys are more honest than women, that men aren't as competitive as women, that men don't gossip, and that men are more intelligent than women. A lot of straight Chicanas are now dealing with this betrayal. We dykes are past that. We've already recognized that we've been oppressed by men.

What's got to happen now is not concentrating so much on that kind of victimhood but concentrating on how we're liberating ourselves, how we're emancipating ourselves, and how we're empowering ourselves as Chicanas. We do this not only by going back and rewriting the myths but also by creating a new culture, by saying, "From now on, when a little girl is born into the Chicano culture she's going to have the choice—to run and climb trees, to dress in blue, to go to college. She has as much right as the little guy." We're trying to change the culture. We're rewriting the culture.

For me rewriting culture was speaking about what was forbidden, what was hidden. It was sort of to say, "Hey, these are fictions! You say women are inferior to men. That's a fiction. That's a myth." The stuff around sexuality is very hidden in all cultures. In my culture—our culture, Carmen's and mine—there's a different tactic to hiding sexuality: it's by not allowing women to use certain words or by not having certain words for sexual acts or sexual body parts. We grew up without knowing what these words were; the only words we knew were the ones derogatory about sexuality. I don't know what words you grew up hearing, Carmen, but I didn't hear any of the pretty ones.

CA: No, I didn't hear any of them in Spanish. They were mostly in English—ugly words created by men to describe my body. I knew that my breasts were called "breasts"—not "tits" or "boobs" or ugly words that I heard white guys talk about and later heard my brothers using.

GEA: A lot of our writing exposes what's been hidden from us in terms of our sexuality and our bodies and exposes how women are conditioned and controlled. Making a connection between all these oppressions and figures like la Llorona helps me to formulate theories about where the oppressions connect and where I can create empowering ways—whether physical, emotional, derived from activism or from writing. So the figures are a shorthand for me.

Essentializing, Universalizing, and the Autobiographical

DB: I'd like you to address the issues of essentializing and primitivism that come up in relation to the use of Amerindian goddesses and ideas of Earth Mother and women as closely related to nature. I find these ideas alluring, interesting, and creative, but I also recognize the dangers in them.

GEA: Some women writers when using these figures may tend to essentialize, but from the beginning I've been aware of the dangers in attributing innate qualities to women—for example the idea that it's genetic for women to be nurturing. I don't believe those things. I think we're born with certain predispositions towards ways of being, but the environment also has a lot to do with it—our surroundings, our growing up, and the way ideologies control how we act and think. In my own writing I'm not talking about all races. When you universalize something, when you essentialize something, you say, "All races are this way in all of these historical periods." What I'm saying is that "In this particular community, in this particular race, in this particular time, these are the experiences I'm writing about."

When I say "I," usually I mean "I in a plural way." If you come from a Chicana/Latina identity, it's an identity that's in part collective and relational, so that the "I" doesn't stand by itself. Behind the "I" is the community, it's a plural kind of I. When I say "we" I don't mean a universalized we, I mean a singular we: People from this particular group—whether they're women of color, whether they're Chicanas—experiencing in this time, in the city or the country, these relationships with men or with the society. The "we" becomes singular and the "I" becomes plural.

I've been doing these kinds of talks on the "we" and the "I" since about '88. I have an essay that's part of a book I'm working on, *Lloronas, mujeres que lean y escriben: Producing Writing, Knowledge, Cultures, and Identities*. All the ideas I've been talking about come from this particular book. I've been working on it for six years and only three of the chapters have been published. A lot of it I've been living with and telling other people about. One of the things that happens with my work is that because I share it with everybody people use it and don't credit me.

CA: Right. They don't footnote you.

GEA: Other people have picked up on this "I" and "we" concept I've been talking about at conferences and are now taking credit for originating the ideas. In some cases people independent of each other come up with the same ideas—like a zeitgeist. But in a lot of cases they forget they got the ideas from me. In one way I'm flattered that they've taken these ideas and expanded on them, but in another sense there's an amnesia, a short memory loss about what came before. Who were the people that did the work in discourse? Who were the activists in gay and lesbian rights? It's sort of like we have memory loss and we don't historicize. This is the danger of essentializing and of making generalizations and reductions: people don't show a progression of ideas, a progression of theories, a progression of history, a progression of development.

CA: Going back to the "I" and the "we," I always have a disclaimer when I read one of my poems—that the "I" of my poetry was not necessarily me—because I see that I also represent other Latinas and Chicanas. So I understand what you mean.

GEA: This is what I'm talking about with the zeitgeist, that two people independent of each other come up with the same theory. It happens a lot.

CA: Someone asked me, "Why don't you write in the third person?" My response was "I've never been a third person. I've always been me, the first person, so I don't know what it's like to be a third person. I can't write from that experience." I think that person was trying to put me in the margins; I don't want to be put there any longer.

GEA: Carmen, you brought up an important point in that we do a lot of autobiographical writing, the "I." In my own autobiographical writing sometimes the things are so painful to write about that I have to dislocate myself from myself. So I'll say, "This is happening to Prietita," and I'll use the third person. Once I get over the trauma of reexperiencing this thing I'm writing about and putting it in words, the pain is lessened so then I can say, "This was me. Yes, this happened to me." I've written about being mugged, I've had several near deaths, and I can't get to them because when you're working on the personal it's very hard to dive into the writing. It's painful. You're reliving the pain. So one method I use is to give it to la Prieta/Prietita, an alter ego. I give her this autobiographical experience, I write it out and then later I can change it to the "I" if I want to.

A lot of the stuff I write stays in the third person because for me—this may not be true for you—third person gives me more of a license to write without assuming. For example, when you write auto-biographically you assume a lot of things—that people know the landscape, the way the room was, what was on the wall. But if you pretend it's a fiction, you have to recreate all the different specificities of the room, of the culture, for the reader. I pretend it's a fiction because then I can write it up like a story.

Lived Experience/Representation

DB: You've been working on a book called *La Prieta*, originally written as a short story that discussed the racism and sexism in your own community. Is this book autobiographical, too?

GEA: It addresses the same issues my other works, including the anthologies, address. I'm trying to project or reflect what's happening in women's lives—both the oppressions, the traumas, and the positive. *La Prieta* reflects what's strong about us and gives readers different options as models: the strong woman, the sensitive woman, the intellectual, the activist, the spiritual person, la curandera. These are some of the figures in the culture, but they haven't been out there so that young readers—children, young adults—can see themselves reflected in all their body and spirit, in the wholeness of their being.

La Prieta is an elaboration of that short prose piece in *Bridge*. I didn't see "La Prieta" as a short story, though. I saw it as a memoir, an autobiographical prose piece. In *La Prieta* I'm problematizing lived reality and represented reality. The boundaries between what really happened and how I represent what's happening in a story are blurred. I'm saying that fiction is selective. Fiction is constructed and fiction is invented. So are some of these experiences. For example one of the stories, "Dolores en el cuerpo," is autobiographical about my relationship with my sister. Both the lived experiences I had with my sister and the way I'm portraying them in the story are fictional because the ways my sister experienced those events are very different from my experiences. I'm constructing mine from memory. Memory is not infallible. Memory has gaps. Memory has silences. Memory has wrong imprints. I'm reconstructing a memory, but in reconstructing it I'm being true to maybe the psychological experience but not the details: who said what, the exact words spoken, who was wearing what, who was thinking what. Because there's no way I can get into my sister's head to know what she's thinking, in writing about her I'm fictionalizing her. In looking back at my interactions with my sister I'm also fictionalizing them because, in the first place, I'm being selective about what I remember. In the second place, the memories I have may be imprinted wrong. I may have heard them wrong, I may have put the wrong slant on them.

A lived experience and a representation or a theorizing of it are made to seem like two separate things, and in this book I implicate them in each other. The boundaries are blurred. I'm looking at different realities.

For example, I'm looking at imaginal reality, reality of the imagination which is where the writer spends 90 percent of her time—thinking, imagining, visualizing, making up as she goes along. Then there's the reality of the other world, the theory world, the nahualismo, the world of the Nahuatl, the world of the shaman, which is a parallel universe to this one we're living in. Certain people—like the Native Americans, the hechicera, curandera, the shaman—have access to this other world. In my life that other world has bled into this one, impinged on this one, collided with this one.

A lot of what I write is about el mundo mas allá, the other world. Then there's what I call "electronic reality," films, books. You're reading a book and you get into the world of that book. If it's Toni Morrison, Isabel Allende, or whoever, if you're watching a video, *Jurassic Park* for example: during the time you're watching that video you're in the reality of the video. Then there's the reality of the dream world, the reality of the daydreams. In *La Prieta* I'm exploring all these worlds— the events of my life, the events of my fantasies, the events of my fiction. So it's all autobiography because whatever comes from me—from my experience—is autobiography. If I have a dream, that's my lived experience. If I fantasize some erotic fantasy, that's also mine. I problematize what's autobiography and what's lived experience and what's made up fiction, fantasy.

The social setting is South Texas, California, the different cities I've lived in, the landscapes I know. And then the goddesses, these cultural figures (I hate to call them "goddesses," I like to call them "cultural figures" because it works better for me to think of them as cultural figures). They're interwoven in this series. There are about twenty-five stories that hopefully will have enough connections between them so that the book can be read in two ways: as cuentos and as novela.

Making Soul: Writing the Coatlicue State, Nepantla, Llorona

DB: I'm interested in this process you're talking about, the Nahuatl world, which seems to be similar to what you described in *Borderlands* as "the Coatlicue state."

GEA: The Nahuatl world and the Coatlicue state are different stages of the same terrain. When you come out of the Coatlicue state you come out of nepantla, this birthing stage where you feel like you're reconfiguring your identity and don't know where you are. You used to be this person but now maybe you're different in some way. You're changing worlds and cultures and maybe classes, sexual preferences. So you go through this birthing of nepantla. When you're in the midst of the Coatlicue state—the cave, the dark—you're hibernating or hiding, you're gestating and giving birth to yourself. You're in a womb state. When you come out of that womb state you pass through the birth canal, the passageway I call nepantla.

DB: And *then* do you enter the Nahuatl world, or is this all part of the whole process?

GEA: The Nahuatl world, yes. It's being hit with that otherworldliness, with that alienness, with that strangeness. For example, if you're walking through a park and you see a snake crossing your path and something about that experience strikes you: that snake is so significant. It's trying to tell you something. It takes you out of your everyday world into a kind of nahualtismo. Or when you've had, say, a near-death experience or severe illness, you're not just in this reality but in the others too. For me the writing reproduces that kind of shock that comes when encountering a snake or being near death. This is why writing is very much a tearing apart of who I am, pulling me—who I was—into little pieces. It's as if something was being worked inside me. The writing is trying to put certain experiences into order, but before it can put them into order it has to take me apart. This is why part of writing the personal is so agonizing for me, so painful. Because I feel like I'm being dismembered. It's like Coyolxauhqui being dismembered.

This process or struggle, where a piece of experience is worked on, is connected to the soul, connected to making soul. It's where the spiritual, psychic component of writing comes in for me, in the creative act. You have to destroy, tear down, in order to put together and rebuild. That's why writing has saved our lives, because it makes sense out of this chaos. But the process is painful. I think other writers might have an easier time. In general most women-of-color writers have a really hard time of it. It's like looking inside at your innards and pulling them out one by one. Does that resonate with you, Carmen?

CA: Yeah, the whole thing of writing being very painful. I have to go into seclusion to find a safe space to write. I've never been able to write at my parents' home. I've gone through the process of getting the paper inside the typewriter and all that and I can't write because it's not my house, it's my parents' home. In Iowa City I've chosen to go into seclusion to be able to write because I've found a safe space here. I don't have the distractions I had in Chicago—meaning the Latino community, which I miss a lot—but at the same time I'm doing what I always wanted to do which is to write.

GEA: I have to leave home in order to write. I'm going home on Tuesday for fourteen days; I may be able to do some reading and revising but I won't get to the writing because it goes against everything my family believes in. I'm not supposed to be telling these secrets. In exposing my family and my culture I'm betraying it and them.

CA: And also you aren't being with the family because you want to be secluded in order to write and you're supposed to be with the family having fun or just being there. You're not partaking in family activities. I was always called rude because I'd go upstairs to my room and just start reading because I found everything so boring.

DB: I can relate to that.

GEA: I was called selfish. I was reading and writing, I wasn't doing housework, I wasn't helping, I wasn't socializing. I was selfish.

CA: Yes, egoista. Especially during the Christmas holidays at home it's always tamales. To this day, I don't know how to make tamales. All I remember was a group of women making tamales and me saying, "No. I'm never going to do that because I'm never going to have a husband to do that for."

GEA: I'll make you some tamales, Carmen. [Laughter]

CA: I always found myself buying books and reading.

GEA: It gave us access to the world outside from our very limited cultural and class world.

DB: Yeah, it's an escape.

GEA: But you know writing is a very solitary activity.

CA: Yeah, you're there with your computer, typewriter, or journal.

GEA: But when I moved away I started going to coffeehouses as a grad student. Now I can write in coffeehouses and the place kind of insulates me. I have these comadres in writing and we have these dates to go to a coffeehouse to write. Here in Santa Cruz there are several dyke-owned coffeehouses and bookstores. I also have dates with my writing

227

comadres to walk and talk about the writing projects. But otherwise it's very solitary; I can only do some stages of the writing in coffeehouses. For other stages I need complete solitude, no interruptions. I turn off the phone. And if you're in an intimate relationship, there's the lover, the novia. A lot of times in my life they've felt excluded or secondary to the writing and that's always been a problem. They want to spend more time with me, they want me to spend more time with them when I know that I have to do this work, I have these deadlines. But they feel that's time taken away from them.

CA: I know. The process of writing is a solitary act. It's almost like taking a shower or a bath: You do that only by yourself and it's a very intimate act. It's almost like masturbation.

GEA: Yes, it's very intimate and very pleasurable, and at the same time it's a pleasure that hurts.

CA: People ask me, "Can you write when Rusty is in the house?" I say, "No because I know she's there. I have to be by myself." Even though we have such a big house, I can hear her footsteps.

GEA: The presence impinges. In order to open up that world of writing you have to secure your walls, your boundaries. You have to insulate yourself so that you can allow yourself to expand and be exposed in the writing. It's sort of like getting in the bathroom to take your clothes off. You need to have the door shut to prevent all the strangers from looking in. For me, when that process includes speaking about the writing and speaking about my theories, it's sort of like going on stage without any clothes on. I think sometimes that's what puts me off and I don't do such a good job. Speaking and writing are very similar. When I'm speaking it's kind of like I'm writing in process, orally, so that I have to expose myself. When the audience is too large (like the audience in Iowa City at the queer conference was very large), or if it feels like there's a lot of potential misunderstanding or hostility it's like you're in your bathtub taking a bath and there's an auditorium of people staring at you.

DB: This seems to me to be a lot about silence and utterance which you talked about in relation to la Llorona and your current writing project.

GEA: Yes. In fact she appears in three different projects. First, I have a children's bilingual story, the second in the *Prietita* series; it's called

Prietita Encounters La Llorona. Instead of presenting the traditional Llorona story I'm rewriting her in a different light. Second, in *La Prieta,* the novela/cuentos collection, a lot of the stories use la Llorona. For example in "She Ate Horses" Llorona appears as a woman with a horse's head. And third, in *Lloronas, mujeres que lean y escriben* (the theoretical book that's a sequel to *Borderlands)* I use the cultural figure of the serpent woman, la Llorona, through all the chapters, through all the theoretical writing.

Llorona was the first cultural figure I was introduced to at the age of two or three years old. My grandmothers told me stories about her. She was a bogeyman. She was the horrific, the terror, the woman who killed her children, who misplaced her children. She was used to scare us into not going out of the house at night, and especially to scare the little girls into being good little girls. If you were a bad little girl la Llorona was going to come and get you. To me she was the central figure in Mexican mythology which empowered me to yell out, to scream out, to speak out, to break out of silence. To me she's very important.

Impact on Readers

DB: How do you view the impact of your books on different audiences—feminist and lesbian studies, the academic audience, and the community as another audience?

GEA: With some of the books I've attempted to present a dismantling of certain ideologies—of racial ideologies, of Euro-American culture that wants to determine what's real, what counts, what's fictitious, what's subversive, what's inferior. The dominant culture has created its version of reality and my work counters that version with another version—the version of coming from this place of in-betweenness, nepantla, the Borderlands. There's another way of looking at reality. There are other ways of writing. There are other ways of thinking. There are other sexualities. Other philosophies. At the same time the Borderlands—the nepantla, the in-betweenness, the mestizaje—borrows from the white dominant culture because in the United States this is the world we live in: English is the dominant language and whites are the dominant culture, although not for much longer. And so my version of reality, my ideology, has vestiges of the Euro-American ideology.

In these works I'm trying to present another way the senses can perceive reality. This belief that you can perceive reality in other ways is what has impacted the feminist community, the lesbian community, and the communities of color. These communities which have been marginalized—relegated to the sidelines, displaced, oppressed—can see themselves reflected in my books. They see the dykes, the Chicanas, the campesinas, the battered mothers, the intellectuals, the activists. These works are like tiny pieces of a mirror in which they see an aspect of themselves. Previously, they and we and I would read texts, see movies, and watch television shows but we wouldn't see ourselves in them, at all.

A lot of what passes for ethnic writing or ethnic art or ethnic thinking is actually regurgitated white stuff. What writers call ethnic is actually Eurocentric. What they call Mexican is really a whitewashed agringada kind of concept. They think they're divorced from the Western ideology, but we can never be divorced from it. We're contaminated with it because we live in this country—in these United States—which is Eurocentric. It's a danger for some of us to think that we can one-up them. Ellos—los gringos, the Euro-Americans—read the ethnic, the Chicana, mexicana, and it's not that simple. I have to be careful in my writing that I acknowledge that the white community, the white world, the white ideology is also part of my world. I write in English as well as in Spanish. This whole interview has been conducted mostly in English, but you see how hard it is for me to separate out. It's impossible. People say they have, when they haven't.

DB: There's a lot of debate about whether academic writing, creative writing, can change the material circumstances of oppressed groups. Have you published only through academic circles? Do you feel some of your works have reached the community and if so what impact have those works had on the Chicano/Chicana community?

GEA: Well, the Chicano community would not publish me and has been the last to read me. In fact the people now reading me are mostly young Latinas and Latinos working on their B.A.'s. The people who first started reading me were not academics. When *This Bridge* came out a lot of people in the activist community, in the grassroots community, in the dyke community read it. Then it got going with the academic community. I've always felt very comfortable with my intellectual class as a reader and a writer; that's not the identity that gives me problems. It's the class identity that is critical of the intellectual, artistic identity. I feel like I do write for academics, I do write for intellectuals, and that there's a difference between intellectuals and academics. You can be an intellectual academic and you can be an intellectual nonacademic. I think the artists—writers, visual artists, performing artists, video artists—fall somewhere between the academy and the community and many of us depend on the community to show our work, to give us grants, to allow us to teach.

I'm fortunate that the academic community and the intellectual community are reading me because a lot of the changes in the Chicano and the Latino cultures result from having more access to knowledge. So for the first time these chicanitos and chicanitas are being exposed to the work of Chicanas and the work of Chicana dykes. They're seeing little pieces of their faces in the mirror I'm presenting in these texts. Hopefully these little pieces will be honest in terms of portraying what really has happened, the oppressions and the traumas. And hopefully they also will show how we could be stronger, how women really are strong people and we survive, how we need to be working towards self-economy and need to change the culture so that it accommodates not just the guys—who in some ways are just as oppressed as women because they're trained to be macho and trained to kill off the feeling, the emotional part of themselves—but also the Chicanas, who have been denied their bodies, a language, respectability, and integrity.

The impact has been more of a dissemination of information that enables people to be more culturally sensitive to other groups of people. It also makes them more aware of their own internalized workings, more aware of the world they live in. Hopefully they're better able to arm themselves against the oppressive parts of that world and celebrate those parts which empower them.

"Doing Gigs"

DB: You mentioned earlier that you're working on a new project called "Doing Gigs: Speaking for a Living." Let's end this interview by having you briefly discuss this project.

GEA: Conferences are a very particular site. First of all they usually take place in a university. A university is a private space that's been made public so that it offers a kind of safety and containment to draw in students. It will say, "OK you students, you teachers, you conference-goers: come into this space and be safe and be secure and feel at home." In reality, that space is only secure and safe and comfortable for people complicit in the system. But if you're a resister, a challenger, if you're an activist it's a very uncomfortable place, an alienating place.

So here I go to these insular cities, these universities. I'm thrown in with several hundred or several thousand people and my goal is to make some connections, make some alliances, talk about where we can make connections and how as a group we can make changes in the culture, either through the writing or the speaking or the activism. For three or four days we're building a bond together, me and these other people with each other and amongst ourselves. At the end of the three or four days we're jerked out of this very intense emotional, intellectual space and when you're jerked out of it you realize that this little space was—or is to me—analogous to what happens out in the greater world. It's a little microcosm of the greater macrocosm. Whatever race issues, class issues, knowledge/power issues are talked about and dealt with and which we get emotional about, they're the same issues people in the cities, in the other parts of the world are also involved in.

I go to a conference with the hope of transferring and receiving certain knowledges, made aware of certain ideas, certain ways of working together. My part is in communicating, writing, and speaking about some of these issues and struggles. In that sense I feel like these conferences are minialliances, coalition-type activities, and that we're working together toward one common goal.

The Akron, Ohio, NWSA conference is the focus of this particular paper on gigs. That was the conference with the blow-up and split between women of color and white women in the National Women's Studies Association. Race was what broke the camel's back and exploded in our faces: the fact that we'd been working against racism for so many years and every conference we had to start all over again with Racism 101. There was no continuity from one conference to another. The white leaders of the NWSA weren't getting their shit together to fight against racism. That was kind of what happened later in L.A. with the violence surrounding the Rodney King verdict. I see these conferences as sites of microcosms and believe that some of what goes out in the greater world can be tested and articulated in these conferences.

Since 1981 I've been doing gigs. Some years I do twenty. This year I only did thirteen because I'm getting older and I'm diabetic. I can't do as much. I'm also seeing a lot of new activists, a lot of new writers out there, so I'm sitting back and letting the young try out their stuff. I'm at the stage in my life where I want to be more at home doing the writing than I want to be out there as a visible presence.

The issues of feminism come up at these conferences. Sometimes the conference, like the Kentucky Women Writers Conference, will be on writing. Sometimes it will be some kind of anthropological conference. I went to the Latina Symposium in Amherst in 1983 where the Latinas from Central America, Mexico, and South America attended in great numbers and the Chicanas attended in very small numbers, and we got pretty marginalized. We're not recognized as Latina writers. I've been to conferences in Mexico, Canada, Amsterdam where the issues have been different but they all happen to be feminist issues: dissemination of knowledge, power struggles, race, class, gender and sexual preference, environmental racism, or eco-feminism—they all get played out at these conferences.

So conferences are very rich for me because they give me a chance to bring my thoughts together on specific topics and try them out on the audience or try them out in a workshop. I also walk away saying, "Oh yeah, this is going on in Massachusetts, Florida, Seattle. . . ." I get a general idea of what's going on in this country because of traveling so much. I can chart where people are at in terms of, say, Proposition 187 which is actually about the national identity of the U.S., which is changing. People who see themselves as the "real Americans" are very scared of this change in identity because of the Latinos coming in or the Asians coming in or the blacks getting stronger.

I feel privileged to travel and do these gigs but it's also very tiring. I get home and it takes me a week to recover, catch up, and get over the shock of being jerked out of that insular city where I was making bonds with people for four days. The umbilical cord gets severed and I'm left as if I'm bleeding.

CA: Yeah, it's very draining and you have to take care of yourself.

DB: Speaking of which, this interview has gone on a long time and we don't want to drain your energy any further. Thank you very much.

GEA: Oh, I love doing interviews.

8

....

Writing

A Way of Life

An Interview with María Henríquez Betancor (1995)

....

ALK: In this interview and elsewhere in this volume and in your published works you take issue with the term "Hispanic," which you view as a "whitewashed" government-created label that erases the many differences among so-called "Hispanics." I used to agree with you, and I'd *always* avoid using the term "Hispanic." But now I wonder if, at times, it's not situationally useful. For instance many of the students where I used to teach—in Portales, New Mexico—identify as "Hispanic." When I first moved there I'd insist on referring to "Chicanos" and "Chicanas" and, if asked, would explain the assimilationist "white"-identified nature of the term "Hispanic." But they found this explanation insulting. So I'm no longer sure that simply rejecting the term "Hispanic" is always appropriate. What do you think?

GEA: I think I agree with you that if they want to go with that "Hispanic" label they should. But writers like me need to point out that we have far more indigenous blood in us than we do Spanish. I'm there to remind these Chicanos and these Mexicans of their Indian ancestry and the part of the globe they live in. The younger generation always ends up naming themselves, so it's up to them to name themselves. But that doesn't mean that I should stop stressing the indigenous. This need for an umbrella term was one of the reasons I wanted to emphasize "mestizo" instead of "people of color." But I don't think the term has taken off.

ALK: I think it has! Certainly among many academics.

GEA: When we started *This Bridge*, Cherríe and I had to decide on a label. We decided to use the term "women of color" to be in solidarity with colored people. We never thought it would take off the way it did. It wasn't so much that the term designating all people of color originated with us, but we put it forth. I don't know what other umbrella term to use.

ALK: I think "mestiza" is a really good term because, yes, it's an umbrella term, but the word itself means "many different mixes."

GEA: Yes, it can be applied to Canadians, to people from the Carribean, and so on.

"Writing: A Way of Life"
An Interview with María Henríques Betancor (1995)

Chicana Writers

MHB: Perhaps we could start by talking about the history of Chicana writers in the past twenty years. I'd like you to tell me tu visión of Chicano women's writing in this country.

GEA: When I decided to become a writer I had to give up the idea of doing visual art—not enough time to practice and be good in two art forms, to buy oil paints, brushes, and other art materials. At that time I looked around to see what other Chicanas were writing and I found very little. Since then Chicana feminist scholars have rediscovered earlier nineteenth-century and twentieth-century writers, but at that time the only writers I knew were John Rechy, a gay writer from El Paso who wrote *City of Night*, Verónica Cunningham, a Chicana lesbian poet, Corky González, and Estella Portillo. Later, in the eighties, I found Alma Villanueva's books of poetry, *Bloodroot* and *Mother May I*.

When I started writing I was influenced more by Spanish Euro-American and English literature. I read some of the classics, Dostovieski and Tolstoi. García Lorca was a great favorite of mine, also Cortázar, Faulkner, Poe, Hawthorne. I was really hungry for Chicana or mexicana writers. Later, in the eighties and nineties, I found Elena Poniatoska, Elena Carro, Cristina Peri Rossi, and Angeles Maestreta. By then I was already a writer and had gone through the initiation of practicing, studying, and learning writing on my own. Ahora si hay muchas escritoras Chicanas. I'm particularly impressed with Cherríe Moraga, Sandra Cisneros, and María Elena Viramontes. Have you read her latest novel, *Under the Feet of Jesus*?

MHB: No.

GEA: She has very good technique, I like the lyricism in her writing. I also found that I was very picky and critical of Chicana writers— more so than of black, Native, Asian-American, or white writers. I think it's that I want my gente to do good. Writers of theory I like are Chela Sandoval, Norma Alarcón, Emma Pérez, Antonia Castañeda.

I started doing *This Bridge Called My Back* in 1978, as a reaction to experiences I had in graduate school. Before I entered the Ph.D. program here at Santa Cruz I had almost completed one—all but the dissertation—in Austin. I wanted to write my dissertation on feminist studies and Chicano literature but was told that there was no such thing as Chicano literature or feminist studies. So in '77 I left Austin. I was really upset because I was finding that the experiences of people of color weren't out there in the world and those that were were discredited. That's why I decided to do *This Bridge*: it was a way of giving voice to other people who didn't have a voice. I worked on *This Bridge* for about a year and then asked Cherríe to help me. It came out in '81. Since then more women of color have started writing and publishing their creative and academic work.

MHB: In your eyes, how is feminist Chicana literature developing now?

GEA: It's very strong. In fact, there are now Chicanas enrolled at the University of California, Santa Cruz, doing their dissertations on identity, films, and popular culture—all with Chicanas as the focus. I see this interest at universities when I lecture and do keynoters at conferences. Everywhere I go Chicanas, other women of color, and white students are doing border studies or working on several themes that incorporate my work or the work of other Chicanas.

MHB: What do you think defines Chicana women's writing? Are there any common characteristics?

GEA: A lot of Chicanas use the personal as well as the collective in talking about literature, writing literature, and doing theory. That was one of the things I wanted to bring up in the interview. In your letter you said you were focusing on Chicanas' search for identity, but I wanted to tell you that for most of us now writing it's not really a search *for* identity because we haven't really lost an identity. Instead, we're figuring out how to arrange, componer, all these facets of identity: class and race and belonging to so many worlds—the Chicano world, the academic world, the white world, the world of the job, the intellectual-artistic world, being with blacks and Natives and Asian Americans who belong to those worlds as well as in popular culture.

So here we are in a Borderlands—a nepantla. Nepantla is a Nahuatl term meaning "el lugar entre medio," el lugar entre medio de todos los lugares, the space in-between. The work I'm doing in my dissertation, estoy componiendo los pedazos, los fragmentos, estoy rearranging them ... trying to make sense, trying to organize and make meaning out of all the pieces and come up with a different identity, labels, and terms for myself and for other Chicanas. There are some Chicanas, like those of the X Generation or younger, who may be searching for their identity because it's been so whitewashed and repressed by the dominant culture. It's particularly been whitewashed with the term "Hispanic" which I really hate! They identify as "Hispanic" and subsume particular nationalities like puerto-rican, salvadorean, nicaraghense, cubana under its umbrella. In many of my lectures I review the terms "mexicanos" and "mexicanas," terms my mother and grandmother called themselves. I describe our struggle as anticolonial because the dominant culture is still colonizing our minds by giving us all these identities that we didn't choose!

Younger people may be searching for their identity, but people like Emma Peréz and Norma Alarcón and me—the identities are already there. Sometimes they're hidden or whitewashed. You have to think them out and theorize them. Our work has that in common and the fact that we're border people, estamos en ese lugar entre medio, en nepantla. Chicana feminists deal with border studies and with linguistic code-switching, as well as cultural code-switching. We use cultural figures like la Virgen de Guadalupe, la Llorona, la Chingada, and indigenous Mexican myths to describe Chicana thought and experience.

Identity-in-Process: A "Geography of Selves"

MHB: How would you define identity—as a process, as a rearranging process perhaps?

GEA: I think identity is an arrangement or series of clusters, a kind of stacking or layering of selves, horizontal and vertical layers, the geography of selves made up of the different communities you inhabit. When I give my talks I use an overhead projector with a transparency of a little stick figure con un pie en un mundo y otro pie en otro mundo y todos estos mundos overlap: this is your race, your sexual orientation, here you're a Jew Chicana, here an academic, here an artist, there a blue-collar worker. Where these spaces overlap is nepantla, the Borderlands. Identity is a process-in-the-making. You're not born a Chicana, you become a Chicana because of the culture that's caught in you. Then as you go to school you learn about other cultures because you meet kids from other races. By the time you get to grad school you've become acquainted with all these worlds. So you shift, cross the border from one to the other, and that's what I talk about in *Borderlands*.

Let me draw you a picture of how identity changes. So aquí tienes a particular identity at this little train station which is maybe when you were five and lived in this particular community. At ten you were another person, you stopped at this other way station for awhile and your identity was pretty stable. Then you got on the train again and when you reached this station you're twenty and another station when thirty. Bueno, you're no longer the same person at thirty or twenty that you were at five or at ten. When the train is between stations you struggle and all is chaos: you don't know what you are, you're a different person, you're becoming a new person, a new identity. This in-between space is nepantla, the liminal stage. You're confused, you don't know who you are. Every time you settle in a particular place— either a state of mind or a physical location—you become comfortable and you look back to your past from the perspective of this location. So if I'm now a feminist I look back to my growing years and say, "I was really fucked up when I was twenty. My culture told me that women were not as good as men, I felt women were liars and gossips." But from this present perspective I can say, "No, we were *taught* those beliefs. Women in my life have always been there for me." I look at my mother's and grandmother's lives in a different way. In *Borderlands* I have a poem about my grandmother que se llama "Immaculate, Inviolate" where I look at her sexuality with my grandfather from my present point of view, that of a politicized Chicana feminist who happens to be a dyke.

Relational Identities

GEA: You're constantly reconfiguring your identity, and your past changes as your interpretation of yourself changes. For me, identity is a relational process. It doesn't depend only on me, it also depends on the people around me. Sometimes I call this "el árbol de la vida." Here's el árbol de la vida [while drawing] y tiene raíces y cada persona is her own árbol. Y estas raíces son la raza—the class you come from, the collective unconscious of your culture and aquí tienes a little body of water I call "el cenote." El cenote represents memories and experiences—the collective memory of the race, of the culture—and your personal history. For me el cenote is indigenous, is Mexican; in it you find the cultural myths and histories—pre-Columbian history as well as colonial history. The tree of your life is embedded in the world, y este mundo es el mundo de diferentes gentes. It's also the world of nature, the trees, and the animals. How do you relate to the environment, to white people, to other people of color, and to Chicanas? As a writer, my identity is especially relational to other writers. How do I relate to people like Cortázar, Faulkner, and Elena Poniatoska who have influenced me through their work?

Identity is not just a singular activity or entity. It's in relation to somebody else because you can't have a stand alone; there must be something you're bouncing off of. The whole tree of the person is embedded in the world of TV, popular culture, film, commercials, malls, education, the world of information, even computers and the Internet. When I try to identify and name myself it's always how I see myself as similar to or different from groups of people and the environment. Identity is not just what happens to me in my present lifetime but also involves my family history, my racial history, my collective history . . .

MHB: So, your previous and entire history goes into your identity.

GEA: Sí, y luego acá, las ramas del árbol y las hojas y la fruta are all the good works I do—whether teaching or writing. I don't consider inferior teaching or writing a good work.

MHB: What do you call inferior writing?

GEA: Inferior writing results from working only on the surface. It's risky to examine a lot of these experiences and feelings, to write about them in theoretical ways, to explore them in a poem or to fictionalize them in a story. It means getting into emotional states and facing truths about yourself when you would rather not. Surface writing means easy formulas and plots, information that everybody knows, repeating what others have said. Doing good art means going below and beyond the surface. The deeper you go, the more scared you become because you deal with politically incorrect emotions. Chicano presses rejected my work. Maybe they didn't want to hear about feminist or lesbian topics, they didn't want women to critique the Chicano culture. The deeper you dig with the poem or the story or the theory, the more uncomfortable you get. So doing art has a lot of anxieties with it and you always risk exposing yourself to other people. When *This Bridge* came out I sent a copy to my mom and my sister. My sister tore it up and threw in the trash can and wouldn't speak to me for three years; my mother didn't want me to bring my queer friends home. My brother didn't want me to be around his kids . . . It still hurts! It's risky when you write really deep, it's safer to explore the same old symbols and cliches.

It's better to find original images, words, or theories that you're passionate about. I explore borders and Borderlands, now everybody's doing it! It isn't that they don't live that kind of Borderlands life, but nobody highlighted it the way I did. Y ahora estoy con eso de nepantla. When I originate concepts I never know if people are going to attack me for them or whether they're going to say, "Oh yeah, that speaks to my life and I want to write about it." Some ideas ripen to bear fruit. Certain ideas already exist in the world so they are not really mine! The ideas in *Borderlands* and my pieces and vision in *This Bridge* are not really mine; I just happen to be the channel. Everything I read, all the movies I saw, all the people I encountered influenced me. I processed them through my mind and my vision—and that's the way a style becomes you—but the books and images are of the world! So when people attack me or critique my work I often don't take it personally. Some of it I do, but some of it is part of the zeitgeist and belongs to everyone. The Borderlands metaphor and concept are up in the air, anybody can work them.

María, you're doing your dissertation, you're probably going to deal with border issues, with the in-between spaces. You take el árbol tuyo acá,—your roots are in the Canary Islands and you have that African influence. Your collective history is very different from mine but you're a cultural mestiza—somebody who's lived or been influenced by other worlds through research and reading. You're getting something from my árbol about mestizaje and Borderlands. You have all these influences, everything you read from the time you were in first grade until now will be part of it. Identity is like a work of art: you take from all the influences and worlds you're inhabiting and . . . los compones, haces una composición with different stages. Your dissertation is going to be your fruit.

I'm writing an essay on nepantla which explains the different stages of acquiring an identity and the process of how one composes one's identity, as well as the different stages of the creative process, how one composes a work of art, and how one solves any kind of puzzle or problem in life. It's similar to the way the scientist also goes about making discoveries. There are analogies between how one compiles, arranges, formulates, and configurates one's identity and how one solves problems and how one creates a work . . . Todo eso! Everything and everyone is in relationship with everything else. Subjective life is relational as well. We all have many different selves or subpersonalities, little "I's": this self may be very good at running the house, taking care of the writing as a business, making a living from the writing, and figuring out expenses. This other self is very emotional and this other self is the public figure who goes out, does speeches and teaches. Whatever subpersonalities you have (and some are antagonistic to others)—they all make up el árbol, which is the total self, and it's embedded in this ground which is the world and nature. So it's all relational. Does this make any sense to you ?

MHB: Oh yes. It connects very much with what we were talking about concerning personal experience and the creation of literature. . . . You're talking about all these ramas of your árbol and all these different selves that really embody the tree . . .

GEA: Every few years you pull up the roots, get on the train, and move. Some of it changes pero las raíces como culture, race, class—some of that stays. For example, my roots are campesino, from a farmworking class. Later I became working class, and now I'm close to middle class. Though I've joined the ranks of an artistic intellectual class, I emerged from a farming and ranching community where people don't read and aren't intellectual. La Gloria que vive aquí en 1995 en Santa Cruz is different from the one who takes center stage when I visit South Texas, but you always pick up your roots and take them with you.

"Autohistorias, Autohisteorías"

GEA: One of the essays I'm writing focuses on what I call autohisteorías—the concept that Chicanas and women of color write not only about abstract ideas but also bring in their personal history as well as the history of their community. I call it "auto" for self-writing, and "historia" for history—as in collective, personal, cultural, and racial history—as well as for fiction, a story you make up. History is fiction because it's made up, usually made up by the people who rule.

La *Prieta* stories are part fiction and part autohistorias, and the *Lloronas* book is "autohisteorías" as I use my life to illustrate the theories. *La Prieta* consists of autobiography that's fictionalized, true stories I treat like fiction, parts of my life which are true but which I embellish with fiction.

MHB: To what extent do you think personal experience becomes a part of the collective experience?

GEA: It kind of has a boomerang effect. People pick up a book like *Amigos del otro lado*, my first children's book, and they'll say, "Oh, yeah, I used to know some illegal immigrants, some mojaditos like Joaquin and his mother," or "I had an encounter with la migra," or "I lived in a little town like that." You don't need to be Chicana; you can be from Chile and have that experience of the border, of being here illegally or going through the immigrant experience. Say you're Cuban, you come to this country, you've never been with Mexicans and suddenly you have to deal with "What's the difference?" We're all Latinas but there are differences. Or they'll pick up *Borderlands* and say, "Oh yeah, you're writing about me. I know this life. It's just that I never articulated it until you gave me the words." They take these ideas or metaphors and add to them, and begin writing their own poems, books, and dissertations.

MHB: So personal experience really gets into the collective through publishing?

GEA: Sí. Women of color and especially Latinas used to go to leaders of the movement to get a sense of who they were, of their people, their heritage. Now they go to the writers: they look at the writing and artwork about la Llorona, la Chingada, y la Virgen de Guadalupe— lo que sea—and identify with it. The writing and art become part of their cultural history which they didn't get directly from their culture or their parents. Maybe their parents never talked about la Malinche or la Llorona so they read my book about these cultural figures or view them in art and incorporated them into their lives by doing some of the rituals we do: burning a la Virgen de Guadalupe candle, creating a Day of the Dead altar. Aquí en Santa Cruz even the gringos celebrate el día de los muertos.

MHB: Y cómo así?

GEA: The gringos here may have lost their cultural heritage, or other

243

people's spirituality seems more exotic. Some appropriate in the wrong way, but others really appreciate it and want to make these rituals part of their lives. They'll do the Virgen de Guadalupe and then go to the ocean to Yemanja y avientan allí un watermelon—or other rituals for the orishas in the santería religion.

Many artists and writers introduce parts of Chicano culture to younger Chicanos. My personal experiences with la Virgen de Guadalupe and la Llorona become part of their collective experience.

MHB: And what about everyday things? For example, in *The House on Mango Street* Sandra Cisneros talks about the barrio, women, and things like how you do your hair or your nails, cook, clean house. I find the domestic world very interesting and at the same time very much part of Chicanas' writing, how they claim and validate the little things.

GEA: Yes, the little things . . . Well, ella se crió en Chicago, Illinois, not in the Southwest, and midwestern Chicanos have their own history. For me the symbol of the self has always been the house, so actually she's writing about herself and also about becoming a writer. The dominant culture in this country looks down on some of our eating habits, dress, speech, and so we try to validate them. That's what Cisneros does with the little day-to-day things. We're trying to say, "These are our lives. This is part of what some Chicanas do." We're trying to give meaning to the common activities by writing about them. Other people say, "Yeah, my family does that" or "I do that," and they feel good about themselves because there's a mirror reflecting them back. When I went to school all we had were white books about white characters like Tom, Dick, and Jane, never a dark kid, una Prieta. That's why I write for children, so they can have models. They see themselves in these books and it makes them feel good!

Your whole life as a Mexican you're dumb, you're dirty, you're a drunkard, you beat your wife and children, you can't speak correct Spanish, you can't speak correct English, you're not as intelligent as whites, you're physically ugly, you're short. ¡Todo! You yourself may not have had these experiences because you're a legitimate citizen and lived in a country where Spanish is your native tongue, whereas we grew up in a country that used to be Mexican territory, a Mexican state that was sold to the U.S. All of a sudden we Mexicans became Mexican Americans, became foreigners in our own country. What and who we were was not valued, was treated as inferior. From kindergarten through college we were bludgeoned with these views. Reading and writing books that show Chicanos in a positive way becomes part of de-colonizing, disindoctrinating ourselves from the oppressive messages we've been given.

MHB: When I read *Friends from the Other Side* I thought, "Who's her audience here? Is it a children's book?" You've answered that question already, but is it a book for Chicano children or is it for the Anglos as well, to let them know what's happening?

GEA: There are different levels. I wanted to reach the Chicano kid, the mexicano kid, the immigrant kids straddling these borders. But I also wanted to reach kids of color: blacks, Natives. And I wanted to reach their parents. This book is taught in college courses—can you believe that? It's taught in children's literature courses. Professors buy it for their kids or nietos or sobrinos or for themselves! So it's for both adults and children. It's also for whites, to educate them about Chicano culture. On the primary level it's for the Chicano kids because it's written in Chicano Spanish. If the others get it, fine, and if they don't, fine. I have to struggle against the standards and marketing strategies in children's book publishing. My publishers also have to struggle against these. When I submitted *Prietita and the Ghost Woman/Prietita y la Llorona* (the children's book coming out in February) the publishers wanted to make it comfortable for the white reader. It's in both languages, but I wanted to put "la curandera" in the English side as well because it doesn't translate and at first they objected but later accepted. They also didn't want a real scary Llorona. The Texas public schools have a different set of taboos than the other states so we had to try to get past all these restrictions and taboos.

Language Conflicts

MHB: I wanted to return to an earlier comment you made about the language conflict.

GEA: There's pressure on Chicanas and Chicanos from both sides: there's pressure from the Spanish-speaking community, especially the academic community to speak "correct" Castillian standard Spanish and not to assimilate. Then there's pressure from the Anglo society to do away with Spanish and just speak English because English is the law of the land. My use of both languages, my code-switching, is my way to resist being made into something else. I'm resisting both the Spanish-speaking people and the English-speaking white people because I want Chicanos to speak Chicano Spanish, not Castillian Spanish. We have our own language, it's evolving and it's healthy. A lot of the stories I'm writing use Spanglish, also known as Tex-Mex or caló, a pachuco dialect. This resistance is part of the anticolonial struggle against both the Spanish colonizers and the white colonizers.

I wasn't the first person to code-switch or incorporate Nahuatl, but I think I was one of the first to write theory como en *Borderlands*. Chicanas are using a language that's true to our experience, that's true to the places where we grew up—New Mexico, Arizona, Texas, the Midwest. We all have that in common. Even people like Cherríe Moraga who learned to speak Spanish later as adults are code-switching. Las mexicanas y las Chicanas que sus padres no les enseñaron el español, tuvieron que tomar cursos en los colegios, are now code-switching. To me it's a political as well as an aesthetic choice—code-switching to politicize people about a situation. It's a way of resisting this new colonization. Does that make sense to you?

MHB: Oh yes, absolutely. I read "Linguistic Terrorism" in *Borderlands*, where you say that many Chicanas speak English to each other because they feel more comfortable, it's like a natural language for them. And I thought, "But why? They've got their own language; they can switch into one language or another. They shouldn't be ashamed of it." For us, as Canarians, we get messages from many people in the mainland that our Spanish is not the proper Spanish. . . . We're told that our language is not good enough.

GEA: ¿También ustedes?

MHB: We speak Spanish but we just have a different accent and some words which are not common. You reach a point when you say, "No yo hablo bien, y donde yo vivo no existe este sonido o no se pronuncia la c." So I think in a way I know what you mean. I've been getting that message all my life every time I went to Madrid or to other places in Spain, outside the islands.

GEA: ¡Qué feo!

MHB: Now I see lots of words we use in the Canary Islands in books by Chicana writers. It's amazing, the connections from so far away.

"On the Edge, Between Worlds"

MHB: In *Borderlands* you state that "being a writer feels very much like being a Chicana, or being queer—a lot of squirming, coming up against all sorts of walls. Or its opposite: nothing defined or definite, a boundless, floating state of limbo." Could you talk a bit about this statement?

GEA: The writing process creates anxieties. When you sit down to write your dissertation, you know, le sacas la vuelta. It's hard to talk about stuff! That's the squirming you come up against. Being a Chicana or being queer is also that same feeling of anxiety: You're in this limbo state of nepantla porque you're this but you're that, estás en medio de todos estos identity states of minds or states of consciousness; you're caught in a liminal stage, in nepantla. This country doesn't value its writers or artists, so if you're a writer or an artist already eres algo extraño en este mundo. If you're an artist it's not like going to the office and working, it's not like working for a corporation or any of these jobs that people do. It's more than just a job, it's more than a vocation. It's a way of life!

   OK, this society doesn't value you if you're a person of color, a Chicana. They certainly don't value you if you're queer of any color, so there are parallels between being an artist, being of color, being queer—there are similarities. You always feel on the edge, between worlds: not all of you fits into this world, only a little bit, but you don't fit entirely into that other world either. Your language doesn't fit into English or Castillian Spanish. An oyster makes a pearl out of sand by rubbing, rubbing, rubbing, rubbing. You're the little pearl and you're being irritated on all the sides of your identity.

The Ethnic Test: Who's the Real Chicana?

MHB: Do you think there's discrimination among Chicanas, against each other?

GEA: Oh yes! Tengo un ensayo en *Haciendo Caras* que se llama "En rapport, In Opposition: Cobrando cuentas a las nuestras," where I talk about how Chicanas and Latinas critique each other, saying, "Esta no sabe español." We look down on her: "She's whitewashed, agringada." Or "This one looks middle class, she looks down on the Chicanos who come from a campesino or working class." We have what I call "the ethnic test": Who's the most Chicana? Who's the best Chicana? Quien es la más mexicana? People actually come up to me and say, "You're a real Chicana because you never lost your Spanish, whereas we did." And I say, "No! You're just as real a Chicana as I am but we've had different experiences!" They judge each other about who's the most real.

MHB: What's real, Gloria?

GEA: It all is! Your experience is real: coming from your island and not being part of the mainland. Me as a seventh-generation tejana: when they made the border fence they split up Tamaulipas, a state in Mexico that's now Texas, and they split up los Anzalduás. It's like, "What side of the fence do I belong to?" I am from Texas, formerly part of Spain and part of Mexico, I'm three-quarters Indian but belong to a culture that has negated its indigenous part. Which is the real Chicana? They *all* are. The one who speaks Spanish but doesn't know English, the one who knows English but doesn't speak Spanish, the one who lives in Chicago and not the Southwest, or the one who lives in New York and not California: they're all real. It's just that the experiences and the way we figure our identity and the names we call ourselves are different. So I keep telling these chicanitas, "No, I'm not more real than you!" Just because I write these books they think I'm the more real Chicana. . . . No!

Writing/Reading as Survival and Healing

MHB: Is writing a need for you? Es una necesidad?

GEA: Yes. It's the only way I could survive emotionally and intellectually in this society because this society can destroy your concept of yourself as a woman, as a Chicana. I survived all the racism and oppression by processing it through the writing. It's a way of healing. I put all the positive and negative feelings, emotions, and experiences into the writing, and I try to make sense of them. Reading and writing are almost the same activity for me. When reading you create meaning out of what you're reading, you put your personal experience into it. Writing is the reverse: you're putting your personal experience in the writing and then when you read it for editing you keep revising it and moving it around. Writing is partly cathartic. In talking about certain experiences I have to go back into the wound, and it hurts! But every time I do it, it hurts less; the wound starts to heal because I've exposed it. So for me writing is a way of making sense of my realities. It's also a way of healing my wounds and helping others heal theirs. There are times when I was really sick with the diabetes que no podía beber and I was suffering from mental distraction and a foggy state of mind: estoy escribiendo sobre un concepto y luego se me olvida lo que estoy escribiendo, or I'll be driving and when I come home I forget to put the car on park. Having a hypo (low blood sugar) is like being drunk, you can't function.

The blood sugar in my body and brain descompuso todo! I'd get dizzy and hear ringing in my ears, I'd be deaf and lose the equilibrium, me caía. Not enough oxygen and blood were getting to the capillaries around my eyeballs so I was getting these flashes of light and everything would go blank. I couldn't watch TV, read a book, or work on my computer. So I thought, "God, my whole life is writing and reading, es todo lo que hago!" Well, I suppose I could probably do other things with my life, but 90 percent of the time I'm either reading or writing or fantasizing or watching a movie or listening to music or thinking. The other 10 percent I don't know where I am, maybe I'm asleep. But even when you're asleep you're dreaming and working with images. I thought I was going to die. The doctor was amazed that I wasn't dead because my blood sugar was so high! I went through periods of depression y no podía hacer nada! I couldn't stay with a task because my eyes were bothering me. Dealing with my illness took all my energy.

9

Toward a Mestiza Rhetoric

Gloria Anzaldúa on Composition, Postcoloniality, and the Spiritual

An Interview with Andrea Lunsford (1996)

(1998–1999)

ALK: In this interview you equate "the writer part" of yourself with "the spiritual part." Could you say more about the interconnections between writing and spirituality?

GEA: It's related to my idea of the artist as shaman. While we can't go back thirty thousand years to the original forms of shamanism, artists practice a type of shamanism through the imagination. You fly to these distant worlds in your imagination—in what you paint, sculpt, dance, or write. I translate shamanistic tasks that were practical twenty thousand, ten thousand, or five hundred years ago into artistic tasks or techniques, into tasks accomplished through art: writers switch identities when we concentrate on different characters. Often our stories, ideas, and art enact psychological healing, healing that's much like that performed by traditional shamans.

The "spiritual" part of myself as a writer is also concerned with traveling to other realities, with change, with transformation of consciousness, with exploring reality, with other possibilities and experiences, and with recreating other experiences. You do these tasks through the imagination, through your creative self, creative unconscious—which to me ties in with spirituality and with the spirit. That's why I wanted to find a word for spirituality that would incorporate the imaginal, the imagination. When you're praying, meditating, or having an ecstatic trance, it's an inner experience; the imagination facilitates it. So if you're an artist and you're working with the imagination, that to me has to be spiritual. For me, writing is a spiritual activity just as it's a political activity and a bodily act. It's got all these dimensions to it, all these aspects.

"Toward a Mestiza Rhetoric:
Gloria Anzaldúa on Composition, Postcoloniality, and the Spiritual"
An Interview with Andrea Lunsford (1996)

Early Memories of Writing

AL: What are some of your very early memories of writing? I'm using "writing" very broadly here to include drawing, marking, any kind of language use that seems like writing.

GEA: I attribute my writing to my grandmothers who used to tell stories. I copied them until I started telling my own, but I think it was my sister who forced me to find an outlet to communicate my feelings of hurt and confusion. My whole family is very verbal. We'd talk and fight and quarrel a lot, in some ways like your average family in the U.S.: abusive verbally, or not aware of the vulnerabilities a child might have. I was criticized for being too curious, for reading, for being selfish because I was reading, and I wanted to fight back and yell. Sometimes I did, but I'd watch my sister have temper tantrums so severe that she'd pee in her pants. I started shutting down emotions but I had to find a release for all these feelings and so I started keeping a journal.

AL: Did you keep them throughout school?

GEA: Yes. I have all of them lined up on top of my closet, but the earlier ones are still back home. I always keep journals, and I do both my little sketches and some texts.

If you define writing as any kind of scribble, any kind of trying to mark on the world, then you have the oral, dance, choreography, performance art, architecture. I had a feminist architect help me design this addition to my study. Some of us want to take those marks already inscribed in the world and redo them, either by erasing them or by pulling them apart—which involves deconstructive criticism. Pulling them apart is looking at how they're composed and the relationship between the frame and the rest of the world. In this country the frame of reference is white, Euro-American. This is its territory, so any mark we make has to be made in relationship to the fact that they occupy the space. You can take any field of disciplinary study, like anthropology: that frame is also Euro-American; it's western. Composition theory is also very Euro-American. Thus any of us trying to create change have to struggle with this vast, very powerful territory. It's kind of like a fish in the Pacific Ocean, with the analogy that the Pacific Ocean is the dominant field and the fish is this postcolonial, feminist, queer, or whoever is trying to make changes. Before you can make any changes in composition studies, philosophy, or any other field, you have to have a certain awareness of the territory. You have to be able to maneuver in it before you can say, "Here's an alternative model for this particular field, for its norms, rules, regulations, and laws." Especially in composition these rules are very strict: creating a thesis sentence, having some kind of argument, having logical step-by-step progression, using certain methods like contrast or deductive versus inductive thinking. It goes all the way back to Aristotle and Cicero with his seven parts of a composition.

It takes a tremendous amount of energy for anyone like me to make changes or additions to the model; it's like you're this little fish going against the Pacific Ocean. You have to weigh the odds of succeeding with your goal. Say my goal is a liberatory goal: to create possibilities for people, to look at things in a different way so that people can act in their daily lives in a different way. It's a freeing up, an emancipating. It's a feminist goal. But then I have to weigh things: OK, if I write in this style and I code-switch too much and go into Spanglish too much and do an associative kind of logical progression in a composition, am I going to lose those people I want to affect, to change? Am I going to lose the respect of my peers—other writers, artists, and academicians—when I change too much? When I change not only the style but also the rhetoric? Then I have to look at the young students in high school and elementary school who are going to be my future readers, if my writing survives that long. And I look at the young college students, especially those reading *Borderlands*: How much of it is a turn-off for them because it's too hard to access? I have to juggle and balance, make it a little hard for them so that they can stop and think, "You know, this is a text; this is not the same as life; this is a representation of life." Too often when people read something they take it to be the reality instead of the representation. I don't want to turn those students off. So how much do you push and how much do you accommodate and be in complicity with the dominant norm of a particular field?

Nos/otras

AL: So if you're a fish in this vast ocean, which is the Anglo-European framework, you can't just reject the water outright but rather try to change it?

GEA: Yes. Let me show you a little graph, a little visual, so that you can understand what I'm saying, because a lot of times it's hard for me to say everything in words. I want to speak of the nos/otras concept. It used to be that there was a "them" and an "us." We were over here; we were the "other" with other lives and the "nos" was the subject, the white man. There was a very clear distinction. But as the decades have gone by, we—the colonized, the Chicanos, the blacks, the Natives in this country—have been reared in this frame of reference, in this field. All of our education, all of our ideas come from this frame of reference. We're complicitous because we're in such close proximity and intimacy with the other. Now "us" and "them" are interchangeable. Now there's no such thing as an "other." The other is in you, the other is in me. This white culture has been internalized in my head. I have a white man and woman in here, and they have me in their heads, even if it's just a guilty little nudge sometimes. I try to articulate ideas from that place of occupying both territories: the territory of my past, my ethnic community—my home community, the Chicano Spanish, the Spanglish—and the territory of formal education, the philosophical, educational, and political ideas I've internalized just by being alive. Both traditions are within me. I can't disown the white tradition, the Euro-American tradition, any more than I can the Mexican, the Latino, or the Native, because they're all in me. And I think that people from different fields are still making these dichotomies.

Living in a multicultural society, we cross into each others' worlds all the time. We live in each other's pockets, occupy each other's territories, live in close proximity and intimacy with each other at home, in school, at work. We're mutually complicitous—us and them, white and colored, straight and queer, Christian and Jew, self and other, oppressor and oppressed. We all of us find ourselves in the position of being simultaneously insider/outsider. The Spanish word "nosotras" means "us." In theorizing insider/outsider, I write the word with a slash between nos (us) and otras (others). Today the division between the majority of "us" and "them" is still intact. This country does not want to acknowledge its walls or limits, the places some people are stopped or stop themselves, the lines they aren't allowed to cross.

Hopefully sometime in the future we may become nosotras without the slash. Perhaps geography will no longer separate us. We're becoming a geography of hybrid selves—of different cities or countries who stand at the threshold of numerous mundos. Forced to negotiate the cracks between realities, we learn to navigate the switchback roads between assimilation/acquiescence to the dominant culture and isolation/preservation of our ethnic cultural integrity.

Navigating the cracks between the worlds is difficult and painful, like going through the process of reconstructing a new life, a new identity. Both are necessary to our survival and growth. When we adapt to change we come out with a new set of terms to identify with, new definitions of our academic disciplines, and la facultad to accommodate mutually exclusive, discontinuous, inconsistent worlds. As world citizens we learn to move at ease among cultures, countries, and customs. The future belongs to those who cultivate cultural sensitivities to differences and who use these abilities to forge a hybrid consciousness that transcends the "us" versus "them" mentality and will carry us into a nosotras position bridging the extremes of our cultural realities.

AL: Would you describe yourself as being in one or more "fields"?

GEA: Composition, feminism, postcolonialism . . . I didn't even know I belonged in this postcolonial thing until Patricia Clough said in a bookflap that I'm a feminist postcolonial critic. Then there's me the artist, me the teacher, and all the multicultural stuff. It's hard to keep up with the reading, so I don't even try anymore. In preparation for this interview, one of your questions was "Who has influenced you as a postcolonial critic?" I couldn't think of anyone. All the reading I've done has been in terms of particular articles for class. When Homi Bhabha was here I did some reading and went to his lecture, which I couldn't understand. When Gayatri Spivak was here I did the same thing. I took a class with Donna Haraway in feminist theory and when I had to read Spivak's "The Subaltern Speaks" it took me a long time to decipher her sentences. I've read a few of Abdul JanMohamed's essays, and a long time ago when I was taking education courses I read parts of Frantz Fanon's *The Wretched of the Earth* and Paolo Friere's *The Pedagogy of the Oppressed*. For your interview I got a copy of this postcolonial studies reader. But I didn't have time to study a lot, so I made little notes about the things I wanted to think about and maybe respond to in writing.

Postcolonial Studies, Composition Studies

AL: One of the reasons Lahoucine and I wanted particularly to talk to you about postcolonial studies is that we don't completely understand why there hasn't been more confluence between postcolonial studies and composition studies. One reason is no doubt the historical association of the English language with colonialism. Another reason may well be that postcolonial studies has very quickly theorized itself into highly abstract language that's inaccessible. Homi Bhabha is a very good example of the kind of scholar speaking on a level of abstraction that just seems completely foreign to a student in a first-year writing class, who may come from southern Texas and be a speaker of Spanish as a first language. Yet, it seems a shame that these fields don't talk more to one another. In our perspective, you're a person who does talk to both fields, but in ways that are accessible. My first-year students read parts of *Borderlands*, for example, and they're more threatened than they are puzzled. They're threatened because they think they can't imagine you. Many of my students are from small farming communities in Ohio. Most of them are Anglo, and they say things like, "She sounds so mad. Is she mad? Who is she mad at?" That's one of the reasons we wanted to talk with you, and to see if in doing so we could find some means of getting both composition and postcolonial studies to think about their own discourses, and the ways in which some of those discourses are very exclusionary—they shut people out.

GEA: You came at the right time because the first half of one of the book projects currently on the back burner is about composition and postcolonial issues of identity. Most of the questions you've asked are there, plus others. I have about four different chapters of notes and rough drafts that have to do with the writing process, with rhetoric and composition. I'm also taking it into how one composes one's life, how one creates an addition to one's house, how one makes sense of the coincidental and random things that happen in life, how one gives it meaning. So it's my composition theme, compostura. In fact, that's the title of one of the chapters. For me, "compostura" used to mean being a seamstress; I would sew for other people. "Compostura" means seaming together fragments to make a garment which you wear, which represents you, your identity and reality in the world. When you and Lahoucine called me, I thought, "Yeah, there's finally somebody out there who's making the connection."

Writing: Difficulties and Practices

AL: You've already talked about the risks you take and about the stylistic borders you cross. Are there any things about writing that are particularly hard for you? Or easy?

GEA: Yes there are. One problem is getting into a piece of writing, whether it's theory, a story, a poem, a children's book, or a journal entry. I'm always rethinking and responding to something that I or somebody else values. If the value is competition, then I start thinking about how when you compete there's a certain amount of violence and struggle. OK, behind that violence and struggle I experience some kind of emotion—fear, hesitancy, sadness, depression because of the state of the world, whatever. In order to backtrack to the theoretical concepts, I have to start with the feeling. So I dig into the feeling, which usually has a visual side while I'm pulling it apart. One of the visuals I use is Coyolxauhqui, the Aztec moon goddess and first sacrificial victim. Her brother threw her down the temple stairs and when she landed at the bottom she was dismembered. The act of writing for me is this kind of dismembering of everything I'm feeling—taking it apart to examine and then reconstituting or recomposing it again but in a new way. So I really have to get into the feeling—the anger, the anguish, the sadness, the frustration. I have to get into this heightened state which I access sometimes by being very quiet and doing some deep breathing, or by some little meditation, or by burning some incense, or by walking along the beach, or whatever gets me in there. I get all psyched up, and then I do the writing. I work four, five, six hours; and then I have to come off. It's like a withdrawal. I have to leave that anger, that sadness, that compassion, whatever it is I'm feeling.

So that's one problem of writing for me: engaging in an emotional way and then disengaging. To disengage you have to take another walk, wash the dishes, go to the garden, talk on the telephone, just because it's too much. Your body cannot take it.

Some of the other things that come up for me—I wrote them down, because I knew you were going to ask me this—one other problem is the problem of avoidance, of not doing the work. You procrastinate. It takes a while to go to the computer. You circle around the stuff over and over. You don't want to get to the dissertation, to the master's thesis, to that paper that's due, because you're going to be struggling. Every day I have to recommit myself with the writing. It's like making a date with myself, having an appointment to do this writing. Some days I don't feel like going to meet that appointment. It's too hard on my body, especially since I have diabetes; it takes out too much.

AL: Do you try to write at a regular time? Every day?

GEA: Not in terms of clock time but in terms of my routine because my internal clock changes. I get up later and go to bed earlier; sometimes I write at night and sometimes I write during the day. But yes, I have a certain routine. I get up, inject myself with insulin, and have my food. Generally after that I have some activity like this interview or maybe a few hours of writing or home office stuff—filing and returning people's calls, answering faxes or letters—things I don't like to do. Then I have a snack and go for my daily walk. I look at the ocean, the trees, or the field and I think about some writing concern, whatever's occupying my mind that day. As I let my thoughts mingle with what I'm observing often the writer part of myself—the spiritual part—makes some connections, sorts through images, flashes of sudden fantasy, little snippets of scenes, characters, or ideas for the theoretical book. When I get home I dive into four, five, or six hours of writing. Sometimes I can only do two or three hours and other times I can do it around the clock. Sometimes it's hard to keep this daily appointment with myself. There are distractions; other matters vie for my attention. My illness has changed the way I work. I have diabetes, so I need to eat more often—every two and a half to three hours to keep my blood sugars balanced. I need to rest more and to exercise. I can't be a workaholic anymore. After writing I take a break for lunch or the second meal, whenever that is, and then I do some reading: serious theoretical stuff for maybe an hour or two and then some escapist reading. I love mysteries and horror.

AL: Do you compose at the word processor?

GEA: Yes I do, at my desk, and sometimes I take my powerbook to the coffeehouse, the beach, or out to my patio.

AL: Do the words seem to come out as well from the ends of your fingers typing as they did when you were scripting?

GEA: Yes. I prefer writing directly on the computer, especially the first few drafts when I'm still imagining the story or if I'm writing nonfiction, discovering what I'm trying to say and trying out different directions. With electronic writing I can try out different points of view, scenarios, and conflicts. I like to edit on the computer too, though I need to do the last few edits on paper. When I was at the Norcroft writer's retreat my hard drive crashed and I had to resort to handwriting for four weeks. I was surprised to find that I could achieve a smoother flow by writing on paper. I'd gone there to revise *La Prieta, The Dark One*, a collection of stories. I had nineteen of the twenty-four stories in hard copy, so I was able to revise on paper, but the rest of the time, much to my surprise, I wrote poems and worked on my writing guide— exercises, meditations for writing, the elements of writing and fictive techniques. I also spent a lot of time thinking and writing about composition, composition theory, and creativity—things I hadn't planned on doing. I just wanted to do the stories but not having a computer forced me to switch over. Basically I'm a several-projects-simultaneously type of writer.

So anyway, those are two problems: the problem of engaging and disengaging, and the problem of avoidance. Then there's the problem of voice. How am I going to write the forward for the encyclopedia I agreed to do? What voice, tone, am I going to take? How much can I get away with the Spanish and the Spanglish? This is a pretty formal reference book. Another example is the bilingual series of children's books: How much can I get through the censors in the state of Texas in any particular children's book? Texas has more stringent censorship rules than the other states and most publishers can only do one book for all of the states. So the publishers tend to be conservative because they want to get these books into the schools. How much can I get away with pushing at the norms, at the conventions? That's another problem and sometimes it's my biggest problem: if I can't find a voice, a style, a point of view, then nothing can get written. All you have are those notes, but you don't have a voice to speak the style. The style is the relationship between me, Gloria, the author; you, the person reading it, my audience, the world; and the text. So there are three of us. Or are there more than three?

AL: A lot more, probably. At least four, I think, when you bring the text in.

GEA: Well, in the author there's the outside author, the author who's the writer, and the narrative-voice author; in the reader there are all these different readers. And then the text changes according to the reader because I think the reader creates the text.

So I'm grappling with this voice: How much I can push in order to make people think a little bit differently or to give them an emotional or intellectual experience when they can go and say, "Oh, so that's the Pacific Ocean?" Not quite that blatantly. Another example is Toni Morrison's *The Bluest Eye*. You never quite look at another black child without what you took from that text. It's changed your way of looking at black children. The problem of voice is the third problem.

Another more external problem is one of censorship. With the very conservative path that this country has taken in terms of the arts, these times are hard. I know artists who can't exhibit nude photographs of their children because it's considered an obscenity. When you apply for the NEA or any of these grants, you're limited. That's external censorship from the right, of morality and family values. Then there's the external censorship from my family: "Gloria, don't write about that; it's a secret." You're not supposed to devalue the Chicano culture. I was disloyal to my mother and my culture because I wrote about poverty and abuse and gender oppression. So there's a kind of weightiness to not write, to not do your art in as honest a way as possible. You're supposed to make nice, like you were talking about being Southern girls.

AL: The kind of good girls we in my Southern neighborhood learned to be.

GEA: I write a lot about sexuality in my stories. I don't know if you read "Immaculate, Inviolate" in *Borderlands*, but when I sent my brother the book and he read it, he had a fit. He was going to show it to my uncle, and my uncle was going to sue me because that's his mother I was talking about, my grandmother. I talked about how my grandfather lifted her skirt to do his thing, and how he had three other mujeres con familia. The children from all the families played together and my grandmother was ashamed and humiliated. I'm not supposed to write about it. I'm constantly asked by my family to choose my loyalty—to myself or to them. I'm supposed to choose them. I don't and I never have, and that's why I'm accused of betraying my culture, why I'm a bad girl—selfish, disobedient, ungrateful.

AL: And also why you're a writer.

GEA: To take the problem of censorship one step further, there's also internal censorship. I've internalized my mom's voice, the neoconservative right voice, the morality voice. I'm always fighting those voices.

AL: I was just going to ask you about that again. The visual you showed me earlier had "us" and "them," and you said very beautifully that both of these—the "them" and the "us"—are now in you. You're very aware of that mixture of voices inside yourself. Many people in composition studies would like to be able to find ways to help our students recognize their own multiple voices, especially the Anglo students who don't see themselves as having any race, any ethnicity, and often they don't even think they have any range of sexuality. They're just "man" or "woman," that's it. How do we help those students get to those other voices? How do we help them get Gloria's voice in them? They have the "nos" so much in their head that they don't have any other voices. One of the reasons work like yours is so important to the future of composition studies is that it gives concrete evidence of many voices in a text, many voices speaking out of who you are, many voices that you allow to speak. Many of our students, on the other hand, are not only monolingual in the strict sense of English being their only language, but they're deeply, internally monolingual as well. And composition really hasn't done much of anything in the past to help them out of that. That's one part of my field that I would most like to change somehow.

Teaching Composition: Assimilation, Resistance, Liberation

GEA: The only recourse is a kind of vicarious move: immersing them in the texts of people who are different. The fastest way for them to recognize that they have diversity, that they have these values, that they have these experiences and beliefs, is to jerk them out into another country where they don't speak the language. It's like taking a fish out of water. The fish doesn't know that it lives in the element of water until it jumps onto the beach and can't breath. You can't do that to every student. Sometimes a traumatic experience can open up a window. What education and the schools can give is this vicarious experience via the text, via reading *The Bluest Eye* or *Borderlands*.

In terms of composition, I think teachers need to look at alternate models. I want my textbook—the writing, reading, speaking, dreaming book I've been talking about—to offer other ways of considering how to write a story, a poem, or a paper. And again, that alternate way is colored by the western frame of everything. I'm trying to present another way of ordering and composing, another rhetoric; but it's only partly new. Most of it is cast in the western tradition because that's all

I was immersed in. Symbolically, the university is this city and somebody brings the Trojan Horse, the Trojan Burra, into the city gates. At night the belly of the burra opens and out comes the "other" trying to make changes from inside. It's kind of hard because the university wall or city is very seductive, you know? There's something very seductive about fitting in, being part of this one culture, forgetting differences, and going with the norm. Western theory is very seductive and pretty soon instead of subverting, challenging, and making marks on the wall, you get taken in.

AL: Certainly some in composition studies have thought that's what the university was for, that's what the composition teacher was for: to help the students become assimilated into the university, rather than to help them challenge the reality of the university.

GEA: Yes. This is also what traditional therapy tries to do. It tries to assimilate you to life, to reality, to living.

AL: So here, in the night, out of the burra, come the challengers?

GEA: Yes, these different ways of writing: the inappropriate ways, the bad girls not making nice. It's really hard because you're one of only a few.

AL: One of the good things about teaching composition is that you can make a place, as a teacher, for students to do dangerous and experimental kinds of writing. But then they have to go and pass the tests and pass the history essays and do the inside-the-lines kind of writing.

GEA: This is what I was talking about earlier: in order to make it in this society you have to know the discipline, if it's teaching, if it's composition, if it's carpentry. Whatever field it is, you have to know your way around. You have to know how to wire the house before you can be an innovative electrician. The question is, how can you change the norm if the tide is so tremendous against change? But you can do something. You're in the field of composition, right? And somehow you respect my ideas and my writing. Otherwise you wouldn't be here. So for me to be effective in making whatever little changes I can, I have to get this respect, this acceptance, this endorsement from my peers. All these academics who teach my writings are endorsing me, and they make it possible for me to reach a wider audience. Whatever little changes I can make in people's thoughts, it's because they first allowed me through the gate. If you absolutely hated my stuff and everybody else hated my stuff, no matter how innovative it was, nobody would ever see it because it wouldn't get through the peer gate. I couldn't do any of this without you.

AL: Well, you could do it and you have done it; but reaching the very largest audience in the United States at least does take that.

GEA: Which is my next step. One of my goals is to have a larger audience, which is what I'm trying to accomplish with this book of fiction. Fiction is a genre that can be accepted by more people than just those from the academy. Community people do read my books—the children's books and *Borderlands* go into the community, but it's still beyond the scale of most people. My family doesn't do any serious reading. They'll look at my writings—my sister and brother will read a little bit of it, but they don't do serious reading. They don't sit down on a daily basis like you and I do and read texts on composition and theory.

AL: But they might read a book of stories.

GEA: Yes, and what I'm trying to convey to you about composition and postcoloniality I'm trying to do through story. You can theorize through fiction and poetry; it's just harder. It's an unconscious kind of process. Instead of coming in through the head with the intellectual concept, you come in through the backdoor with the feeling, the emotion, the experience. But if you start reflecting on that experience, you can come back to the theory.

AL: I wonder if that's partly why the boundaries between fiction and nonfiction seem to be so permeable right now. It's hard sometimes to say what's a short story and what's an essay.

GEA: The way one composes a piece of creative nonfiction and the way one composes fiction are very similar. In composing nonfiction, you're very selective: you take little fragments here and there, and you piece them together in a new way. So right off the bat you're not being true to the nonfiction. It's fiction already, just in manipulating it.

AL: And then the representation itself—you said earlier that the representation is not the same as the experience; it's the representation.

263

GEA: The borders are permeable. I like the fact that at the turn of the century these borders are transparent and crossable. When we get past the millennium, the fin de siècle, some of these things will settle down into another kind of reality. At the turn of each century everything is up for grabs: the categories are disrupted; the borders can be crossed. Then you get to another plateau where things become more fixed, but not really. Then you wait for the next period of insurgency when everything is up for grabs again. It goes in cycles. So this is why I'm so hopeful and so glad that I'm alive right now, because I can partake of this confusion. But still, back to your students, what's going to help them?

AL: Well, the book you're working on may help, but I find students so anxious to be able to work within the framework and to be part of the system and so fearful of what will happen if they're not part of the system, that they resist taking risks and they resist trying to get in touch with things that might hurt.

GEA: Yes, we come back to the same thing: fear of being different. You don't want to stick out: you don't want to be different—especially at their age. You and I have already passed midlife. We can have a sense of identity that's not so much based on other people's reactions anymore. But theirs is very much a relational type of identity, so that if this group of people disapprove of them and find their difference to be problematic, they won't be able to function. They won't be able to get their degree, they won't get the grant, they won't get the job. So how do you teach them to take risks? How do you teach them to stand up and say, "I'm different and this is who I am; your way is maybe a good way, but it's not the only way." How do you get them to do that? I think that writing and postcolonial studies are trying to do that in terms of getting people to think about how they are in the world.

Writing is very liberating and emancipatory; it frees you up. In the process of writing you're reflecting on all the things that make you different, that make you the same, that make you a freak. You're constantly grappling with identity issues. Postcoloniality looks at this power system—whether it's a government, anthropology, or composition—and asks, "Who has the voice? Who says these are the rules? Who makes the law? And if you're not part of making the laws and the rules and the theories, what part do you play? How is that other system placed in your mind?" You get into the neocolonization of people's minds. You get into the erasure of certain histories, the erasure of ideas, voices, languages, and books. A lot of the Mayan and Aztec codices were burned and a whole system of knowledge wiped out. Post-coloniality comes and asks these questions. What reality does this disciplinary field, or this government, or this system try to crush? What reality is it trying to erase or suppress? Writing is about freeing yourself up, about giving yourself the means to be active, to take agency, to make changes. So I see both writing and postcoloniality as emancipatory projects.

Language, Domination

AL: May I ask a question about English? One of the first things that brought me to your work was your mixture of languages. As a teacher of writing who believes that writing and literacy can be liberatory, it was very frightening and disorienting and hurtful when I began to realize the degree to which writing and language could be just the opposite—the ways in which they could enslave, keep down, exclude, hurt, silence. To have to face my own doubleness within the discipline of writing was hard for me because I wanted to do the liberatory thing, and I didn't want to face the fact that teaching any kind of a system involves constraints and hurts. After I started trying to figure that out, it began to dawn on me the degree to which English is hegemonic and silencing, and the way in which English tends to drown out. I also think about the way in which English, throughout its whole history as a language, has been like a sponge, sucking up words from Norse, or German, or French, or I think now of Spanish from which English is absorbing enormous amounts. I don't know how I feel about that. I don't know whether I think it's good that the language is alive and growing, or whether I think English is exerting its power once more and trying to surround Spanish, let's say, and take it in. Those are very confusing issues to me. I'm also very much aware that students quite often fear other languages in the same way that they fear people they perceive as different. So how are you feeling about the state of English today? How do you feel about the English-only legislation which passed in the Congress this summer?

GEA: Languages are representational systems and English is the dominant symbology system in the United States. Language displaces the reality, the experience, so that you take the language to be the reality. Say you had Hindi, or Spanish, or Hopi, or whatever the language happens to be. That language attempts to create reality. Not just shape it but create it, not just mold reality but create it and displace it. I think all languages do that. Then you take a country like the United States, where via the industrial age and the electronic age and the age of the Internet, the dispersal of English is faster and more widespread than any other language thus far. It's going to become the planetary language if we're not careful. Other countries are going to become—I don't want to say "Americanized" because I don't want to use the word "America" to represent the United States—but it's going to have this United Statesian-culture-swallowing-up-the-rest-of-the-world kind of mouth. I like English and I majored in English at a time when I wasn't allowed Spanish. I never took any Spanish courses other than a Spanish class in high school. I took some French and Italian—which didn't do any good because I can't remember any of it now. The way I grew up with my family was code-switching. When I'm most my emotive self, my home self, stuff will come out in Spanish. When I'm in my head, stuff comes out in English. When I'm dealing with theory it's all in English because I didn't take any classes where theory was taught in Spanish. So the body and the feeling parts of me come out in Spanish and the intellectual, reasoning parts come out in English.

AL: Do you dream in Spanish?

GEA: I day and night dream in both Spanish and English. What's happening more and more with English is that I get the ideas in Spanish and in visuals. One of the ideas I'm working with is conocimiento, the Spanish word for knowledge, or ways of knowing. Those ideas come to me in Spanish and in visuals. So when I think "conocimiento" I see a little serpent for counterknowledge. This is how it comes to me that this counterknowledge is not acceptable, that it's the knowledge of the serpent in the Garden of Eden. It's not acceptable to eat the fruit of knowledge; it makes you too aware, too self-reflective. So how do you take this conocimiento and have the student speculate on it when all the student knows and is immersed in is the kind of knowledge that crosses this one out? For a student to do this, there has to be some kind of opening, some kind of fissure, gate, rajadura—a crack between worlds is what I call it—the hole, the interfaces.

Thought activity is actually a type of dreaming, a flash fantasy, the mind capturing flashes of the imagination. You have to be fast, alert, aware to catch these little flashes, these images which are sometimes visual, sometimes auditory, sometimes linguistic—unconnected sentences or words like overheard dialogue that doesn't make much sense and so you're forced to "dream" it onward, make it up. Only sometimes I wonder if it's not just another kind of information that I already have, that you don't really "make it up" but just translate, just act as medium for transporting the information from that hard-to-access realm to the conscious mind to the artistic or theoretical product and finally to the world via the reader. Nepantla can be seen in the dream state, in the transition between worlds, as well as in transitions across borders of class, race, or sexual identity. Nepantla experiences involve not only learning how to access different kinds of knowledges—feelings, events in one's life, images in-between or alongside consensual reality; they also involve creating your own meaning or conocimientos.

AL: Before we began taping you remembered that people generally assume you've read a lot of theory since your books enact so many of the concepts poststructuralism has espoused. You must have read Foucault, Derrida, Irigaray, or Cixous. You said that you hadn't read them before you wrote *Borderlands* but that the ideas are "out there."

GEA: Yes, the ideas are out there because we are all in more or less the same territory. We occupy the world of the academy and of the late twentieth century. We've read some of the same books, seen some of the same movies, have similar ideas about relationships—whether we're French or born in the United States or born elsewhere but raised here. In reflecting on what we know and on our experiences we come up with these paradigms, concepts of what life is about, how interactions and power struggles work. Those theorists give it different terms than I do; a lot of my terms are in Spanish, like conocimiento. A lot of my concepts about composition and postcoloniality are attempts to connect pre-Columbian histories, values, and systems with the postcolonial twentieth century. Often I'll start with a precolonial cultural figure—Coatlicue or la Llorona. Then I look at the experiences Chicanos and Chicanas are going through today, in 1996, and try to see a connection to what was going on then. I want to show a continuity and a progression. I try to give a term, find a language for my ideas and concepts that comes from the indigenous part of myself rather than from the European part, so I come up with Coatlicue, la facultad, la frontera, and nepantla—concepts that mean: "Here's a little nugget of a system of knowledge that's different from the Euro-American. This is my hit on it but it's also a mestizo/mestiza, cognitive kind of perception, so therefore this ideology or this little nugget of knowledge is both indigenous and western. It's a hybridity, a mixture, because I live in this liminal state between worlds, between realities, between systems of knowledge, between symbology systems." This liminal borderland, terrain, or passageway, this interface, is what I call "nepantla." All my concepts about composition and postcoloniality come under this umbrella heading of nepantla, which means el lugar en medio, the space in between, the middle ground. I first saw that word in Rosario Castellano's writings. When they dug up the streets of Mexico City to build the subway system, they found the Templo Mayor. In it they found the statue of Coatlicue, and they found all these artifacts, and they found murals on the walls, and one of the murals was nepantla. There are also all these words in Nahuatl that begin with "nepantla" and have different endings. One of them is "between two oceans"; that's the nepantla. Whenever two things meet, there's the nepantla, so they have tons and tons of words with the root word nepantla. *Borderlands* falls into that category, but it's just one part of this overall umbrella project that's my life's work, my life's writing. *Borderlands* is just one hit on it. This new book on composition, the writing process, identity, knowledge, and the construction of all of these things, is like a sequel to *Borderlands*.

When the mind is restricted to a narrowing of attention it tends to shift to another mode of functioning. This other way of functioning is a nepantla state—an other or "altered state of consciousness"—which may include the meditative state, the hypnotic trance, daydreaming, and even ordinary sleep. When you're in this mode you can extract more information than you ordinarily would. Also, the information you get is from a nonhabitual source.

With the nepantla paradigm I try to theorize unarticulated dimensions of the experience of mestizas living in between overlapping and layered spaces of different cultures and social and geographic locations, of events and realities—psychological, sociological, political, spiritual, historical, creative, imagined. I see the mestiza as a geography of selves—of different bordering countries—who stands at the threshold of two or more worlds and negotiates the cracks between the worlds. La artista is the mediator between various communities in the "normal" worlds and nepantla in the "other" worlds.

AL: And the book of short stories you're working on, too.

Composing the Work, the Self, the World

GEA: Yes. My process for composing all these projects is very much Coyolxauhqui. In composing, you take things apart and everything is fragmented, then you struggle to put things together.

AL: Is there any sense of weaving in what comes after the tearing apart, from the language? I also think of weaving as a metaphor for what happens at some points in writing.

GEA: Yes there is—a kind of weaving, a rearranging. Anyway, I'm enumerating the different stages of my writing process. And what's funny is that I started out just talking about writing and then I branched off into other art forms: into musical composition, choreographed dances, film, video—these arts all have elements in common. Even architecture and building construction have something in common with composition, although in the construction of a building you have to have all the details first—where the electrical outlets have to be, where the windows are, what the dimensions are. Then you're allowed to be creative; you can manipulate things, move the light switch a little bit. But with writing, you can approach it from an outline, from something that's already framed for you; you can start composing with a loosely held-together frame; or you can jump into it and start anywhere. You can start in the end and go to the beginning or you can start in the middle and go both directions, towards the beginning and the end. The frames for all of these art forms vary a little bit, but a lot of the composition process is very similar.

When I realized this similarity I started looking at how I create aspects of my identity. Identity is very much a fictive construction: you compose it from what's out there, what the culture gives you, and what you resist in the culture. This identity also has a type of projection into a future identity. You can say, "Here's the image of Gloria, or here's the image of Andrea that I want to project in the next seven years, the kind of person I'd like to be in the future," and then you start building that person. You can start building that Andrea by saying, "I'm going to make more time for myself, I'm going to value solitude, I'm going to get rid of the clutter, I'm going to find out what my own goals and agenda are and I'm going to follow that agenda instead of what my mother, or my family, or the academy, or my husband wants, and these are the projects I'm going to concentrate on." You reshape yourself. First you get that self-image in your head and then you project that out into the world. When you look at it ten years later, you won't recognize yourself. When you go back home to your mom and to your brothers and sisters, you'll be an entirely different person and they won't see how you came from there to here. So you keep creating your identity this way.

Then I took all of this knowledge a step further, to reality. I realized that if I can compose this text and if I can compose my identity, then I can also compose reality out there. It all has to do with the angle of perception. Say all your life you've perceived Andrea to be this one kind of person, you've perceived an essay to be this one kind of composition, you've perceived the United States and the planet Earth to be this kind of country and this kind of reality. Then you find out that you don't have to be the Andrea you've been all your life, that you don't have to write the essay this way, and that if you see that shed, that sky, that sea, and all that happens in it from this other angle, you'll see something else. You can recreate reality. But you're going to need some help because it's all done in relationship with other people. When we're born we're taught by our culture that this is up and that is down, and that's a piece of wood, and that's a no-no. To change the tree, the up and down, and the no-no, you have to get the rest of your peers to see things in this same way—that's not a tree and that's not a no-no. We all created this physics, this quantum mechanics; now we all have to recreate something different. A scientist will be the first to give us an idea of this other universe, of this other atom; the writer will be the first to give us an idea of this other emotional experience, this other perception, this other angle. One of the members of the tribe has to start making that aperture, that little hole, that crack. One of the members of the community has to say, "Yeah, this is a different way of looking at reality." Then everybody else will say, "Yeah, why didn't I think of that? That's true." All of a sudden you'll have a consensual basis for this reality you're observing. And once you have this consensual view of reality, along comes Anzaldúa who says, "No, that's just the reality of your particular people—who are Indo-European, or Western, or Inuit, or whatever. Here's a different way of looking at reality."

AL: When you were talking about your architect, it made me think about what you later said about the importance of other people and always having other people around you. When I think of the feminist architect you worked with for the addition to your house, that person brought a lot to the project but you were important to the project, too. And then the electricians and the plumbers. Was it a deeply collaborative project?

GEA: Yes. They consulted with me but knew that I didn't have the know-how. They said, "What kind of space do you want to live in?" and I said "Tall, a lot of opening, a lot of window space." Then there's the city code. You have to have a certain amount of free territory in your lot; you can only build so many square feet. I was limited to that, so I said, "I'll go up." Then there are the neighbors. I had to get permission because some of these windows overlook them. There's a public hearing if you build a two-story because you're impinging into somebody else's space. So anyway, all of those people and the architect had their visions of what they wanted the space to be like and I had mine. I wanted them to cocreate it with me. I didn't want it to just be me. There's always negotiating. The corner windows are two or three hundred dollars more expensive than the regular windows and I said, "I can't afford that." But the architect was invested in having these corner windows—which had been my idea in the first place—so I said, "Well this is your project, too, so we'll go with that." I wanted only one door, because I felt that French doors were not as secure, but then I talked to the carpenter who said, "No, this glass is very durable." It's all very collaborative.

AL: I was just looking at your children's book: obviously you collaborated with the artist on that project, too.

GEA: Well, it wasn't quite a straight collaboration because I did the text first and then gave it to the artist. But now I'm doing a book for middle-school girls, and I'll be working with an artist friend. I also think that there's no such thing as a single author. I write my texts but I borrow the ideas and images from other people. Sometimes I forget that I've borrowed them. I might read some phrase from a poem or fiction and I like the way it describes the cold. Years and years go by, and I do something similar with my description, but I've forgotten that I've gotten it somewhere else. I show my text in draft form to a lot of people for feedback: that's another level of cocreating with somebody. My readers do the same thing. They put their experiences into the text and change *Borderlands* into many different texts. It's different for every reader. It's not mine anymore.

Claiming Author(ity)

GEA: Traditional western notions of the "author" don't include the part of the author that's the dreamer, the unconscious watcher, the soul or nagual, that which is not you but was born with you, that keeps vigil, that guides you, an internal companion or nagual. And this brings me to another construct: the text and who constructs it—the author or other forces from the environment. The assumption that only they (imperial critics) can know the other underpins the imperial imperative. The postmodernist construction posits that I'm not writing the text but rather that I am the text and that my self-awareness allows me to present the multitude of historical and cultural perspectives that are written through me. This is a new form of domination, another way of reinstating the old practice of appropriating the work of the "outsider" by saying that writers like me are "being written through by my cultural matrix" and only they—the imperial critics—can deconstruct and own my meaning. But I can know. I can read and speak and write myself (to the extent that anyone can). I can "selve" myself.

Western theories of composition force formerly colonized people to read and write according to western conventions situated in broader ideological systems. Composition practices continue to emphasize the centrality of rationality to the writing process. Not only did I have to invent a new or mestizaje style of writing, a border aesthetics, but in speaking I also use precolonial symbols and images which I modernize and precolonial myths which I rewrite. I also had to refashion my own reading practices and, through my texts, teach my readers to read differently.

Reading, writing, and speaking are not just about the verbal or written text but about how reality is constructed—not just about explaining or reflecting on reality but shaping it. It's about reading, writing, dreaming, and speaking the social. It's about deconstructing oppositions—such as reality and fantasy, fiction and history—maintained by disciplinary knowledges. These are examples of contentions over authority and the desire to end oppression and exploitation, a desire for carnalidad—a kinship beyond kin, beyond race, class, and gender, a desire for meaningful life, a desire to make public my own self-reflections on my processes, and a desire to construct or produce knowledges.

In inventing the text, the fiction, I invent the (my)self and the reader. I may be fooling myself here. I know I can't ward off the influences and pressures of these master discourses, and I don't want to ward off all their influences. It's difficult to escape using and being used by dominant discursive practices. How does an internal postcolonial writer rewrite the dominant ideology from within to produce a different conocimiento of different versions of reality? She can't. But I'd like to think that a community of writers can. A single author is doing pretty good just to resist reincribing dominant discourse. Yet, I don't want to be a production of somebody else's legal, political, or aesthetic text. I'd like to think that my cultural productions—reading, writing, speaking, dreaming—are acts of resistance to that production.

Style

AL: You don't feel possessive about your writing as your "property?"

GEA: No I don't. I've always felt nonpossessive about writing. I do the composing but the writing is taken from little mosaics of other people's lives, other people's perceptions. I take all these pieces and rearrange them. When I'm writing I always have the company of the reader. Sometimes I'm writing with my friends in mind and sometimes for people like you who teach writing. In writing, I'm just talking with you without your being here. This is where style comes in. Style is my relationship with you, how I decide what register of language to use, how much Spanglish, how much vernacular. It's all done in the company of others while in solitude—which is a contradiction.

AL: Have you read Borges?

GEA: Yes. I have his entire collected works.

AL: I was thinking about the story "The Aleph" and that certain spot where, if you lie down and you put your eye there, you can see everything.

GEA: Yes. When I talk about borders with my students I use a visual of the Aleph. Style is a very difficult concept. Often I go to visuals to clarify my concepts, as I've said. For example, I think what's going on now at the turn of the century is exemplified by the remolino, the whirlwind, the vortex. North of the equator, the movement is clockwise so all of our knowledge on this side moves clockwise. South of the equator, the movement is counterclockwise. The rivers flow the other way. As a mestiza, I'm living on the equator. Some of my culture, the indigenous and the Mexican, pulls me counterclockwise. This comes with its own perception of being. And over here, in North America, all the knowledge I learned in school, all the ways I've learned to look at life, pulls me the other way. I'm pulled in two different ways. I think that postcoloniality is situated right here. If you consider the counterclockwise to be the colonized cultures and the clockwise to be the colonizing cultures, then there's this tension: you're trying to accommodate both cultures and still be comfortable. It's a struggle to find this peace, this settlement. You have to change the clockwise movement to be counterclockwise once in a while, and sometimes you have to change this counterclockwise movement to move like the North. It's a very unsettling state. It's also the state writers are in when composing. Moving clockwise is everything that has been written: the literature, the norm, the genre laws. As a writer, you're trying to add to those genre laws, to that knowledge, to that literature, to that art. You have to go along with it in some ways, but to create some changes you have to go counterclockwise. This is the struggle for a writer like me: How much can you get away with without losing the whole thing? All of these metaphors come around and around—to style, to composition itself, to identity, to the creation of knowledge, and to the creation of experience.

AL: When I look at your writing, I think yours is a mixture of styles. Have you seen other people mix things up the way you do?

GEA: Well, other Chicanas were mixing Spanglish in poetry but not in theory, not in academic writing. I think of style as trying to recover a childhood place where you code-switch. If I'm fictionalizing a certain experience, I go back to the reality of the experience in my memory and it takes place in both languages. So I get into that style. But I think by code-switching I was trying to inject some of my history and identity into this text that white, black, Native American, and Asian-American people were going to read. I was trying to make them stop and think. Code-switching jerks the reader out of his world and makes her think, "Oh, this is my world; this is another world; this is her world where she does this, where it's possible to say words in Spanish." It's like taking the counterclockwise and injecting it into the clockwise. That's why I started code-switching. Now a lot of Chicanas are doing it.

AL: Injecting the discourse of lesbianism or alternative sexuality of any kind into traditional heterosexuality does the same thing. It insists that we go this way and it helps readers to inhabit other ways of being, other ways of knowing. I think that's very important too.

GEA: And you know, we live in the remolino, the vortex, the whirlwind; and in this time everything—values, ideology, identity—is very much confused. The student is caught in her own little vortex. I'd like to do what Carlos Castañeda was told to do by don Juan the shaman: to stop the world. The world is both this reality and the description we have of it in our heads. How do you say, "No, this other world exists, this other possibility, this other reality. You have to stop this world a little bit to get the other one in." So I'd like to stop the remolino for just a second, the second that it takes the reader to say, "I didn't know that Chicano Spanish was the bastard language. And if Chicano Spanish is a bastard language, what registers of English are also bastards and not allowed into the academy?" They start looking at British English, Australian English, Canadian English, United States English. Then they look at all the dialects and registers: academic, formal, slang. And then maybe the reader will say, "I'm a redneck and this is my language and maybe I should write about this language for this particular class." Just for that little second it stops them. Does this make sense to you? Or maybe I'm being too presumptuous and I don't really do that. Anyway, I think that writing has that faculty, but it has to be honest writing and it has to be writing that struggles.

AL: When bell hooks says that language is a place of struggle, I think that's what she means: You're struggling to get language out of the clockwise just for a second and into the counterclockwise, and it's a terrible struggle. It goes on your whole life—if I understand her correctly. Generally English in colleges and in universities has been a gatekeeper, functioning to keep the gate closed. Only in the last fifteen years or so have people in English, and mostly people in composition, said, "We don't want to do that anymore. If we're going to be gatekeepers we want to be opening the gate." That is a very, very big change.

GEA: It was a great shock to me several years ago, when the CCCC conference invited me to speak. The very same discipline, the very same teachers who had marked me down and had said that I was writing incorrectly, all of a sudden invited me to speak. Then I started getting requests for reprints in composition readers. That was such a shock to me. Finding that composition people were reading me was a bigger shock than finding that anthropologists or women's studies people were reading me. Just a few days ago I was sent a textbook for students. One of the sections is on place, and they took a little segment of chapter 7 in *Borderlands*, "La Conciencia de la Mestiza," where I talk about returning to the valley. The students are supposed to take that little piece of writing and write a letter assuming my place, signing the letter "Gloria Anzaldúa." I'll show you the book if you don't believe it. I don't know how students are supposed to do this.

It was only a slightly smaller shock to find Spanish and Portuguese modern language people putting my stuff in their readers because we Chicanas were not part of Latino writing. They just included Mexican, South American, and Central American writers, not Chicanas. They put Sandra Cisneros and me in there. I am now a Latina writer. Can you believe that?

Activism, Working for Change

AL: Before our time is over would you talk at least a little bit about activism and working for change? Because in your writing, it's very clear that you see writing and activism as related. I think that it's less clear how we engage others in doing that kind of activism.

GEA: A lot of the activism for writers and artists stems from trying to heal the wounds. You've been oppressed as a woman or oppressed as a queer or oppressed racially as a colonized people, and you want to deal with that oppression, with those wounds. Why did this happen to you? Why is it so hard? Who are these people oppressing you and why do they have a license to oppress you? For me, it started as a child. I was such a freak, such a strange little thing, that I felt all of the ill winds that were blowing. I really felt them. I had a very low threshold for pain. The differences that I felt between myself and other people were so excruciating. I was trying to make meaning of my existence and my pain, and that in turn led me to writing.

I'm trying to write about these moments where I took things into my own hands and said, "This is not the way things are supposed to be. Girl children are not supposed to be treated this way. Women are not supposed to be battered; they're not supposed to be second-class citizens. Chicanos shouldn't be treated in this way in society." I started grappling with those issues and writing became a way of activism, a way of trying to make changes. But it wasn't enough just to sit and write and work on my computer. I had to connect the real-life, bodily experiences of people who were suffering because of some kind of oppression or some kind of wound in their real lives, with what I was writing. It wasn't a disembodied kind of writing. And because I'm a writer, voice—acquiring a voice, covering a voice, picking up a voice, creating a voice—was important. Then you run into this whole experience of unearthing, discovering, rediscovering, and recreating voices that have been silenced, voices that have been repressed, voices that have been made a secret—and not just for me, but for other Chicanas. Look at all these women who have certain realities similar to mine yet don't really see them. But when they read a text by Toni Morrison or when they read *Borderlands* they say, "That went on in my life but I didn't have the words to articulate it. You articulated it for me, but it's really my experience." They see themselves in the text. Reading these other voices gives them permission to acquire their own voice, to write in this way, to become an activist by using Spanglish, or by code-switching. Then they read the book to their little girls or to their neighbor's kids or to their girlfriend or to their boyfriend.

AL: It's like links in a chain or a circle that keeps expanding?

GEA: Yes. As with my children's book *Prietita y la Llorona*, it's really very much a cultural story. All these Chicanitos read is white stuff and then along comes *La Llorona* and they say, "Yeah, my grandmother used to tell me stories like that." It feels really good for them be in a book. There's this young kid who never sees himself represented, so unearthing and nurturing that voice is part of the activism work. That's why I try to do so many anthologies. That's why I promote women, especially women of color and lesbians of all colors, and why I'm on editorial boards for magazines. I want to get their voices out there. Making these anthologies is also activism. In the process of creating the composition, the work of art, the painting, the film, you're creating the culture. You're rewriting the culture, which is very much an activist kind of thing. Writers have something in common with people doing grassroots organizing and acting in the community: it's all about rewriting culture. You don't want a culture that batters women and children. By the year 2005, 50 percent of the group labeled "poverty stricken" is going to be women and children. It's a reality that we need to speak of. Twenty years ago, incest was not part of consensual reality. Writers who wrote about it, feminists who talked about it, made films about it, and did art about incest and child abuse, changed reality. Before that, it was just a given: You beat your wife, that's part of it; forcing your wife to have sex is not rape. Consensual reality has been redefined by these people rewriting a culture. Now it's part of culture that when you batter someone you're responsible. It's not something you can get away with unless you're a psychopath.

AL: What you just said makes me think that one of the things that's important about your work for postcolonial studies is that it goes beyond the deconstructive—which has been a large part of the very important work postcolonial studies has done—to show what colonialism has done and been. But the kind of work that you're talking about creates a new reality. It goes beyond the deconstructing and the showing of old oppressions and hurts.

GEA: When you get into reading and writing the "other," into assuming some kind of authority for the "other"—whether you're the "other" or the subject—there's a community involved. And I think what you're saying is that postcolonial theorists sometimes forget what's going on here in the community, in the world we inhabit.

AL: And so do teachers of writing, I hasten to add.

GEA: There's a responsibility that comes with invoking cultural and critical authority, and I think you could call that responsibility being open to activism and being accountable for your actions.

AL: I want to ask one other thing. Suppose you and I had a little girl-child here, and we wanted to watch her grow up and be a writer. What would be your wildest dream for that little child? What would you most hope for?

GEA: I think what I'd most hope for is probably not something that's possible. I would hope for her to have a peaceful community in all the different worlds, in all the different cultures, in all the different realities. I would hope for her to be a true mestiza, and I don't think it's possible right now because the powers that create and implement the laws are still pretty much males who don't want to share the power. It's not an equal kind of thing.

AL: Do you have any hopes that the situation might change in the future?

GEA: Yes I do. I think we're drifting towards that. The distinction between the people with power and the people without power will get erased, so that the people without agency take on a little agency and the people who were all-powerful become a little powerless. There will be a hybridity of equal parts instead of a graft and a major tree.

I'd also like her to be able to explore the world without fear of being attacked or wounded. To live is to be in pain. To live is to struggle. Life hurts but we can mitigate that hurt a little bit by having a society where the little girl child can pursue her interests and her dreams without being too much constrained by gender roles or racial law or the different epistemologies that say, "This is the way reality is." I don't know if that's ever going to happen but I hope it will. Sometimes I think it will.

Additional Bits

GEA: "Being a crossroads" feels like being caught up in remolinos, vortexes. In intercultural encounters, people, communities, and cultures are swept up in a maelstrom of controversy and whirled around and then pulled in different directions by radically different perspectives, ways of life. We occupy positions that oscillate in a to-and-from movement—mobile, migrating, liminal. We basically live in in-between spaces (nepantlas).

We are experiencing cognitive dissonance, hit by discordant stimuli on all sides. We no longer know who we are and what our lives are about. It's hard to come to terms with change and new ideas if they make us doubt and distrust our sense of self. And change always threatens our identity. We have a choice: We can retreat back to our comfort zones, prisons of familiarity, habitual thought patterns and behaviors rather than risk changing; it's easier to remain in entrenched systems and erect defenses to keep out new ideas. Or we can learn to navigate through the whirlwinds.

Intelligence is the ability to make adaptive responses in new and old situations. It is our ability to recognize order in the form of new patterns, cycles, sequences, processes, tendencies, shapes, similarities, behaviors, and probabilities.

Being in the grip of these whirlwinds of change causes us and our societies to feel fragmented. Our struggle is always to know the worlds we live in, to come to grips with our problems and present horrors, to cope with the external state of affairs at the same time as we cope internally, and to pull ourselves back together as a nation. How do we pull ourselves together?

Culture is the "story" of who we are and our ideas about reality. In other words, culture is an ideology—a series of images and representations that reflect the beliefs a people have about reality.

Culture is rooted in the patterns of the past; thus culture is the last system to change and adapt. We are experiencing demographic and cultural changes that result in shifts in perception of self and others. Changes that usually take more than two generations to assimilate we have to assimilate in less than ten years. Right now the who-we-are is undergoing disintegration and reconstruction. This disintegration (being pulled apart, dismembered) and reconstruction (putting all the pieces back together in a new order), for me, are symbolized by Coyolxauhqui, the Aztec moon goddess. She was the first sacrificial victim, decapitated by her brother Huitzílopochtlí, flung down the temple steps, her body dismembered.

When we experience boundary shifts, border violations, bodily penetrations, identity confusions, a flash of understanding may sear us, shocking us into a new way of reading the world. The ideological filters fall away; we realize that the walls are porous and that we can "see" through them. Having become aware of the fictions and fissures in our belief system, we perceive the cracks between the worlds, the holes in reality. These cracks and holes disrupt the neat categories of race, gender, class, and sexuality.

Change is constant and unrelenting. It's a source of tension. With no sense of closure or completion, it is overwhelming. The who-we-are is changing. Living in the midst of different vortexes makes it hard for us to make sense of the chaos and put the pieces together. But it is in the cracks between worlds and realities where changes in consciousness can occur. In this shifting place of transitions, we morph, adapt to new cultural realities. As time goes by things start to solidify again and we erect new walls. They stay in place until the next generation kicks holes in them. When the dust settles, who knows what the new structures will look like?

10

....

Last Words? Spirit Journeys

An Interview with AnaLouise Keating (1998–1999)

....

(1998–1999)

Dealing with Criticism and Controversy

ALK: Is there anything that's been said about you in print that you'd like to address?

GEA: I kind of welcome criticism and controversy. At the time it may sting a little, but it enables me to step back and look at things without getting caught up in the emotions. At first when I was accused of being essentialist I thought, "How could they think that?" Then I thought, "OK. This accusation maybe is motivated by something negative, like envy." When somebody calls me on my shit in a real way, it's not negative. It's only negative when I react as though I'm attacked unjustifiably. I used to say that I only wanted to be critiqued honestly and openly but now I don't care. They can attack me if they want because what they're attacking is not so much me but my ideas, and ideas don't belong to anyone. They're part of the collective consciousness. The information is out there, it's just the way I organize ideas and put them together that's unique to me. The Borderlands— not only the literal borders but the metaphoric borders as well—for example, is what many people experience. I was aware of this experience and tried to pull it together in a way that I could explain. Many of the people who criticize me attribute too much power to me, they're giving me too much credit for the ideas. If people get jealous

281

or if they think that it's a false idea they can blame part of me, but they can't blame all of me because these ideas are out there. So I don't take it personally. As a matter of fact, if it generates dialogue it gives me more energy. It puts my writing out there more. In the past, before I disengaged, there were a few times when I did take it personally, especially when people used my ideas without citing me.

ALK: In several interviews you mention being annoyed when people use your ideas without citing you, but here you're saying you don't mind?

GEA: It doesn't sting as much because the baby is grown up. When *Borderlands* was first published I felt vulnerable towards it and noticed its vulnerabilities, but now it's been out in the world almost twelve years so they can throw rocks at it if they want.

Ignoring the Spiritual

ALK: Why do you think the spiritual dimensions in your work have been downplayed?

GEA: This whole society is premised on the reality described by the scientific mode of observable phenomenon, while whatever is imagined or subjectively lived doesn't have any credence. Spirituality is subjective experience.

ALK: It's ironic, when you think of these scholars who believe they're so "cutting edge" yet ignore the spiritual . . .

GEA: They're about to fall out of favor, very soon, in the next few decades.

ALK: You think so? You mean like poststructualist and postmodernist theorists?

GEA: It's already happening! Remember the stricture against personalizing your essays? Now all these academics are writing personal essays and putting themselves in the text. Women have been doing it for a while—women like Ruth Behar, the people in *This Bridge*, your kind of work. For a few years deconstruction and poststructualist theory reigned, but it's about to fall off, if it hasn't done so already. There's a time lag where the corpse is dead but you don't know it yet. Some of us have left that corpse. We're already into this new way of functioning, in the inner world and spirituality. We're already growing a new body.

ALK: Don't you think that another reason the spiritual aspects of your work are downplayed is because some scholars don't understand what you're talking about? Especially scholars who focus on the material dimensions and view the spiritual as escapist.

GEA: They have a very narrow range. They see one dimension, that of concrete reality, but nothing else because other dimensions are invisible or because they haven't learned to focus on the other dimensions. But as soon as their perception changes and they address it, they'll acknowledge the spiritual dimension. I've seen many people convert and turn away from the traditional scientific paradigms of concrete reality. As they get older they know the emotional and the spiritual life. I've seen them do a complete change: they'll start doing poetry or art or they'll start meditating. I think the artist's work is to open herself or himself to these other realities.

A person can't make changes in a discipline unless she has some sort of support or acceptance from others; you can't be the lone hero. You're an experimenter, yes, you take the risk and are in the front line but without the cheering crowd behind you, you won't move a foot. Some disciplines in the academy are invested in deconstruction, in postmodernist thought, ideas, and assumptions. But there's a loosening up and these disciplines will change. Innovators in science, in certain fields like mathematics, physics, and neurobiology are presently changing their fields.

ALK: But I like deconstructionist theory when it's used for progressive, liberatory goals.

GEA: I like it too because it challenges assumptions, but it leaves certain elements out.

Shapeshifting

ALK: You discuss shamanism and shapeshifting in *Borderlands* and several interviews. Do you believe that people can *literally* transform into other shapes—into animals, for example?

GEA: One of the common threads running through all human groups is shamanism. There's Korean shamanism, Chinese shamanism,

Mexican shamanism, Celtic shamanism, and so on. Almost every human group has had some form of shamanism. Shamans believe that their souls, their spirits, leave the body, travel long distances, and have encounters with other spirits. You can do this traveling in a trance state or in a dream state. When I'm trancing and if my familiar, my totem animal, my nagual, is a jaguar, then in this other body I become the jaguar. I become the serpent, I become the eagle. I have this visionary experience where I'm flying in the sky as an eagle—a she eagle maybe. I gather information from looking down at the ground. Now, how did I get that information if my body is just here?

It goes back to the three bodies which I think people have. This other body, the second or the third body, can leave my physical body and become a jaguar. I'm working on a were-jaguar story where Prieta literally transforms from a woman to a jaguar and becomes caught in between: She's half human and half jaguar, a were-jaguar, as in a werewolf. But that's fiction; in actuality I don't think that my hands can become flesh-and-blood claw and my mouth a jaguar mouth. I can't do it in my flesh-and-blood body but in my other body, I can. I also think that you can *lose* that body, just like people can misplace their souls. It can stay in the jaguar reality, in the jaguar form.

ALK: What happens then—you'd never become conscious again?

GEA: You'd literally become a jaguar; you wouldn't come back to the human body. But maybe some part of human consciousness would remain.

ALK: So the human body would just—not be human anymore?

GEA: The human body would only have two, instead of the three selves I mention in the Weiland interview. I'd be missing part of myself.

ALK: Would you be able to function?

GEA: Many people have lost part of their souls; they function but they don't function properly. They go to psychotherapy and self-help seminars to get back what they've lost. This age of speed, of rushing, scatters us and it's hard to pull back together unless you make a firm intention to get off the world, or as Carlos Castañeda put it, "to stop the world" and be there with the tree, or the sky, or the water. Then all your selves come rushing back. When your attention gets taken away and you're caught in the middle of a hundred things that need to be done and dozens of people who claim your attention, you get scattered again. Neither the physical self nor the physical body is the totality of a person. My ideas tie in together. It depends on perspective, on that blink of the eye. Like the picture that looks like two faces and a vase, which I mentioned in our discussion of the Weiland interview. Blink this way and you'll see the faces; blink and focus that way, you'll see the vase. Have you looked at the eyes of birds—how their focus changes? Their eyes get opaque and then translucent. That image was my metaphor for the switch in perception in "El Paisano Is a Bird of Good Omen." The main character, this particular "Prieta,"* is able to regulate her perception. She's looking out into the lagoon half a mile away and suddenly she's right there with the lagoon, the water, the plants.

ALK: This is a very literal question, so I'll apologize in advance. But is she really there? Is her body really at the lagoon?

GEA: Her physical body is still sitting on top of the fencepost, but her other bodies have traveled to the lagoon. There may be a time when we can actually move the physical body like that, but right now we don't have the skills. Maybe a few people have the skills: they can imagine they're in New York City and at the blink of an eye, they're in New York City, body, flesh and blood. Today the only way most of us do that is through the imaginal. A lot of the science fiction stuff like *Star Trek* (I've been reading this book on the science of *Star Trek*), have actually come true—like medical injections and the cell phone. There's tons of these things—you create them in your imagination first. So . . . I don't see why in the future I can't literally transform my body into a jaguar. But right now such transformations are limited to the beliefs of the majority of people and they don't believe it can be done. I think this is the great turning point of the century: we're going to leave the rigidity of this concrete reality and expand it. I'm very hopeful.

Interconnections

ALK: In several interviews you discuss feeling an intense inter-connectedness with people and things. Do you still have this sense of interconnectedness?

GEA: Yes. Sometimes I'll bump into a chair and I'll say, "Excuse me."

---

* In "El Paisano" this Prieta's name is Andrea. [ALK]

I'll go for a walk and I'll stare at a tree, the way it's silhouetted, and I feel such a connection to it, as though its roots grow out of my feet and its branches are my arms rising to the sky. Other times, when I'm so into the tasks I need to do, I lose that connection. Then when I walk I become oblivious to the sky, the trees, the sea otters, the whales, and whatever is out there in the sea. I have to bring myself back, and as soon as I put my attention on a little leaf or on the way the waves are coming in, I again feel that deep connection. This society doesn't encourage that kind of thing. Because we live in an accelerated age, we have so much thrown at us that there's no time to just look at the sky. Many people will schedule their walks, but instead of just walking and observing, they'll have their walkman on or they'll walk with a friend and be so busy talking that they won't even see the sky or Monterrey Bay. It's a constant struggle for me to bring myself back to connecting with things.

ALK: The connections are there, but you need to be in a certain frame of mind in order to recognize them.

GEA: The connections are there, the signs I read in the environment— if a snake crosses my path when I'm walking across Lighthouse Field, it means something to me. I'll look at that tree silhouetted by the sun, and its design says something to me, to my soul, which I then have to decipher. We get these messages from nature, from the creative consciousness or whatever you want to call the intelligence of the universe. It's constantly speaking to us but we don't listen, we don't look. At this point in my life it's hard for me to listen and look because there are so many things demanded of me. I need to simplify my life and slow it down so that I have these moments of connection. The same thing happens when I relate to people: if I'm talking to you but not really listening or observing your body language and I'm not really empathic with you, I don't really hear or see you. It's a multilevel kind of listening—not just to inanimate objects or animals, but to people. You listen with both outer ear and inner ear. This is the spiritual dimension of "la mano zurda," which combines activism with inner, subjective listening. It's a different way of being in tune with people and the environment.

ALK: Your statement now is quite different from the Smuckler interview, where you talk about putting up a wall inside yourself so that you don't get overwhelmed by the interconnectedness. Now you're talking about the necessity to become *more* aware.

GEA: Well, it goes both ways. At this time in my life, I need a lot of solitude. I live in my imagination, in my inner world. There has to be a balance: I need a community of people, I need to go out into the world, I need that connection. So it's either extreme. When I find myself being too much out in the world I have to put shields around myself so that I can come home, recuperate, recharge, and reconnect. But if I'm in my little womb of a house (for me, the house is always a symbol of the self), if I'm too protective, too much of a hermit, I have to take those shields off and let people in. That's why I like doing gigs: it allows me a way of earning a living and opens me up to different communities.

Anger

ALK: In an interview which we couldn't include in this volume, you state that you're "a very angry person." And certainly that anger comes through in *Borderlands*. In the most recent piece of yours I read— "Putting Coyolxauhqui Together: A Creative Process"—I didn't notice the same type of anger that you describe in this interview and express in *Borderlands*. Am I mistaken, or has your anger/your relationship with anger changed? If so, how?

GEA: Sometimes it's really healthy to be angry or to be sad, to plumb the depth of a particular emotion. But when the emotion possesses you and becomes a way of life, you have no autonomy. The feeling takes over and colors everything. In the last twelve years I started getting disembroiled from these emotional states, but I felt that *Borderlands* needed that angry voice. Just as it needed the different styles and genres, it needed the different emotional states. I purposely allowed the negative emotions in, sort of like singing with a full range of notes and with both lungs. In the past twelve years I've been able to look at the issues, groups, and people I used to be angry with and see their humanity. I was angry at them for being so oppressive or so wrongheaded or so narrow-minded. Now I look at their oppressive attitudes, their wrongheadedness, or their narrow-mindedness—what I call "desconocimientos"—and I see their humanity—how they came to be this way, what made them racist or homophobic. These oppressive ways are caused by fear, the strongest of all human emotions. When I see that vulnerability I can detach and say, "They're fucked up, they're ignorant, they'll come to their senses, and—if not—they'll die like this and just let it go." Parts of me are angry but they're angry at different things. I spent a year or so being angry at the world because

I got diabetes. I thought I'd already had my share of physical pain. The anger doesn't stop but the object of my anger changes.

ALK: Has the *quality* of your anger changed?

GEA: Yes. It's become softer. As soon as I emote the anger I stop and say, "Wait a minute, look at what you're doing! What is this anger serving? Am I a better person for it? Is it helping make the world a better place?" I look at the dynamics of what's happening and who's to blame, and it softens. I think this change of perspective on emotions comes from just living.

Physical Health, Bodies, and Identity Formation

ALK: How would you say your experiences with physical illness/disease—like the very early and painful menstruation and now diabetes—has impacted the ways you define and think about *other* aspects of your identity—like being Chicana, being queer, being female, being spiritual . . . ?

GEA: They have impacted me totally. My body has played a large role in shaping my identity.

To move from the physical illness and pain to the spiritual I had to have that concrete physiological experience. It set me apart from the herd. I had to figure out "Why was I so different? Do I want to go with the herd or should I resist and rebel?" My resistance to gender and race injustice stemmed from my physical differences, from the early bleeding and my early growth spurt. I was extremely shy and vulnerable, and it all stemmed from the fact that people saw me as "flawed."

Part of my resistance was escape from the physical world that was so harsh, but the other part was a survival mechanism, a capacity I had to use to survive the physical world; I had to be able to go to the fantasy, the imaginal, and the spiritual. I was a dreamer, but I was the firstborn and my mom discouraged everything unpractical because she wanted me to help her with the household chores and with the other kids. She tried to force me—like the culture forces all women—to be a practical person connected with concrete reality when much of my life was really in the imaginal world. This is where I got the idea that spirituality is the ultimate resort of people who are extremely oppressed.

I developed this way of being in my mind, my imagination, and my spirit. It was a result of having a particular body and my interactions with other Chicanos—especially my family. I found that whenever I got "normalized," when I began to fit in, something would slap me down again. I'd have another near death or I'd have horrendous pain with my menstrual periods, pain so horrendous that I'd fall on the floor and go into convulsions. These experiences kept me from being a "normal" person. The way I identify myself subjectively as well as the way I act out there in the world was shaped by my response to physical and emotional pain.

The diabetes also has had a large impact on me. Here I was: I bought this house, I was finishing up my second attempt at a Ph.D., I was traveling all over the world, I was gone six months out of the year, I had all this energy, my writing was going great, and then—POW! Diabetes. I had to stop everything. For a year I could hardly function other than to take care of myself. I was doing some reading and writing but I had to withdraw from people. At the beginning my friends got pissed because I wasn't interacting with them. I was so busy just surviving from day to day. One thing that prompted the diabetes— besides the genetic component, my early environment, and a viral infection I'd had in 1980—was stress. I realized I was going too fast and overextending. I love to be involved with everything but when I'm doing too many things I don't do anything justice. I might have been getting too ambitious, I might have been thinking myself a "Big Shot," as a writer on the fringes of the academy. I never got into the "Star" mentality but there were certain temptations. The diabetes just knocked all that out. I had to go back to basics: "What do I want from life? What do I really want to do?" I wanted to stay home, write more, and not travel as much. Now I can't travel as much because my neuropathy causes my feet to swell. I get dizzy and mentally foggy when I'm having a hypo. I lose my equilibrium and fall. Gastrointestinal reflex has me throwing up and having diarrhea—sometimes simultaneously. At one point I thought I was going to have to start wearing diapers. I tell you, things like these change your image of yourself, your identity.

Some greater self or total self is guiding me to be a certain way; it has instructions for how I should live my life, instructions that the "little me" subselves don't know. Now I'm trying to get information on which way to go, I'm trying to listen more to my inner voice because before diabetes I was too much out in the world. But it's also not good when I hide in my castle. I have to find balance, so I go back and forth. Evidently I haven't balanced my body because my blood sugar keeps changing. No matter how well you're taking care of yourself, no matter how controlled your diabetes is, there's always that percent that's failing. The whole thing with diabetes is having a balance in your blood sugar; if you don't have a balance it affects your eyes. I had blood clots, I had hemorrhaging in my eyes almost two years ago and had to have laser surgery or I'd go blind. The immune system killed the thyroid-producing hormone cells. I gained thirty pounds which I haven't been able to lose. I have to be on a supplement. I walk around like a duck, my metabolism is so low. How do I balance all this? I have to have some exercise, the food has to be nutritious, the amount of insulin has to be in conjunction with how much I eat and exercise. Sometimes I have to take more insulin and eat less, other times I have to eat more and exercise less or exercise when my blood sugar is higher.

ALK: That's what I thought! Since first reading your work I've believed that your body played an enormous role in shaping other aspects of your identity.

GEA: The importance I place on the body may also be a reaction against the New Agers who want to transcend the body. You have to work everything from the body. They're trying to do the opposite, they ignore the body.

ALK: Sometimes New Age people believe that they can immediately materialize whatever they want just by visualizing it.

GEA: Some have no idea of the full script they've programmed for themselves or been programmed with. You have to work through all the layers.

The Importance of Listening

ALK: OK. You have the last words. How would you like to end our book?

GEA: I want to end by saying that we must have very concrete, precisely worded intentions of what we want the world to be like, what *we* want to be like. We have to first put the changes that we want made into words or images. We have to visualize them, write them, communicate them to other people and stick with committing to those intentions, those goals, those visions. Before any changes can take place you have to say and intend them. It's like a prayer, you have to commit yourself to your visions.

I'd also like to emphasize that we can't ignore the body, because we live in a physical world. We're not here as just disembodied spirits, we're here as embodied spirits. Also, we should open our hearts to people through empathic connection, a connection that sometimes our minds don't understand because our perceptions are so limited. Sometimes the heart understands without any rational explanations or causes. We have to let go of hurt, of the wounds of controversy. We have to let go of hatred, of pointing the finger at people all the time.

ALK: Your comments here sound like a shift in your thinking from *Borderlands*.

GEA: In *Borderlands* I said that you have to point your finger at yourself first. We do enough of that, we're always blaming ourselves. I want my last words in this book to emphasize being empathic to people. Listen to people, be open to people or to any experience, open your hearts, stop being so busy that you don't have time to listen to other people and to the world. I guess the only way to stop being so busy is to stop consuming or to consume other things like information and knowledge and learning rather than material things. It's taken a toll on our bodies.

Some of these messages may sound too much like "New Age spirituality," but this is what I've learned in my life. We need to do the things we want to do, the things we have passion for, instead of spending twelve hours attending to somebody else's agenda, hours and hours doing things we have no love for.

Primary Works Cited

Borderlands/La Frontera: The New Mestiza. San Francisco: Spinsters/Aunt Lute, 1987.

"Bridge, Drawbridge, Sandbar or Island: *Lesbians-of-Color Hacienda Alianzas.*" *Bridges of Power: Women's Multicultural Alliances*. Ed. Lisa Albrecht and Rose M. Brewer. Philadelphia: New Society, 1990. 216–31.

"En rapport, In Opposition: Cobrando cuentas a las nuestras." *Making Face, Making Soul/Haciendo Caras: Creative and Critical Perspectives by Women of Color*. Ed. Gloria E. Anzaldúa. San Francisco: Aunt Lute Foundation, 1990. 142–48.

Friends from the Other Side/Amigos del otro lado. San Francisco: Children's Book Press, 1993.

"La Prieta." 1981. *This Bridge Called My Back: Writings by Radical Women of Color*. Ed. Cherríe Moraga and Gloria E. Anzaldúa. New York: Kitchen Table; Women of Color Press, 1983. 198–209.

Making Face, Making Soul/Haciendo Caras: Creative and Critical Perspectives by Women of Color. Ed. Gloria E. Anzaldúa. San Francisco: Aunt Lute Foundation, 1990.

Prietita and the Ghost Woman/ Prietita y La Llorona. San Francisco: Children's Book Press, 1995.

"Putting Coyolxauhqui Together: A Creative Process." *How We Work*. Eds. Marla Morris, Mary Aswell Doll, William F. Pinar. New York: Peter Lang Publishing, 1999.

"She Ate Horses." *Lesbian Philosophies and Cultures*. Ed. Jeffner Allen. New York: State University of New York, 1990. 371–88.

"Speaking in Tongues: A Letter to Third World Women Writers." 1981.

This Bridge Called My Back: Writings by Radical Women of Color. Ed. Cherríe Moraga and Gloria E. Anzaldúa. New York: Kitchen Table; Women of Color Press, 1983. 165–74.

This Bridge Called My Back: Writings by Radical Women of Color. 1981. Ed. Cherríe Moraga and Gloria E. Anzaldúa. New York: Kitchen Table: Women of Color Press, 1983.

"To(o) Queer the Writer—*Loca, escritora y chicana.*" *Inversions: Writing by Dykes, Queers, and Lesbians.* Ed. Betsy Warland. Vancouver: Press Gang, 1991. 249–64.

The Interviewers

Carmen Abrego is a mexicana Chicana poet whose work has been published in a number of anthologies and journals, including *Chicana Lesbians: The Girls Your Mother Warned You About* (Third Woman Press) and *The Iowa Review*. She conducts writing and self-esteem workshops for Latinas and women of color. In the summer of 1999, for the second year, she taught Latina literature and writing for "El Encuentro de Cultura y Conocimiento," a college-preparation program for young Latinas from high schools around the country, held at St. Mary's College of Notre Dame. Presently she is the director of the Puerto Rican Cultural Center's Family Learning Center, a high school diploma-granting program in Chicago primarily serving Latinas with young children.

Jeffner Allen is the author of *r e v e r b e r a t i o n s across the shimmering CASCADAS* (SUNY Press, 1996), *Sinuosities, Lesbian Poetic Politics* (Indiana University Press, 1996), and *Lesbian Philosophy: Explorations* (Institute of Lesbian Studies, 1991). She has edited *Lesbian Philosophies and Cultures* (SUNY Press, 1990) and coedited *The Thinking Muse: Feminism and Recent French Thought* (Indiana University Press, 1989). Jeffner is professor of philosophy and women's studies at SUNY Binghamton. Among her favorite activities are walking on the beach, scuba diving, and gardening—along with conversations with friends.

Born in the Canary Islands, Spain, María Henríquez Betancor graduated from the University of Barcelona in 1990 and completed a master's degree at Leeds University, UK in Commonwealth Literature. Subsequently her main interest has developed in the area of contemporary Chicana literature. She is currently preparing her doctoral thesis at the University of La Laguna on Chicana autobiography.

Debbie Blake is a visiting assistant professor of English at the University of Iowa, where she specializes in Chicana/o literary and cultural studies. She has published an interview with Denise Chávez in the *Iowa Journal of Cultural Studies* and articles on Chicana/o literature and oral histories in *a/b: Auto/Biography* and *Frontiers: A Journal of Women's Studies*. She is currently working on a book manuscript, *The Right to Passion: Chicana Sexuality and Gender Roles Refigured*, and is editing a collection of oral histories by Chicanas from Iowa, Texas, and Arizona.

Jamie Lee Evans is a thirty-two-year-old Hapa Haole dyke feminist who lives in Oakland, Calif. She's written a few good things published in various feminist and lesbian periodicals and she spends most of her time teaching and organizing young women to resist the patriarchy at San Francisco Women Against Rape. She is also the lead facilitator of Breathing Fire Productions, which offers antioppression workshops for nonprofit organizations. She is ever so grateful for the work and spirit of Gloria Anzaldúa.

Inés Hernández-Ávila is Nimpu (Nez Perce) of Chief Joseph's band and Tejana. She is a poet and an associate professor and former chair of the Department of Native American Studies at the University of California, Davis. Her scholarly and creative work looks at issues of identity, community, culture, and spirituality, with a focus on U.S./Mexico connections, Native women, Native literature, and Native belief systems.

Andrea Abernethy Lunsford, distinguished professor of English and director of the Center for the Study and Teaching of Writing, teaches undergraduate and graduate courses in composition, rhetoric, literacy, and intellectual property at Ohio State University. Currently also a member of the Bread Loaf School of English faculty, Professor Lunsford earned her B.A. and M.A. degrees from the University of Florida, and she completed her Ph.D. in English at Ohio State University in 1977. Andrea's scholarly interests include contemporary rhetorical theory, women and the history of rhetoric, collaboration and collaborative writing, current cultures of writing, style, and technologies of writing. She has written or coauthored thirteen books, including *Everything Is an Argument: Essays on Classical Rhetoric and Modern Discourse*; *Singular Texts/Plural Authors: Perspectives on Collaborative Writing*; and *Reclaiming Rhetorica: Women in the History of Rhetoric*.

Linda Smuckler is the author of two collections of poetry: *Normal Sex* (Firebrand Books, 1994) and *Home in Three Days. Don't Wash*, a multimedia project with accompanying CD-ROM (Hard Press, 1996). Her work has been widely anthologized, and she is the recipient of numerous awards in poetry and fiction including the 1997 Firecracker Alternative Book Award in Poetry. She has also received fellowships from the New York Foundation for the Arts and the Astraea Foundation. She currently lives in Tucson, Arizona. *Normal Sex* is dedicated to Gloria Anzaldúa, Smuckler's first writing teacher.

Christine Weiland has known Gloria since the early 1980s.

The Authors

Gloria E. Anzaldúa is the author of *Borderlands/La Frontera: The New Mestiza, Friends from the Other Side/Amigos del otro lado*, and *Prietita and the Ghost Woman/Prietita y la Llorona*, editor of *Making Face, Making Soul/Haciendo Caras: Creative and Critical Perspectives by Women of Color*, and coeditor of *This Bridge Called My Back: Writings by Radical Women of Color*. Anzaldúa has played a pivotal role in redefining U.S. feminisms, cultural studies, Chicano/a issues, U.S. American literature, ethnic studies, queer theory, and postcolonial theory.

AnaLouise Keating is Associate Professor of English at Aquinas College. In addition to *Women Reading Women Writing: Self-Invention in Paula Gunn Allen, Gloria Anzaldúa, and Audre Lorde*, she coedited *Perspectives: Gender Studies* and has published articles on critical "race" theory, queer theory, Latina writers, African American women writers, and pedagogy.

Index

academics, 18, 140–42, 230–31, 236, 262–63
academia, 144, 161, 275, 283. *See also* university
activism, 221, 278, 286. *See also* anthologies; spirituality; writing
affirmation(s), 98
African, 37, 181, 192
African Americans, 40, 67, 147, 181, 254
agency, 10, 75, 179, 183, 189, 218, 221, 265, 278
AIDS, 127, 213
Alarcón, Norma, 237
Alfassa, Mira, 99–10. *See also* Aurobindo, Sri
Allen, Paula Gunn, 171, 174
alliances, 195–99, 201–202, 209, 217, 232; lesbian, 203–205
alliance–making, 196, 198, 218–19
almas afines, 9–10, 120, 164
anger, 58, 66–67, 103, 124, 183, 287–88
Anglos, 23, 31, 55, 75, 87–88, 130, 157, 182, 189–90, 209, 213, 261
anthologies, 155, 202, 206, 277. *See also Making Face, Making Soul/Haciendo Caras; This Bridge Called My Back*
"Antigua, mi diosa" (1987), 213
Anzaldúa, Gloria, adolescence, 13, 27; childhood,13, 22–26, 29, 30, 34–35, 78–94, 112, 168, 252, 276; college years, 30–33, 42, 170; dealing with criticism, 281–82; graduate school, 46, 49–50, 52, 54, 153, 175, 237, 255; mugging(s), 74, 103, 107, 111, 159, 223; spiritual development, 25–27, 48, 71, 97–99, 103–12, 124–25. *See also* diabetes; gigs; menstruation; near–death experiences; sexual identity; writing process
apparitions, 105–6, 126
arbol de la vida/tree of life, 240–42
artist, 19, 49, 247, 251, 268
assimilation, 39, 185, 262
astrology, 8, 38, 50, 61, 70, 108, 117, 120, 149
audience, 60, 65, 229–30, 245, 262–63. *See also* reading
Aurobindo, Sri, 100–101, 120–21, 125–26
autobiography, 5, 25, 225. *See also* autohistorias; autohisteorías; personal
autohistorias, 243
Autohisteorias, 242–43
Aztec(s), 11, 24, 49, 60, 64, 123, 159, 184, 265; calendar, 69–70, 193

Aztlán, 216
"Basque Witches," 53
belief(s), 71–73, 151–52, 162,
    229–30
bisexual(s), 33, 47, 115, 117, 205,
    213. See also queers
body/bodies, 40–41, 71–72, 75,
    94–95, 121, 158, 164, 213, 257;
    female, 220; and health, 30; and
    identity formation, 288–91; and
    mind, 64, 151; reclaiming,
    124–25; and soul(s), 20–22, 220;
    spiritualized, 9, 103, 151–52; 161;
    three, 284–85. See also diabetes;
    health; yoga of the body
Boehm, David, 9
Borderlands, 5, 6, 14, 176, 215,
    219–20, 229, 238–39, 241, 281
Borderlands/La Frontera, 2, 4–5, 7,
    12–13, 18, 53, 73, 131–32, 159,
    165 167–69, 172, 183, 192, 215,
    219, 225, 229, 239, 241, 243,
    246–47, 253, 256, 260–61, 263,
    267–68, 271, 276–77, 282
Borges, Jorge Luis, 36, 50, 273

capitalism, 157, 182, 174, 187
Castillo, Ana, 10. See also Chicana
    writers
Castañeda, Antonia, 237
Castañeda, Carlos, 96, 275, 284
categories, 215, 280. See also labels
Catholicism, 94–97, 180. See also
    Christianity, religion
censorship, 19, 259–60; internalized,
    260–61
change, 72, 73, 75–76, 98, 179,
    192–93, 253, 262–64, 283, 290;
    in consciousness, 280; inner/outer,
    101; social, 9–11. See also identity
    formation/construction; nepantla;
    transformation
changing culture, 221, 270, 277
Chicana(s)/Chicano(s), 31, 41, 48,
    51, 54, 67, 156–57, 179, 181–83,
    191–93, 219, 221, 230–31,
    244–45, 254; culture, 83, 93–95,
    115, 183, 220, 239, 260; indige-
    nous connections, 24, 35, 49,

96–97, 182, 184, 215, 235, 248,
    267–68. See also Chicana writers;
    Chicano movement; "Hispanic"
    label; Latinas/os
Chicana writers, 130–31, 219,
    236–38, 244, 246. See also writing
Chicano movement, 43, 45, 145,
    185–87, 214.
children, 204, 244, 277–78. See also
    Anzaldúa, Gloria
children's literature, 190, 244. See
    also censorship; Friends from the
    Other Side/Amigos del otro lado;
    Prietita and the Ghost
    Woman/Prietita y la Llorona
Christianity, 71. See also
    Catholicism; religion; Chicanas/os,
    culture
Chrystos, 146–17
"Circuit City Song," 49
Cisneros, Sandra, 237, 244, 276. See
    also Chicana writers
class, 51, 57–58, 77, 130–31,
    134–35, 137–40, 143–44,
    152–53, 165, 168–79, 171,
    200–201, 204–205, 208, 213,
    230, 232, 248, 277
coalitions. See alliances
Coatlicue, 11, 168, 192, 219,
    267–68. See also goddess figures;
    myth
Coatlicue state, 225–26
code-switching, 202, 246, 253, 266,
    274, 277; and readers, 274–76.
    See also language
Collins, Patricia Hill, 12, 14–15
colonialism, 179–81, 184, 188–89,
    216, 256. See also Conquest;
    Columbus, Christopher; Cortés,
    Hernán
Columbus, Christopher, 180–81,
    189
commonalities. See differences, and
    commonalities
composition studies, 253, 256,
    261–64, 268, 272, 275–76, 278
compostura, 257
conferences. see gigs

Connor, Randy, 45–46, 48, 54, 59, 60, 66, 181, 105–106, 115, 126

Conquest, 180–82, 190, 194. See also colonialism

conocimiento(s), 5, 14, 177–78, 183, 206, 212, 216, 218, 266–67, 273. See also desconocimientos

consciousness, 76, 79, 102, 160; collective, 20, 281; universal, 73, 112. See also conocimiento(s); desconocimientos; facultad; imaginal

Cortázar, Julio, 36, 50, 105, 236

Cortés, Hernán, 180–81

Coyolxauhqui, 11–12, 19, 219–20, 226, 257, 269, 280. See also goddess figures, myth

creativity, 35, 61, 77, 123–24, 194, 226. See also imagination; writing

culture, defined, 279–80. See also belief(s)

curandera, 19, 224–25, 245

"Del otro lado" (1987), 169–71

desconocimientos, 177–78, 197, 200, 287. See also conocimiento(s)

desire, 101, 160, 166; for carnalidad, 270

diabetes, xiii, 6, 74–75, 152, 207, 232, 249, 258, 289–90

"Doing Gigs," 213

difference(s), 29, 138, 169–71, 203, 261, 264; and commonalities, 76, 123, 129, 157–58, 178, 197, 255, 272. See also identity; identity formation/construction

divine, 9, 39

dominant culture, 173, 181–82, 188, 198, 202, 217–18, 220, 229–30, 244, 254, 261–62, 273. See also Anglos; class; privilege; 'whiteness'

dreams, 18, 21, 72, 75, 101, 120, 125–26, 143–44, 159, 163–64, 225, 266–67, 284

drugs, 6–7, 19, 36, 94, 106, 124, 127

ecofeminism, 193

education, 143–45. See also Anzaldúa, Gloria; composition studies; gigs; university

ego, 39–40, 102, 120–21, 179. See also identity formation/construction

el cenote, 240

El Mundo Zurdo, 51, 63, 68, 183, 196

"El Paisano Is a Bird of Good Omen" (1981), 24, 49, 61, 161–62, 285

"El segundo corazón/The Second Heart," 71

emotion(s), 22, 27, 77, 91–92, 101, 103, 121–22, 144, 177, 206, 213, 257, 263, 266, 287; politics of the emotions, 199–200. See also anger; body/bodies; fear

empathy, 27, 91, 178, 290–91

"En rapport, In Opposition" (1990), 155–56, 217, 247

environment, 20, 26, 38, 41, 89, 100, 102, 134, 140, 159–60, 162, 182, 184, 187, 194, 221, 240, 258, 286

epistemology, 18, 266–67. See also consciousness; dominant culture; facultad; intuition; mestiza consciousness; mind; nepantla; rational thought; spirituality

essentialism, 7, 139, 161, 165, 203, 221–23, 281

extraterrestrial, 8, 17, 20, 34

facultad, 4, 122–23, 177, 255, 267

Faulkner, William, 236, 245

fear, 39–40, 121, 134, 15, 264

feminine, 66, 124. See also goddess figures

femininity, 172–73

feminism, 45, 47, 50, 51, 56, 141, 232–33, 253; white, 66

feminist(s), 53, 54, 63, 159–60, 167, 172. See also feminism; Feminist Writers Guild

Feminist Writers Guild, 56–59, 153

fiction, 21–22, 163, 223–24, 243, 263, 272

folklore. *See* goddess figures; La Jila; La Malinche; myth; storytelling

Friends from the Other Side/Amigos del otro lado (1993), 4, 190, 243, 245, 171

"Funeral of Sabas Q," 50

gay men, 41, 81, 97, 134, 167, 105. *See also* homosexuality; mita' y mita'; queer(s)

gender, 20, 129–30, 136, 172, 197–94, 215. *See also* femininity; masculinity

geography of selves, 5, 238–39, 255, 268

gigs, 143, 148, 163, 172, 196–201, 211–14, 228, 231–33, 238–39, 287

goddess figures, 108–10, 194, 221–22, 225. *See also* Coatlicue; Coyolxauhqui; la Llorona; la Virgen de Guadalupe; myth; Oya; Snake Woman; Tonántzin; Yemanja

González, Corky, 40, 230

good/evil, 74–75, 99, 106–107

Guadalupe. *See* la Virgen de Guadalupe

half and half, 122, 113–14, 122, 123. *See also* lesbian(s); mita' y mita'

healing, 19, 151–52, 205–206; and alliances, 199–200

health, 34–35, 66, 69, 74, 92–93, 107,125, 151, 153, 288. *See also* diabetes; healing

heterosexual(s), 124, 130; and women, 135–37. *See also* heterosexuality; homophobia; privilege

heterosexuality, 131, 165–66, 169, 274. *See also* dominant culture; privilege

Hillman, James, 37

"Hispanic" label, 182, 235, 238

history, 160, 182, 184–85, 197, 223, 240–42, 272. *See also* colonialism; Conquest; myth

"Holy Relics" (1980), 56

homophobia, 74, 122, 287

homosexuality, 32–34, 54, 80, 123, 171. *See also* gay men; lesbianism; lesbian(s); mita' y mita'; half and half; queer(s)

"Hummingbird Song," 44

I Ching, 48, 120, 126

identity, 5, 9–10, 129, 130, 143–44, 158, 164, 205, 215; Chicana, 237–38; as relational process, 239–40, 264; multiple, 20, 36, 132, 173; *See also* arbol de la vida; geography of selves; imaginal; masks; New Tribalism; nos/otras; shapeshifting

identity formation/construction, 5, 138, 177, 203–204, 241–42, 255–56, 269–70. *See also* identity

ignorance. *See* desconocimientos

images, 145, 200–201, 241, 254, 257, 266–67, 273

imaginal, 13, 18, 73, 129, 144, 177, 196, 225, 251

imagination, 18, 23, 29, 61, 73, 77, 124, 144, 159, 160, 163, 225, 251–52, 285, 287–88

"Immaculate, Inviolate" (1987), 239, 260

indigenous, 5, 37, 72, 176. *See also* Chicana(s)/Chicano(s); Native peoples

"Interface" (1987),

Internet, 216, 240, 266

interview process, xi–xii, 2, 211

interviews, 3–4, 233

intuition,18, 53, 105

Jane Eyre, 25, 27

Kitchen Table Press, 61–62

labels, 73–74, 76–77, 115–16,

129–33, 236. *See also* categories; "Hispanic" label; identity

la Chingada, 219–20, 238, 243. *See also* Malinche

la diosa, 73, 161, 190. *See also* goddess figures

"La entrada de ajenos a loa casa/The Entry of the Alien into the House," 158

la Jila, 96

la Llorona, 96, 176, 180–81, 191–92, 219–21, 228–29, 238, 244–45, 267. *See also* goddess figures; myth

language, 28, 42–43, 230, 247–48, 265–66, 272; conflict, 244–46. *See also* code-switching

La Prieta, The Dark One, 4, 19, 21, 67, 158, 161, 13, 168, 224–25, 229, 243, 259, 284

"La Prieta" (1981), 53, 224

La Serpiente que e come su cola, 53–54, 61, 68

la Virgen de Guadalupe, 73, 95, 180, 192, 219–20, 238, 243–44. *See also* goddess figures; myth

Latinas/Latinos, 67, 147, 156–57, 243. *See also* Chicana(s)/Chicano(s)

lesbianism, 46–47, 123, 143, 274. *See also* homosexuality; mita' y mita'

lesbian(s), 34, 41, 48, 51, 95, 97, 114–19, 134, 136–37, 139, 142, 147, 166–68, 202, 207; white, 207–209. *See also* writing

Lloronas, mujeres que lean y escriben: Producing Writing, Knowledge, Cultures, and Identities, 222, 229, 243

magical realism, 36–37

Making Face, Making Soul/Haciendo Caras (1990), 4–5, 153–56, 158, 168, 202, 217. *See also* anthologies

making soul, 4, 35, 65, 74–75, 226

Malinche, 192, 242. *See also* La Chingada; myth

masculinity, 172–73. *See also* mita' y mita';

masks, 3, 159, 161

masturbation, 30, 71, 110. *See also* sexuality

Mayan, 159, 161, 192, 265; calendar, 69, 193. *See also* indigenous

media, 157, 216

meditation, 8, 11, 20, 35, 38–39, 68–69, 98, 101, 103, 106, 108–11, 118–19, 125–26, 257

memory, 224, 240. *See also* history; myth

men, 75, 278. *See also* gay men; gender; patriarchy; privilege

menstruation, 9, 19–20, 23, 25, 27, 29–30, 78–79, 87, 91, 94, 169, 287

mestizaje, 5, 14, 197–98, 215, 229; style of writing, 272

mestiza consciousness, 215

mestiza/o(s), 123, 134, 181, 188–89, 235–36, 241, 268, 278; new, 133

metaphor(s), 133, 176, 274

metaphysics of interconnectedness, 9–12, 20, 26–27, 36, 39, 41, 75, 100, 102, 118–19, 160, 162, 164, 195, 285–86

Mexican(s), 25, 42–43, 94–95, 122, 132, 180, 182–83, 191–92, 318–19, 144–45. *See also* Chicana(s)/Chicano(s)

migrant workers, 88–89. *See also* Chicano movement

mind(s), 7, 75, 77, 107, 121, 152, 220, 268

mita' y mita', 4, 172–73. *See also* half and half

Molina, Papusa, 213

Moraga, Cherríe, 6, 56–60, 62, 65, 67, 153, 165, 236–37, 246

Morales, Aurora Levins, 19

Morrison, Toni, 260–61, 277

multiculturalism, 182, 199, 216

multiracial, 186–87. *See also* mestiza/o

myth(s), 11, 12, 238, 240, 272; and agency, 218; creating reality, 219. *See also* goddess figures; Coatlicue; Coyolxauhqui; la Jila, la; la Virgen de Guadalupe; Snake Woman; Tonántzin; Yemanja; storytelling

nagual, 272, 284

Nahuatl, 67, 225–26, 246

naming. *See* labels

nationalism, 118, 156, 214–15. *See also* New Tribalism

Native peoples, 20, 25, 67, 74, 100, 133–34, 181–82, 194–91, 225, 254. *See also* colonialism; Conquest; indigenous

nature. *See* environment

near-death experiences, 8, 14, 19, 34, 66, 74, 112–13, 223, 226, 289

neocolonization, 212, 264–65

nepantla, 5, 7, 14, 168, 176–77, 225–26, 229, 238–39, 241, 147, 167–68, 279

New Age, 8, 14, 20, 144, 160, 290–91

New Tribalism, 5, 178, 185–86, 214–15

nos/otras, 5, 17, 178, 215, 254–55, 261

Olmecs, 64, 159, 161

oppression, 10, 57, 72–73, 95, 98, 116, 122–23, 180, 183, 200, 218, 248, 276; of women, 66, 182, 190–91, 209, 214, 218, 220–21, 231. *See also* colonialism; homophobia; patriarchy; racism

otherness, 39–41, 146, 254, 262, 272, 278

out-of-body experiences, 19, 72. *See also* near-death experiences

Oya, 19

patriarchy, 135, 140, 165, 191, 194, 218. *See also* dominant culture

perception, 74, 76, 107, 159, 160–63, 177–78, 183, 229–30, 270, 280, 283. *See also* facultad

"El Paisano Is a Bird of Good Omen"

Pérez, Emma, 237

Persephone Press, 62–63

perspective, 201, 285. *See also* perception

personal, 2–3, 5, 4, 142–44; as political, 198–200. *See also* autobiography; risk-taking; writing

Piercy, Marge, 46, 50

Poniatoska, Elena, 236, 240

postcolonial studies, 5, 253, 255–56, 263–65, 268, 277. *See also* theory

postmodernism, 272, 282–83. *See also* theory

poststructuralism, 282–83. *See also* theory

power, 125, 182, 196, 204–205, 208, 216

Prieta, 176, 223, 285. *See also La Prieta, The Dark One*

Prietita and the Ghost Woman/Prietita y la Llorona (1995), 4, 228–29, 245, 277

privilege, 165, 212, 220. *See also* dominant culture

psychic readers, 17, 19, 20, 35, 48, 107, 119

publishers, 61–63, 240–41, 259

"Puddles," 72

"Putting Coyolxauhqui Together" (1999), 287

queer(s), 33, 40, 54, 115, 117, 123–24, 166, 171–72, 208, 247. *See also* gay men; mita' y mita'; lesbian(s)

queerness, 170, 203–204

Quincentennial, 188. *See also* colonialism; Conquest

Quintanales, Mirtha, 53, 60, 68

racism, 57, 74, 76–77, 122, 153, 212, 217–18, 287; internalized, 184, 217

race(s), 20–21, 77, 118, 129–30, 137–38, 143–44, 165, 171, 215, 222, 232

rational thought, 8, 12, 22, 162, 196, 272

reading, 21–22, 25, 29, 77, 132, 135, 138–41, 144–45, 148, 174, 227, 243–45, 259, 261, 272, 277; as an act of resistance, 273; and writing, 272. *See also* audience

reality, 143–44, 162, 283; consensual, 270, 277–78; created, 20, 75, 212, 219, 270–72; multi-layered, 18, 21, 23, 36, 104, 159, 163–64, 176, 225–26, 275, 283

reincarnation, 17, 20, 21, 99

religion, 8–9,39–40, 66, 95–98, 100, 103, 111. *See also* Catholicism; Christianity

remolino(s), 273–75, 279

resistance, 180, 183, 185. *See also* agency; spirituality; writing

"Resisting the Spirit," 19

Rewriting Reality, 173

Rich, Adrienne, 53, 62, 204

Richards, Dona, 8

risk taking, 2, 14, 17–18, 142, 207, 257, 264, 283

ritual(s), 11, 68, 98, 160, 163, 243–44

Robert, Jane, 49

Sandoval, Chela, 237

santería, 107, 122

science, 18–19, 163, 270, 282–83, 285

self-esteem, 111–12, 207, 218

separatism, 55, 185. *See also* nationalism

serpents, 64, 102, 178, 266

sexual identity, 29–30, 32, 79–81, 115–18. *See also* sexual preference

sexuality, 47, 66, 215; and Chicano culture, 221; female, 40, 64–65, 104; fear of, 39, 113; and lesbian writing, 146; other, 229; and spirituality, 37–38, 68–69, 79; as a topic in writing, 5–6, 260; *See also* heterosexuality; lesbianism; sexual identity; sexual preference

sexual preference, 115–16, 122–23, 165, 226. *See also* way station

shaman, 19, 72, 132, 225, 251

shamanism, 283–84

shapeshifting, 132, 283–85

"She Ate Horses" (1990), 166, 175, 229

Signs' Theorizing Lesbian Experience (1993), 202

Sledd, James, 51

S/M, 63, 65–66, 134, 172

Snake Woman, 192

social constructionism, 6, 165, 203

social justice, 3, 6,12, 169, 199

soul(s), 19–21, 34, 38–40, 72, 76–77, 94, 97–98, 108, 120–21, 159, 220, 284; creating, 75, universal, 73, 100, 118, *See also* spirit(s)

"Speaking in Tongues" (1981), 61, 64–65

spirit(s), 19–20, 38–39, 60, 77, 96–98, 100, 102–103, 106, 119, 122, 152, 159, 288; disincarnate, 20, 125, interconnected with body, 7, 98, 220; and shamans, 284; as a term, 8; world of 48., *See also* extraterrestrial; spirituality; soul(s)

spiritual activism, 8, 11–12, 38, 178

spiritual-imaginal, 13

spirituality, 5, 7–8, 40, 111–12, 126, 138–39, 158–61, 282–83; and oppression, 10–11, 72–73, 288; politicized, 8, 72–73, 98, 101, 127, 158, 164; as subjective experience, 282; as a term, 73–74; and writing, 251–52. *See also* Anzaldúa, Gloria, spiritual development; metaphysics of interconnectedness; sexuality; spiritual activism; spiritual-imaginal

Star Trek, 99, 111, 285

Stone, Merlin, 55–56, 58–59, 153

storytelling, 22–23, 96, 180, 229, 252
supernatural, 5, 41, 96, 176. *See also*
    reality, multi-layered
survival, 73, 122–23, 231, 248, 255,
    288. *See also* agency

tarot, 48, 107, 126
Tatum, Charles, 202
Teish, Luisah, 19
theory, 3, 137, 140–41, 145, 161,
    166, 178, 213, 221, 262, 267. *See
    also* composition studies;
    postcolonial studies;
    postmodernism; poststructuralism
This Bridge Called My Back (1981),
    4–5, 54–55, 58–59, 61–63, 52–56,
    164, 201–202, 217, 230, 236–37,
    241, 282
"tlapalli," 48
tolteca, 49
Toltecs, 60, 159, 161
Tonántzin, 192
tokens, 202
"To(o) Queer the Writer" (1991),
    129, 208
tradition, 185. *See also* belief(s);
    change
transsexuals, 213
transformation, 1, 5, 8, 11–12, 96,
    189; of consciousness, 251. *See
    also* change; shapeshifting
Tres lenguas del fuego, 53, 55

United States, 157, 163, 188, 244,
    247, 260, 266. *See also* capitalism;
    colonialism
university, 3, 18, 68, 73, 142–43,
    194, 198–99, 216, 231–32, 262

vibration(s), 100, 103–105, 110–11,
    159–60

victimization. *See* agency
Vietnam War, 44–45
Viramontes, María Elena, 237. *See
    also* Chicana writers
Virgin of Guadalupe. *See* la Virgen
    de Guadalupe
visuals. *See* gigs; images
visualization(s), 109, 144, 290
voice(s), 60–61, 259–61, 264, 277

way station, 167–68, 239, 242
'whiteness,' 42, 146, 204, 252–53.
    See also Anglos; dominant culture;
    lesbian(s), white; women, white
Wittig, Monique, 46, 63
women, 56–57, 158, 165–66, 174,
    192–94, 197, 200–202, 207, 217,
    222, 236, 243; white, 152–53,
    155, 168, 201–202, 217
women of color. *See* lesbian(s);
    women
women's studies, 142–43, 232
writing, 41, 51–52, 62, 69, 120,
    174; as activism, 11, 183, 189,
    206, 273, 276; as
    alliance–making, 197; of conver-
    gence, 4, 21, 36–37; and first per-
    son, 222–23; as healing, 248–49;
    inferior, 240; lesbian, 130–31,
    134–35, 138, 142, 146; the
    personal, 223, 226–27; and read-
    ing, 248; style, 137–38, 145, 259,
    273; through/with the body,
    63–64. *See also* spirituality;
    creativity; imagination
writing process, 70, 175–76, 228,
    247, 257–60, 269

Yemanja, 19, 244
yoga of the body, 4, 77, 99